T5-CAI-049

3 2109 00850 3329

CCCC

Bibliography of Composition and Rhetoric

1988

Erika Lindemann
Managing Editor

Mary Beth Harding
Associate Editor

Conference on College Composition and Communication

Southern Illinois University Press
Carbondale and Edwardsville

ISSN 1046–0675
ISBN 0-8093-1669-2
ISBN 0-8093-1670-6 (pbk.)

The paper used in this publication meets the minimum requirements of
American National Standard for Information Sciences—Permanence
of Paper for Printed Library Materials, ANSI Z39.48-1984. ∞

Contents

Preface

Erika Lindemann

The *CCCC Bibliography of Composition and Rhetoric,* published by the Conference on College Composition and Communication, offers teachers and researchers an annual classified listing of scholarship on written English and its teaching. This volume cites 1798 titles that, with few exceptions, were published during the 1988 calendar year. The bibliography lists each work only once, but it descriptively annotates all citations, cross-references them when appropriate, and indexes all authors and editors. A group of 146 contributing bibliographers, whose names appear on pages xi to xii, prepared the citations and annotations for all entries appearing in this volume.

SCOPE OF THE BIBLIOGRAPHY

The *CCCC Bibliography* includes works that treat written communication (whether the writing people do is in English or some other language), the processes whereby human beings compose and understand written messages, and

methods of teaching people to communicate effectively in writing. The bibliography lists entries in five major categories (see the Contents for a fuller description of these categories):

Section 1. Bibliographies and Checklists
Section 2. Theory and Research
Section 3. Teacher Education, Administration, and Social Roles
Section 4. Curriculum
Section 5. Testing, Measurement, and Evaluation

The bibliography makes few restrictions on the format, medium, or purpose of the works it includes, so long as the subject of the work falls into one of the five categories described in the preceding list. It lists only published works: books, articles, monographs, published collections (of essays, conference presentations, or working papers), bibliographies and other reference works, films, microforms, videotapes, and sound recordings. It includes citations for unpublished doctoral dissertations appearing in *Dissertation Abstracts International*. It also includes review articles that discuss several works, define movements or trends, or survey an individual's contribution to the discipline. It excludes masters theses, textbooks, computer software, book reviews, and works written in a language other than English.

SOURCES

The *CCCC Bibliography* cites works from four major sources.

Periodicals. Journals publishing articles on composition and its teaching are the source for approximately 1100 entries. Each journal is identified by an abbreviation; an alphabetical list of Journal Abbreviations begins on page xiii. With few exceptions, the contributing bibliographers preparing entries for journal articles examined the material firsthand.

Publishers. A second source of materials are commercial publishers and university presses. These publishers, whose participation in the bibliography project is voluntary, provided contributing bibliographers with written information for approximately 100 books listed in this volume. By and large, contributing bibliographers were unable to examine these materials firsthand.

This volume also includes scholarly essay collections, books that bring together essays, articles, or papers by several authors. The bibliography annotates these collections, but does not annotate each essay. Unless the annotation for a collection says otherwise, all authors contributing to the collection are listed in the Name Index.

Dissertation Abstracts International (DAI). DAI represents a third source for approximately 420 citations. Not all degree-granting institutions list their unpublished doctoral dissertations in *DAI,* and as a rule, the contributing bibliographers have not examined these dissertations firsthand. The citations in this volume serve only to direct readers to abstracts in *DAI.* Users will want to consult the *DAI* abstracts for additional information, including who supervised the degree candidate's work and which institution granted the degree.

Resources in Education (RIE). A fourth source of materials in the *CCCC Bibliography* is the Educational Resources Information Center (ERIC), a federally funded document retrieval system coordinated by sixteen clearinghouses.

ERIC indexes its materials in two reference works. Journal articles appear in *Cumulative Index to Journals in Education (CIJE). Resources in Education (RIE),* on the other hand, indexes documents in the ERIC microfiche collection, which is available in 2600 regional libraries or directly from ERIC. These documents, frequently published elsewhere, include government documents, research and project reports, bibliographies, and conference papers. Documents indexed in *RIE* receive a six-digit "ED" number (e.g., ERIC ED 269 701) and are cross-referenced under various subject headings or "descriptors."

Some documents may be listed in *RIE* and may become available through ERIC several years after they were written. For convenience and to ensure comprehensiveness, the *CCCC Bibliography* reports ERIC documents cited in *RIE* during the years covered in the current volume; that is, this volume cites over 130 ERIC documents listed in *RIE* in 1988, even though the works themselves may have an earlier "date of publication." Also as a convenience, each ERIC entry includes the six-digit "ED" number.

Contributing bibliographers working with ERIC materials have developed the following criteria for determining what documents to include in this volume:

Substantiveness. Substantive documents of general value to college composition teachers and researchers are included. Representative publications are curriculum guides, federal government final reports, and technical reports from various publication series, such as those published, for example, by the University of Illinois Center for the Study of Reading and the recently established Center for the Study of Writing.

Relevance. Documents that seem to represent concerns of high interest to researchers are included. The topics of functional literacy, computer-assisted instruction, and revision, for example, represent concerns of greater relevance than the teaching of handwriting.

Inclusiveness. All papers on composition and rhetoric available in ERIC and delivered at the annual meetings of the Conference on College Composition and Communication (CCCC) and the National Council of Teachers of English (NCTE—Fall and Spring conventions) are included. Papers delivered at other regional and national meetings—for example, meetings of the American Educational Research Association (AERA), the International Reading Association (IRA), and the Modern Language Association (MLA)—are selected for inclusion on the basis of their substantiveness and relevance.

Reference value. Items for which the ERIC microfiche system might provide unique access are included. Representative of entries meeting this criterion would be books or collections of articles no longer available from their original publishers.

Alternate access. Many professional organizations regularly make copies of book and monograph publications available as ERIC microfiche. And many papers presented as reports or conference talks and available in ERIC are later published as monographs or as articles in journals. When such information is available, the entry in this volume will include ERIC ED numbers to indicate an alternate source of access to the document. However, users of this volume should keep in mind that, although a book in ERIC reflects the exact contents of the published work, an article in ERIC is a manuscript that may see substantial revision before it is published.

The following criteria determine which items cited in *RIE* are excluded from this volume:

Communication theory. ERIC documents broadly concerned with human communication or with language study in general, rather than with college composition and rhetoric, are routinely excluded.

Local interest. ERIC documents concerned with composition and rhetoric but judged to be primarily of local interest are excluded. For example, this volume omits annual evaluation reports of writing programs in local schools.

Availability. Publications of commercial publishers and other organizations that are listed in *RIE* and assigned an ERIC ED number but are not available through the ERIC microfiche system are omitted.

Users of the *CCCC Bibliography* may wish to supplement this resource by consulting *RIE* or various computer-assisted retrieval systems that access ERIC documents. Copies of most documents indexed in *RIE* can be purchased in paper or microform from the ERIC system. ERIC clearinghouses also make available free or inexpensive guides to special topics of interest to rhetoric and composition teachers and researchers. Order forms and current addresses for these clearinghouses appear at the back of each monthly issue of *RIE*.

A few entries in this volume show publication dates earlier than 1988. By and large, these materials have two sources. They represent articles published in 1988 but appearing in journals showing earlier volume numbers, or they represent materials accessioned by ERIC clearinghouses in 1988 but originally published earlier.

Authors, publishers, and editors may send offprints of articles, copies of books and journals, or microforms to me for possible inclusion in the *CCCC Bibliography;* however, I will be unable to return them.

The items listed in the annual bibliography are not housed in any single location or owned by any single individual. The *CCCC Bibliography* lists and describes these materials but does not provide users of the bibliography any additional means of retrieving them. However, users of this volume will find librarians extremely helpful in finding copies of particular works to examine firsthand. Some materials may be available through interlibrary loan, OCLC and on-line catalogues, ERIC and other information retrieval systems, or in state and university libraries. To locate materials cited in this volume, ask your librarian to help you.

CONTRIBUTING BIBLIOGRAPHERS

The reliability and usefulness of these annual volumes depend primarily on a large group of contributing bibliographers, listed on pages xi to xii. Contributing bibliographers accept responsibility for compiling accurate entries in their areas of expertise, for preparing brief, descriptive annotations for each entry, for determining where each entry will appear within one of the five sections of the bibliography, for cross-referencing entries when appropriate, and for submitting completed entries by a specified deadline.

To ensure consistency, contributing bibliographers receive a *Handbook for Contributing Bibliographers* to guide them in their work and fill out a printed form for each entry. Contributing bibliographers agree to serve a three-year term and, thereafter, may request reappointment for another two-year term. In return for their valuable service to the profession, they receive a copy of each annual volume they have helped to prepare. Graduate students, teachers, researchers, or other individuals who wish to become contributing bibliographers may write to me.

ANNOTATIONS

Annotations accompany all entries in this volume. They describe the document's contents and are intended to help users determine the document's usefulness. Annotations are brief: up to fifty words for books and up to twenty-five words for all other documents. Insofar as the English language allows, annotations are also meant to be descriptive, not evaluative. They explain what the work is about but leave readers free to judge for themselves the work's merits. Most annotations fall into one of three categories: they present the document's thesis, main argument, or major research finding; they describe the work's major organizational divisions; or they indicate the purpose or scope of the work.

CROSS-REFERENCES AND INDEXES

This volume cites and annotates each document only once, in one of the five major sections of the bibliography. Every entry, however, re-ceives an "entry number" so that cross-references to other sections are possible. Cross-references are necessary because much scholarship in composition and rhetoric is interdisciplinary. Cross-references appear as a listing of entry numbers preceded by "See also," found at the end of each subsection of the bibliography.

The Subject Index lists most of the topics discussed in the works cited in this volume. Consulting the Subject Index may help users locate sections and subsections of the bibliography that contain large numbers of entries addressing the same topic.

The Name Index lists all authors, editors, and contributors to publications cited in this volume.

ACKNOWLEDGMENTS

A publication of this scope depends on many people, especially those who offer advice, encouragement, and criticism during its planning and preparation. I am grateful to the CCCC Officers, CCCC Executive Committee members, and colleagues in the profession whose confidence in this project have made it possible. The contributing bibliographers also deserve thanks for their significant efforts, work often made troublesome because deadlines were demanding and some materials difficult to locate. The Department of English at the University of North Carolina—Chapel Hill offered generous and welcome financial support. Larry Mason contributed important technical help in computer programming. Mary Beth Harding provided invaluable editorial assistance; an expert, intelligent, and remarkably thorough bibliographer, she has made the daily work of preparing this volume a pleasure. Finally, my thanks to Kenney Withers, Susan Wilson, Chris Bucci, and James Simmons of Southern Illinois University Press for their sound editorial advice and their extraordinary commitment to publishing works important to the profession.

Contributing Bibliographers

Jim Addison
Clara Alexander
Ken Autry
Walter Beale
Richard Behm
Thomas Bidwell
Laurel Black
Virginia A. Book
Jody Brown
Lady Falls Brown
Stuart Brown
Mary Louise Buley-Meissner
Vicki Byard
Barbara Cambridge
Cora Castaldi
James R. Cichoracki
Gregory Clark
John Clifford
Joseph Colavito
Edith Baker Crow
Donneva Crowell
Richard Cummins
Susan Currier
Rick Cypert
Donald A. Daiker

Thomas E. Dasher
Kenneth W. Davis
Susan S. Davis
Dan Dawson
Holly Roberts Dawson
Bonnie Devet
Judith Dobler
William M. Dodd
Robert Donahoo
Suellynn Duffey
Lisa Eary
Marisa Esposito
Chuck Etheridge
Timothy J. Evans
Janis Forman
Richard Fulkerson
Patricia Goubil Gambrell
Roger Gilles
Beate Gilliar
Joan I. Glazer
Judith Goleman
Gwendolyn Gong
Alice Goodwin
Perry M. Gordon
Mary C. Graham

Meredith Green
Barbara Griffin
C. W. Griffin
Nedra Grogan
Evonne Kay Halasek
Anne-Marie Hall
Cynthia Hallen
Judy Halverson
Kathy Haney
Jim Hanlon
Kristine Hansen
Tori Haring-Smith
Jeanette Harris
Sarah E. Harrold
Patrick Hartwell
Gary Hatch
Cozette Heller
John F. Heyda
Dona Hickey
Dixie Elise Hickman
Betsy Hilbert
Deborah H. Holdstein
Sylvia A. Holladay
Pamela Holland
Elizabeth Huettman

C. Mark Hurlbert
David Hutto
Jack Jobst
Patricia Kedzerski
Rose Marie Kinder
Joyce Kinkead
James Kinney
Alexandra R. Krapels
Elizabeth Larsen
Janice M. Lauer
Naton Leslie
Steven Lynn
Kate Mangelsdorf
Stefan E. Martin
Rhoda Maxwell
Ben W. McClelland
Geraldine McNenny
Stephen Merrill
Vincent P. Mikkelsen
Corinne L. Miller
Susan Miller
Nancye Mitchell
Pamela Moravec
Max Morenberg

Joseph M. Moxley
Quin Myers
Neil Nakadate
Terence Odlin
Rory J. Ong
Peggy Parris
Michael A. Pemberton
Elizabeth F. Penfield
Pamela Pittman
Virginia G. Polanski
Deborah Pope
James Postema
John W. Presley
Paul W. Ranieri
Rebecca Rickly
Duane Roen
Audrey J. Roth
Sara Lyles Sanders
Judith Scheffler
Marianne Sciachitano
Cynthia L. Selfe
Yolan Shetty
Barbara M. Sitko

Penelope Smith
Susan Smith
Barbara Stedman
Gail Stygall
Patricia Sullivan
Suzanne Swiderski
Dan J. Tannacito
Josephine K. Tarvers
Nathaniel Teich
Valerie Tencza
Laura Thomas
John Trimbur
Myron Tuman
Elizabeth Vanderlei
Billie J. Wahlstrom
Robert H. Weiss
Jackie Wheeler
James D. Williams
Michael M. Williamson
David E. Wilson
J. Randal Woodland
Mindy Wright
Michael Zerbe

Journal Abbreviations

A&E	Anthropology and Education Quarterly
AdEd	Adult Education
AdLBEd	Adult Literacy and Basic Education
AERJ	American Educational Research Journal
AmP	American Psychologist
ArEB	Arizona English Bulletin
AS	American Speech
ASch	The American Scholar
BABC	Bulletin of the American Business Communication Association
BADE	Bulletin of the Association of Departments of English
BL	Brain and Language
CAC	Computer-Assisted Composition Journal
CalE	California English
CC	Computers and Composition
CCC	College Composition and Communication
CE	College English
CEAC	CEA Critic

CEAF	CEA Forum
CHE	Chronicle of Higher Education
CHum	Computers and the Humanities
CJL	Canadian Journal of Linguistics
CLAJ	College Languages Association Journal
Cognition	Cognition
CollL	College Literature
CollM	Collegiate Microcomputer
CollT	College Teaching
ComEd	Communication Education
ComM	Communication Monographs
CompC	Composition Chronicle
ComQ	Communication Quarterly
ComR	Communication Research
CPsy	Cognitive Psychology
CSc	Cognitive Science
CSSJ	Central States Speech Journal
CSWQ	The Quarterly of the National Writing Project and the Center for the Study of Writing
Daedalus	Daedalus
DAI	Dissertation Abstracts International

DPr	Discourse Processes
EdPsy	Educational Psychologist
EEd	English Education
EngT	English Today
EQ	English Quarterly
ESP	English for Specific Purposes
ETC	ETC: A Review of General Semantics
ExEx	Exercise Exchange
FEN	Freshman English News
Focuses	Focuses
FS	Feminist Studies
GR	Georgia Review
HCR	Human Communication Research
HD	Human Development
HER	Harvard Educational Review
HT	History Teacher
IlEB	Illinois English Bulletin
Intell	Intelligence
IPM	Information Processing and Management
Issues	Issues in Writing
JAC	Journal of Advanced Composition
JBC	Journal of Business Communication
JBTC	Iowa Journal of Business and Technical Communication
JBW	Journal of Basic Writing
JC	Journal of Communication
JCBI	Journal of Computer-Based Instruction
JCS	Journal of Curriculum Studies
JCST	Journal of College Science Teaching
JDEd	Journal of Developmental Education
JEd	Journal of Education
JEdM	Journal of Educational Measurement
JEdP	Journal of Educational Psychology
JEdR	Journal of Educational Research
JEPG	Journal of Experimental Psychology: General
JEPH	Journal of Experimental Psychology: Human Perception and Performance
JEPL	Journal of Experimental Psychology: Learning, Memory, Cognition
JGE	JGE: The Journal of General Education
JMEd	Journal of Medical Education
JML	Journal of Memory and Language
JNT	Journal of Narrative Technique
JourEd	Journalism Educator
JPsy	Journal of Psychology
JPsyR	Journal of Psycholinguistic Research
JR	Journal of Reading
JT	Journal of Thought
JTW	Journal of Teaching Writing
JTWC	Journal of Technical Writing and Communication
Lang&S	Language and Style
LangS	Language Sciences
Leaflet	The Leaflet
Learning	Learning
LSoc	Language in Society
MCQ	Management Communication Quarterly
MEd	Medical Education
MLJ	The Modern Language Journal
MLQ	Modern Language Quarterly
MLS	Modern Language Studies
MM	Media and Methods
MT	Mathematics Teacher
P&L	Philosophy and Literature
P&R	Philosophy and Rhetoric
PhiDK	Phi Delta Kappan
PMLA	Publication of the Modern Language Association
PMS	Perceptual and Motor Skills
PPR	Philosophy and Phenomenological Research
PsyR	Psychological Review
PsyT	Psychology Today
PT	Poetics Today
QRD	Quarterly Review of Doublespeak
Raritan	Raritan
Reader	Reader

RER	Review of Educational Research	TECFORS	TECFORS
Rhetorica	Rhetorica	TESOLQ	Teachers of English to Speakers of Other Languages Quarterly
RR	Rhetoric Review	TETYC	Teaching English in the Two-Year College
RRQ	Reading Research Quarterly		
RSQ	Rhetoric Society Quarterly	TWT	Technical Writing Teacher
RTE	Research in the Teaching of English	VLang	Visible Language
		WAC	Writing across the Curriculum
SAm	Scientific American	WC	Written Communication
SCJ	Southern Communication Journal	WCJ	Writing Center Journal
		WI	Writing Instructor
SFS	Science Fiction Studies	WJSC	Western Journal of Speech Communication
SLang	Studies in Language		
SNNTS	Studies in the Novel	WLN	Writing Lab Newsletter
ST	Science Teacher	WPA	Journal of the Council of Writing Program Administrators
Style	Style		
SubStance	SubStance	WS	Women's Studies

Abbreviations in Entries

ABC	Association for Business Communication	ESP	English for Specific Purposes
ABE	Adult Basic Education	EST	English for Science and Technology
ACT	American College Test	ETS	Educational Testing Service
ACTFL	American Council on the Teaching of Foreign Languages	FIPSE	Fund for the Improvement of Postsecondary Education
ADE	Association of Departments of English	GED	General Education Development
AERA	American Educational Research Association	GPA	Grade Point Average
		GRE	Graduate Record Examination
APA	American Psychological Association	IRA	International Reading Association
		LEP	Limited English Proficiency
CAI	Computer-Assisted Instruction	LES	Limited English Speaking
CCCC	Conference on College Composition and Communication	L1	First Language
		L2	Second Language
		MCAT	Medical College Admission Test
CEE	Conference on English Education	MLA	Modern Language Association
CSW	Center for the Study of Writing	NAEP	National Assessment of Educational Progress
EDRS	ERIC Document Reproduction Service	NCTE	National Council of Teachers of English
EFL	English as a Foreign Language		
ERIC	Educational Resources Information Center	NEA	National Education Association
		NEH	National Endowment for the Humanities
ERIC/RCS	ERIC Clearinghouse on Reading and Communication Skills	NIE	National Institute of Education
ESL	English as a Second Language	NIH	National Institute of Health

SAT	Scholastic Aptitude Test		of Other Languages
SCA	Speech Communication	TOEFL	Test of English as a Foreign
	Association		Language
SLATE	Support for the Learning and	TSWE	Test of Standard Written English
	Teaching of English	WPA	Council of Writing Program
TESOL	Teachers of English to Speakers		Administrators

CCCC
Bibliography of Composition and Rhetoric
1988

1
Bibliographies and Checklists

1 BIBLIOGRAPHIES AND CHECKLISTS

1. Anson, Chris M., and Hildy Miller. "Journals in Composition: An Update." *CCC* 39 (May 1988): 198–216.

   Gives publication information, targeted readership, a brief description of subjects, subscription costs, and addresses for 97 journals, including interdisciplinary ones.

2. Appleby, Bruce. "Word Processing and Beyond." *MM* 25 (September–October 1988): 7–8, 93–95.

   Evaluates recent word processing programs, describing 29 of them in chart form.

3. "Basic Reading List for Cicero's Rhetorica." *Rhetorica* 6 (Summer 1988): 326–328.

   A bibliography of texts and commentaries as well as secondary works.

4. *Bibliographic Guide to Education*. Boston: G. K. Hall, 1988.

   An annual bibliography listing material recorded on the OCLC tapes of Columbia University Teachers College during the year, supplemented by listings for selected publications from New York Public Library. Covers all aspects of education, including composition pedagogy.

5. Book, Virginia A. "1987 ATTW Bibliography." *TWT* 15 (Fall 1988): 244–268.

   Lists entries in eight categories: bibliographies, book reviews, the profession, theory and philosophy, research, pedagogy, and communication in the profession.

6. Caras, Pauline. "Literature and Computers: A Short Bibliography, 1980–1987." *CollL* 15 (Winter 1988): 69–82.

   An unannotated bibliography of 203 entries. Includes books, articles, and journals.

7. Chapman, David. "Checklist of Writing Center Scholarship: April 1987–March 1988." *WCJ* 9 (Fall-Winter 1988): 61–66.

Includes scholarship "of interest to those who administer, work in, or make use of writing centers."

8. Collins, Mary Ellen. *Education Journals and Serials: An Analytical Guide*. Annotated Bibliographies of Serials: A Subject Approach, no. 12. Westport, Conn.: Greenwood Press, 1988. 384 pages

   An annotated bibliography of national and international scholarly journals. Designed to assist scholars and other professionals in submitting manuscripts or choosing journals to read.

9. Cress, Cynthia J. *Bibliography of Vocabulary Frequency and Wordset Analysis Studies*. Madison, Wis.: University of Wisconsin–Madison Trace Center, June 1986. ERIC ED 289 318. 45 pages

   Offers an annotated bibliography of studies of word and letter frequencies and of vocabulary applications based on issues of word frequency.

10. Jones, Nancy. "Bibliography of Composition, 1940–1949." *RSQ* Special Issue No. 2 (1987).

    An unannotated listing of 612 books, articles, monographs, and pamphlets published in the 1940s on the theory, practice, and teaching of composition.

11. Larson, Richard L. "Selected Bibliography of Scholarship on Composition and Rhetoric, 1987." *CCC* 39 (October 1988): 316–336.

    Lists and annotates 70 journal articles and anthologized essays as well as 11 monographs and books.

12. Lindemann, Erika, ed. *Longman Bibliography of Composition and Rhetoric, 1986*. Longman Series in Composition and Rhetoric. White Plains, N.Y.: Longman, 1988. 249 pages

    An annotated list of 2724 works grouped into six categories: bibliographies and checklists; theory and research; the education and professional environments of composition teachers; curriculum; textbooks

and instructional materials; and the assessment of writing and its teaching.

13. Marshall, James D., and Russel K. Durst. "Annotated Bibliography of Research in the Teaching of English." *RTE* 22 (May 1988): 213–227.

    Lists and annotates studies appearing in 1986 and 1987. Groups them in four areas: writing, language, literature, and teacher education.

14. McBride, Donald L. "Twentieth-Century Publications on Richard Whately: A Bibliography." *RSQ* 18 (Fall 1988): 205–208.

    Thirty-seven entries addressing Whately's rhetorical analysis.

15. Morton, Herbert C., Ann J. Price, Jane Rosenberg, Deborah Styles, Carol Tenopir, Bettina Hagen, and Judith Mayers. *Writings on Scholarly Communications: An Annotated Bibliography of Books and Articles on Publishing, Libraries, Scholarly Research, and Related Issues*. Lanham, Md.: University Press of America and the American Council of Learned Societies, 1988. 158 pages

    Seeks to identify the literature of common interest to scholars, librarians, publishers, and others concerned with the advancement of learning in the humanities and social sciences. Annotates more than 100 books and journals.

16. O'Brien, Nancy Patricia. *Test Construction: A Bibliography of Selected Resources*. Westport, Conn.: Greenwood Press, 1988. 320 pages

    Lists over 2700 entries on test development, design, and construction. Includes a section on English testing.

17. "Portfolio Assessment: An Annotated Bibliography." *CSWQ* 10 (October 1988): 23–25.

    Lists 14 entries published from 1983 to 1987.

18. Presley, John W., and William M. Dodd. "Business Writing in the Social Sciences: A

Checklist of Dissertations, 1984–1986." *BABC* 51 (March 1988): 32–34.

An annotated bibliography of dissertations in social sciences that relate to composition and rhetoric.

19. Silva, Tony. "Comments on Vivian Zamel's 'Recent Research on Writing Pedagogy' [*TESOLQ* 21 (December 1987)], A Reader Responds." *TESOLQ* 22 (September 1988): 517–520.

Maintains that Zamel does not differentiate between L1 and L2 composing and is biased toward qualitative research.

20. Stafford, Carl. "Audio Visual Update." *MM* 25 (November–December 1988): 28–31.

Describes new projectors, video cameras, computers, and interactive video discs.

21. Weaver, Barbara. "Bibliography of Writing Textbooks." *WPA* 11 (Spring 1988): 59–76.

An annotated bibliography of 195 developmental, freshman, advanced, and professional writing textbooks published from 1987 to 1988. Includes some computer software sold as texts for writing courses.

22. "Who's Who in Educational Media." *MM* 25 (November–December 1988): 57–67.

Lists names, addresses, and telephone numbers for producers and distributors of educational audiovisual hardware and software.

23. Woods, Donald R. "Books, Courses, Research." *JCST* 17 (December 1987–January 1988): 241–243.

An annotated bibliography of problem-solving research. Also gives suggestions for incorporating problem-solving instruction into the classroom.

24. Zamel, Vivian. "Comments on Vivian Zamel's 'Recent Research on Writing Pedagogy' [*TESOLQ* 21 (December 1987)], The Author Responds." *TESOLQ* 22 (September 1988): 520–524.

Maintains that effective writing instruction goes beyond L1 and L2 differences. Underscores support of ethnographic research.

See also 1083

2
Theory and Research

2.1 RHETORICAL THEORY, DISCOURSE THEORY, AND COMPOSING

25. Anderson, Chris. "Hearsay Evidence and Second-Class Citizenship." *CE* 50 (March 1988): 300–308.

> Defines the essay as democratic, without pedantry, and not professional, allowing a freedom of movement precluded by scholarly writing.

26. Andres, Laura Gay. "The Authentic I: A Theory of Expressive Writing." *DAI* 49 (September 1988): 447A.

> Attempts to define expressive discourse and distinguish it from other aims. Distinguishing features include a three-part phenomenological self, an emotionally valued goal, and features of style.

27. Angus, Ian H., and John W. Lannamann. "Questioning the Institutional Boundaries of U.S. Communication Research: An Episte-

mological Inquiry." *JC* 38 (Summer 1988): 62–74.

> Seeks to define the domain of communication study and research.

28. Aston, Jean Ann. "A Participant Observer Case Study Conducted in a Traditional Developmental Writing Class in an Urban Community College of High Risk, Nontraditional Women Students Who Demonstrate Apprehension about Error Production." *DAI* 6 (December 1988): 1392A.

> Shows that the fear of risking error constrains fluency and that students develop counter-productive strategies to deal with the teacher's corrections.

29. Barnett, Judith Curran. "Toward a Rationale for Teaching Expressive Discourse." *DAI* 49 (December 1989): 1355A.

> Synthesizes Hegel's dialectics of consciousness and self-consciousness and Dewey's conception of reflective thinking. Then situates the discussion in Kinneavy's aims of discourse.

30. Barrios, Michael Vincent. "Writer's Block and Blocked Writers." *DAI* 49 (December 1988): 2369B.

   A descriptive and intervention study of 45 writers. Examines writer's block as a combination of personality, environment, and writing task.

31. Bate, Barbara, and Anita Taylor, eds. *Women Communicating: Studies of Women's Talk.* Communication and Information Science. Norwood, N.J.: Ablex, 1988. 321 pages

   A collection of 14 studies examining the communication of women with other women in a variety of settings: health clinics, political campaigns, a weavers guild, a basketball team, a university tutoring center, an arts organization, a production company, and a feminist bookstore-coffeehouse, among other contexts.

32. Bator, Paul G. "The 'Good Reasons Movement': A 'Confounding' of Dialectic and Rhetoric? [Response to Crusius, *P&R* 19 (First Quarter 1986)]." *P&R* 21 (First Quarter 1988): 38–47.

   Defends Perelman's and Booth's theories, which Bator asserts have been misrepresented and criticized.

33. Baumlin, James S. "Persuasion, Rogerian Rhetoric, and Imaginative Play." *RSQ* 17 (Winter 1987): 33–43.

   Argues that persuasion is impossible in any model of discourse that views the self as a single, fixed entity. Imaginative play and Rogerian sympathetic understanding can mediate between rhetoric-as-opposition and rhetoric-as-identification.

34. Bazerman, Charles. "What Are We Doing as a Research Community?" *RR* 7 (Spring 1989): 223–293.

   Reports on a symposium held during the 1988 CCCC Convention. Explains research methods used to study writing, contrasts their similarities and differences, and proposes further research.

35. Beckham, Jean C., Joyce Lynn Carbonell, and David J. Gustafson. "Are There Sex Differences in Problem Solving? An Investigation of Problem Context and Sex Role Type." *JPsy* 122 (January 1988): 21–32.

   Uses the Bem Sex-Role Inventory and SAT scores to interpret the results of "analytical insight problems" administered to 80 men and 80 women.

36. Bereiter, Carl, P. J. Burtis, and Marlene Scardamalia. "Cognitive Operations in Constructing Main Points in Written Composition." *JML* 27 (June 1988): 261–278.

   Examines this process in skilled adults and less skilled elementary school writers.

37. Berkenkotter, Carol, Thomas N. Huckin, and Jon Ackerman. "Conventions, Conversation, and the Writer: Case Study of a Student in a Rhetoric Ph.D. Program." *RTE* 22 (February 1988): 9–44.

   Examines the acquisition of disciplinary discourse conventions, including both linguistic text features and procedural knowledge.

38. Bernstein, Cynthia G. "The Internal Audience in Literary and Rhetorical Discourse." *DAI* 48 (June 1988): 3099A.

   Identifies three purposes for internal and external audiences, stressing their relationship to how internal audience is used in the discourse genre.

39. Berthoff, Ann E. "Response to Winterowd [*CE* 49 (March 1987)]." *CE* 50 (January 1988): 95–96.

   Challenges Winterowd's claims regarding the origins of vitalist philosophy and his assertion that her textbook exemplifies vitalism.

40. Blankenship, James. "I. A. Richards's 'Context' Theorem of Meaning." *RSQ* 18 (Fall 1988): 153–158.

   Discusses the importance of "global context" in Richards's work.

41. Blau, Sheridan. "Freeing Attention and Focusing Concentration through Invisible Writing: An Experimental Mode of Free Writing." Paper presented at the CCCC Convention, New Orleans, March 1986. ERIC ED 288 201. 15 pages

    Reports on an experiment involving 100 writing teachers. Finds that invisible writing, whereby writers cannot see what they write, focuses attention on content.

42. Bocchi, Joseph. "The Collective Concept of Audience in Nonacademic Settings." Paper presented at the CCCC Convention, St. Louis, March 1988. ERIC ED 293 150. 11 pages

    Treating audience analysis as a social rather than a cognitive process equips students to realize situational and organizational constraints in writing.

43. Bohman, James. "Emancipation and Rhetoric: The Perlocutions and Illocutions of the Social Critic." *P&R* 21 (Summer 1988): 185–204.

    Argues for an intermediate class of speech acts to show how features of both perlocutionary and illocutionary acts function in the rhetoric of social criticism.

44. Branscomb, H. Eric. "A Descriptive Study of the Process of Superordination in Community College Writers." *DAI* 48 (January 1988): 1757A.

    Studies cognitive processes in series drafting. Concludes that separate superordinating processes are not needed by basic or advanced writers.

45. Brooke, Robert. "Robert Brooke Responds [to Hiller and Osburg, *CE* 49 (October 1987)]." *CE* 50 (November 1988): 820–822.

    Defends his style of writing as a product of his discourse community, institutional position, and goal in writing instruction.

46. Brunner, Daniel K. "Case Studies in Two Contexts: Self-Sponsored Writers' Subjective Impressions of Written Fluency." *DAI* 48 (February 1988): 2006A.

    Examines the act of writing and the conditions that facilitate the development of written fluency. Discusses the relationship of language and thought.

47. Burgoon, Judee K., and Jerold L. Hale. "Nonverbal Expectancy Violations: Model Elaboration and Application to Immediacy Behaviors." *ComM* 55 (March 1988): 58–79.

    Compares the model to similar theoretical models, broadening its underpinnings with the results of an experimental study.

48. Burrell, Nancy A., William A. Donohue, and Mike Allen. "Gender-Based Perceptual Biases in Mediation." *ComR* 15 (August 1988): 447–469.

    Finds that trained mediators of both sexes use equally controlling strategies although disputants perceived males as more controlling. Untrained females were more controlling but were perceived as being less controlling.

49. Camitta, Miriam P. "Invented Lives: Adolescent Vernacular Writing and the Construction of Experience." *DAI* 49 (August 1988): 318A.

    Investigates vernacular writing among urban adolescents as it is traditionally and variously practiced as part of everyday behavior.

50. Campbell, J. Louis, III, and Richard Buttny. "Rhetorical Coherence: An Exploration into Thomas Farrell's Theory of Synchrony of Rhetoric." *ComQ* 36 (Fall 1988): 262–275.

    Analyzes rhetorical coherence, the synchronic interdependence of rhetoric and conversation, by examining its failure in a welfare interview.

51. Canary, Daniel J., Ellen M. Cunningham, and Michael J. Cody. "Goal Types, Gender, and Locus of Control in Managing Interpersonal Conflict." *ComR* 15 (August 1988): 426–446.

A study of 434 students examines how the actors' goals, gender, and locus of control affected conflict strategies.

52. Carlson, A. Cheree, and John E. Hocking. "Strategies of Redemption at the Vietnam Veterans' Memorial." *WJSC* 52 (Summer 1988): 203–215.

Analyzes the interplay of goals and strategies in messages left at the Memorial.

53. Carter, Michael. "Problem Solving Reconsidered: A Pluralist Theory of Problems." *CE* 50 (September 1988): 551–565.

Examines the dynamic nature of problems and their corresponding discourse types. Redefines problem solving in composition by critiquing both the information-processing and the epistemic models of what a problem is.

54. Cerulo, Karen A. "What's Wrong with This Picture? Enhancing Communication through Distortion." *ComR* 15 (February 1988): 93–101.

Challenges the assumption that clarity achieves the most effective communication by showing that certain syntactic and semantic types of distortion can enhance communication effectiveness.

55. Chafe, Wallace. "Punctuation and the Prosody of Written Language." *WC* 5 (October 1988): 396–426.

Suggests that certain important aspects of "covert prosody"—auditory imagery of intonation, accents, and hesitations—are part of punctuation.

56. Cherry, Roger D. "*Ethos* Versus Persona: Self-Representation in Written Discourse." *WC* 5 (July 1988): 251–276.

Although *ethos* and *persona* are often used as synonyms, they should be differentiated to improve a critical view of self-representation in writing.

57. Chesebro, James W. "Epistemology and Ontology as Dialectical Modes in the Writings of Kenneth Burke." *ComQ* 36 (Summer 1988): 175–191.

Holds that a solely epistemic view of rhetoric is restrictive and that ontological understandings have been neglected.

58. Cooper, Allene. "Given-New: Enhancing Coherence through Cohesiveness." *WC* 5 (July 1988): 352–367.

Argues that given-new research can be used in process approaches to teaching composition.

59. Cooper, Martha. "Rhetorical Criticism and Foucault's Philosophy of Discursive Events." *CSSJ* 39 (Spring 1988): 1–17.

A critical method for making discursive practice the locus for investigating social processes in constructive functions of discourse.

60. Crusius, Timothy W. "Kenneth Burke's *Auscultation:* A 'De-Struction' of Marxist Dialectic and Rhetoric." *Rhetorica* 6 (Autumn 1988): 355–379.

Presents Burke's critique of Marxist thinking by antithesis and his own complex dialectic of continuity, revealing permanence in change. Contrasts rhetoric with philosophical discourses of modernity.

61. Crusius, Timothy W. "Orality in Kenneth - Burke's Dialectic." *P&R* 21 (Second Quarter 1988): 116–129.

Compares the dialectics of Hegel and Marx. Explains the implications of "print dialectic" and discusses the dialogic dimension of Burke's written discourse.

62. Crusius, Timothy W. "Response to Paul G. Bator [*P&R* 21 (First Quarter 1988)]." *P&R* 21 (Second Quarter 1988): 153–157.

Refutes the claims that he misrepresented the works of Perelman and Booth.

63. Cypert, Rick L. "Readers and Writers: Transacting between Texts in Composition Classes." *DAI* 48 (February 1988): 2006A.

From a reader-response perspective, describes what happens to students between reading and writing about a text.

64. Dasenbrock, Reed Way. "Becoming Aware of the Myth of Presence." *JAC* 8 (1988): 1–11.

   Students need to understand that writing is not speech on paper (Derrida's logocentricism). Tacitly believing such a myth causes many of their errors.

65. Dillard, James Price. "Compliance-Gaining Message-Selection: What Is Our Independent Variable?" *ComM* 55 (June 1988): 162–183.

   Two studies examine the external validity of three analytical approaches.

66. Dobie, Ann B. "Writing Rituals." Paper presented at the CCCC Convention, St. Louis, March 1988. ERIC ED 295 172. 9 pages

   Reports on a study that questioned writers about their writing habits. Explores pedagogical implications.

67. Dryden, Nathan, and Irene June. "The Composing Processes of Five Malaysian ESL-EFL College Writers: A Multimethod Approach." *DAI* 48 (April 1988): 2563A.

   Uses case studies, process-tracing, naturalistic, and quasi-product approaches to examine advanced and intermediate writers.

68. Duran, Robert L., and Lynne Kelly. "The Influence of Communicative Competence on Perceived Task, Social and Physical Attraction." *ComQ* 36 (Winter 1988): 41–49.

   Finds that in dyadic interactions a speaker's communicative competence influenced a stranger's perception of the speaker's attractiveness.

69. Ede, Lisa. "What Is Social about Writing as a Social Process?" Paper presented at the CCCC Convention, St. Louis, March 1988. ERIC ED 293 151. 12 pages

   Criticizes the social constructivist view of writing, finding it questionable in effectiveness and biased in epistemology.

70. Elliot, Audrey Marie White. "Throwing the Well Wrought Urn: The Relationship between Concepts and Evaluation Moves in Revision Processes of Three Writers of Fictional Narratives." *DAI* 49 (December 1988): 1393A.

   Demonstrates a method for understanding the meaning-making aspects of revision. Confirms that revision is a complex of emotional, technical, and rational processes.

71. Englert, Carol, Sharon Stewart, and Elfrieda Hiebert. "Young Writers' Use of Text Structure in Expository Text Generation." *JEdP* 80 (1988): 143–151.

   Examines the ability of writers to generate textually consistent superordinate main ideas and subordinate details for three types of text structures. Better writers possessed more generalized knowledge of text structure.

72. Enholm, Donald K. "The Most Significant Passage for Rhetorical Theory in the Work of I. A. Richards." *RSQ* 18 (Fall 1988): 181–189.

   Discusses the implications of Richards's theory of metaphors.

73. Ewald, Helen Rothschild. "The Implied Reader in Persuasive Discourse." *JAC* 8 (1988): 167–178.

   Counters the common assumption that persuasive discourse is purely addressed to real audiences by using Prince's textual signals of implied readers.

74. Faas, David P. "Rhetorical Antecedents for Persuasive Discourse in the People's Republic of China." *DAI* 48 (June 1988): 3113A.

   Examines rhetorical modes in editorials appearing in two contemporary Chinese newspapers. Finds that traditional persuasive forms date back to Confucian thought.

75. Fahnestock, Jeanne, and Marie Secor. "The Stases in Scientific and Literary Argument." *WC* 5 (October 1988): 427–443.

   Identifying the stases helps determine the rhetoric of disciplines. Scientific discourse usually deals with fact, classification, and cause; literary criticism is problematic.

76. Flower, Linda. "The Construction of Purpose in Writing and Reading." *CE* 50 (September 1988): 528–550.

    Defines purpose for writers as creating complex webs of meaning. Defines purpose for readers as building inferences. Traces the construction and reconstruction of purpose through stages of both processes.

77. Flower, Linda. *Interpretive Acts: Cognition and the Construction of Discourse*. CSW Occasional Paper, no. 1. Berkeley, Calif.: CSW, September 1987. ERIC ED 287 172. 22 pages

    Uses protocol analyses and rhetorical theory to note how readers and writers negotiate meaning.

78. Flower, Linda. *The Role of Task Representation in Reading-to-Write. Reading-to-Write: Exploring a Cognitive and Social Process Series , Report 2*. Berkeley: 1987. ERIC ED 285 206. 41 pages

    Proposes a theory of task representation based on a think-aloud study of how English majors plan to organize their writing. Offers suggestions for teaching.

79. Fontaine, Cheryl L. "The Unfinished Story of the Interpretive Community." *RR* 7 (Fall 1988): 86–96.

    Expresses concern that the original philosophy of "shared authority of social construction" is threatened by a current emphasis on socializing students to academic discourse. Suggests a reconciliation.

80. Foster, David. "What Are We Talking about When We Talk about Composition?" *JAC* 8 (1988): 30–40.

    Compares Hillocks's and Beach and Bridwell's views of composition as empirical science to North's more inclusive view. Sees composition's mixed nature as a strength.

81. Freedman, Sarah W. "Much Composition Research Has Nothing to Do with College Students." *CHE* 34 (1 June 1988): B2.

    Complains that Heller [*CHE* 34 (27 April 1988)] discusses only one area of composition research, college writing. He also presents misinformation about the writing center at the University of California—Berkeley.

82. Fulkerson, Richard. "On Imposed Versus Imitative Form." *JTW* 7 (Fall–Winter 1988): 143–155.

    "Natural order is less effective than imposed order." "All decisions need to rest on audience," including retaining some natural order.

83. Fulwiler, Toby. "Looking and Listening for My Voice." Paper presented at the CCCC Convention, St. Louis, March 1988. ERIC ED 295 161. 7 pages

    Explains whether or not each writer has one authentic voice.

84. Gabin, Rosalind J. "The Most Significant Passage for Rhetoric in the Work of I. A. Richards." *RSQ* 16 (Fall 1988): 167–171.

    Discusses Richards's departure from Aristotle's definition of metaphor.

85. Gannaway, Gloria Jane. "Toward a Critical Theory of Teaching Composition and Cultural Literacy." *DAI* 49 (December 1988): 1393A.

    Argues that "TV culture" hinders the development of thought and language skills. Uses Derrida and Vygotsky to suggest a new paradigm for teaching writing.

86. Gannett, Cinthia Lee. "Gender and Journals: Life and Text in College Composition." *DAI* 48 (January 1988): 1680A.

    Examines the historical and social contexts of journal and diary keeping. Uses three men's and three women's journals to study how gender informs students' attitudes toward language.

87. Garbo, Michael G., and Kenneth N. Cessna. "An Axiological Reinterpretation of

I. A. Richards' Theory of Communication and its Application to the Study of Compliance-Gaining." *SSCJ* 53 (Winter 1988): 121–139.

Analyzes how the concept of choices unites and integrates theories of value and communication.

88. Gates, Rosemary L. "Causality, Community, and the Canons of Reasoning: Classical Rhetoric and Writing across the Curriculum." *JAC* 8 (1988): 137–145.

Treats relationships among *aitia* (scientific causal thinking), enthymeme, example, and *kairos* (right timing).

89. Gaunder, Eleanor P. "Revision Using the Word Processor: Three Case Studies of Experienced Writers." *DAI* 48 (June 1988): 3064A.

Examines the revising patterns of three upper-division college students, illustrating that in the revision process meaning was maintained rather than altered.

90. Gibbs, Raymond, and Rachel A. G. Mueller. "Conversational Sequences and Preference for Indirect Speech Acts." *DPr* 11 (January–March 1988): 101–116.

Prerequests ("Do you sell Marlboros?") serve to remove obstacles to complying with actual requests ("I'll take two packs").

91. Gottlieb, Esther E. "Development Education: Discourse in Relation to Paradigms and Knowledge." *DAI* 49 (October 1988): 969A.

Analyzes functionalist, radical structuralist, radical humanist, and interpretive paradigms of theoretical discourse in development education. Argues that knowledge is constructed by discourse.

92. Griffith, Peter. "The Discourses of English Teaching." *EEd* 20 (December 1988): 191–205.

Explores how the "growth model" of English remains vulnerable to attacks because it has never clearly articulated its ideological and social agenda.

93. Gutierrez, Christine Diane. "The Composing Process of Four College-Aged Ethnic Mi-

nority Basic Writers: A Cognitive, Socio-Cultural Analysis." *DAI* 49 (September 1988): 449A.

Employs ethnographic methods to examine the composing processes of four ethnic minority students admitted provisionally to a postsecondary institution.

94. Haas, Christina. "How the Writing Medium Shapes the Writing Process: Studies of Writers Composing with Pen and Paper and with Word Processing." *DAI* 49 (November 1988): 1081A.

Examines significant differences in the amounts and types of planning during composing.

95. Hansen, Kristine. "Rhetoric and Epistemology in Texts from the Social Sciences: An Analysis of Three Disciplines' Discourse about Modern American Blacks." *DAI* 148 (April 1988): 2561A.

Using three research studies, compares genre, invention, arrangement, and appeals. Then analyzes the authors' arguments for their texts.

96. Harris, Joseph. "The Spectator as Theorist: Britton and the Function of Writing." *EEd* 20 (February 1988): 41–50.

Argues that Britton has isolated the language used in the spectator role. The spectator role should be broadened to include theory development.

97. Haswell, Richard H. "Error and Change in College Student Writing." *WC* 5 (October 1988): 479–499.

Studies impromptu essay performance among college freshmen, sophomores, juniors, and postcollege employees. Students continued to make mistakes, but the errors were part of improvement in writing.

98. Hatlen, Burton. "Michel Foucault and the Discourse(s) of English." *CE* 50 (November 1988): 786–801.

Traces the history of composition and literature as areas of English studies by using Foucault's definition of *discourse*, "a group of rules that are immanent in a practice and define it in its specificity."

99. Hatlen, Burton. "Writing Is a Craft That Can Be Learned, Not an Effortless Outpouring by Geniuses." *CHE* 34 (27 April 1988): B1-B2.

In his youth during the 1950s, Hatlen believed that writing geniuses lived in Paris, producing effortless masterpieces. Now, in middle age, he knows differently.

100. Haught, Kenneth Wayne. "An Analytical and Critical Study of the Function of Contemporary Rhetorical Invention Heuristics with Application to the Theories of Chaïm Perelman and Kenneth Burke." *DAI* 49 (October 1988): 657A.

Creates a taxonomy of four heuristic functions and applies it to Perelman's and Burke's theories to assess their heuristic potential and strength.

101. Hayes, John. "Commentary." *RTE* 22 (February 1988): 99–104.

Reviews Hillocks's *Research on Written Composition*. Finds metanalysis useful but also recommends developing more encompassing theories for writing research.

102. Hays, Janice N., Kathleen M. Brandt, and Kathryn H. Chantry. "The Impact of Friendly and Hostile Audiences on the Argumentative Writing of High School and College Students." *RTE* 22 (December 1988): 391–416.

Analyzes argumentative essays written by high school students and college undergraduates to friendly and hostile audiences. Compares holistic ratings to the Perry Scheme.

103. Heller, Scott. "Growing Field of Composition Research Forges Links to Literature, Psychology, and Other Disciplines." *CHE* 34 (17 April 1988): A4-A6.

Composition teaching and research, long considered unworthy of scholarship, has found its niche by studying composing processes and their importance in other disciplines.

104. Hillard, Van Edward. "The Dialectical Nature of Learning Writing in an Epistemic Rhetoric." *DAI* 48 (April 1988): 2562A.

Discusses language as an imaginative and social construction, particularly as explored by Richards, Langer, and Burke. Examines metaphor as a way of understanding the operation of dialectic.

105. Hillocks, George, Jr. "A Response to the Commentators [*RTE* 22 (February 1988)]." *RTE* 22 (February 1988): 104–108.

Defends his approach in *Research on Written Composition* as a function of the constraints in metanalysis research and of current knowledge about writing research.

106. Hillocks, George, Jr. "Synthesis of Research on Teaching Writing." *Educational Leadership* 44 (May 1987): 71–82.

Synthesizes 20 years of research on the composing process and teaching composition, discussing its implications for curriculum development.

107. Himley, Margaret. "Becoming a Writer: A Documentary Account." *WC* 5 (January 1988): 82–107.

Describes a phenomenological or documentary record of a seven-year-old's writing activity.

108. Hodges, Elizabeth Scott. "Speaking of Writing: A Sociolinguistic Reading of Content and Context in a First-Year College Composition Course." *DAI* 49 (December 1988): 1393A.

Develops a classification system to study how students acquire college-level literacy and what the social workings of a writing classroom are.

109. Horgan, Paul. *Approaches to Writing*. 2d ed. Middleton, Conn.: Wesleyan University Press, 1988. 266 pages

A collection of epigrams from the author's notebooks on the art and act of writing.

110. Huckin, Thomas N., and Linda Hutz Pesante. "Existential *There* ." *WC* 5 (July 1988): 368–391.

A survey of 100,000 words of good writing. Existential *there* is used to "assert existence, to present new information, to introduce topics, and to summarize."

111. Hunter, Paul, and Nadine Pearce. "Reading, Writing, and Gender." *JDEd* 12 (September 1988): 20–26.

A study of 180 drafts written by 10 female college students. Includes suggestions for teaching basic reading and writing.

112. Hunter, Paul, Nadine Pearce, Sue Lee, Shirley Goldsmith, Patricia Feldman, and Holly Weaver. "Competing Epistemologies and Female Basic Writers." *JBW* 7 (Spring 1988): 73–81.

Compares two female groups—10 basic writers and 10 freshman writers—at work on nine drafts. Advocates developing an "intersubjective epistemology" for female writers.

113. Hurlbert, C. Mark. "The Rhetoric of Possessive Individualism." Paper presented at the American Culture Association, New Orleans, March 1988. ERIC ED 296 341. 9 pages

Argues that product and process approaches are both grounded in capitalist ideology.

114. Hythecker, Velma I., Donald F. Dansereau, and Thomas R. Rocklin. "An Analysis of the Processes Influencing the Structured Dyadic Learning Environment." *EdPsy* 23 (1988): 23–37.

Examines the effectiveness of cooperative learning scripts that prescribe a sequence of activities for students working in dyads. Finds that scripts control peer interaction.

115. Isenberg, Joan P., Karen D'Angelo Bromley, and Mary Renck Jalongo. "The Role of Collaboration in Scholarly Writing: A National Survey." Paper presented at the AERA meeting, Washington, D.C., April 1987. ERIC ED 287 873. 43 pages

Surveys 26 scholarly journals and 547 scholars across the curriculum about collaborative writing.

116. Jarboe, Susan. "A Comparison of Input-Output, Process-Output, and Input-Process-Output Models of Small Group Problem-Solving Effectiveness." *ComM* 55 (June 1988): 121–142.

Compares three independent-conditions models with communication models to assess their productivity.

117. Jolliffe, David A., ed. *Advances in Writing Research , vol . 2: Writing in Academic Disciplines*. Writing Research: Multidisciplinary Inquiries into the Nature of Writing. Norwood, N.J.: Ablex, 1988. 258 pages

Six essays report on research that studies how writing functions within academic disciplines. Divided into three parts, the book describes the current state of knowledge about writing in academic disciplines, demonstrates methodologies for conducting writing research in academic fields, and presents three reports of research on writing in English literature classes, the social sciences, and the sciences.

118. Jones, Steven Jeffrey. "The Logic of Question and Answer and the Hermeneutics of Writing." *JAC* 8 (1988): 12–21.

Criticizes cognitivist approaches to composition. Views writing as a language game whose socially contextualized rules lead from statement to question to interpretation to generative response.

119. Juncker, Clara. "Clara Juncker Responds [to Raschke, *CE* 50 (April 1988)]." *CE* 50 (November 1988): 825–827.

Defends her position, that Cixousian writing instruction allows discovery of the "self" and "other" without defining writers by their genders.

120. Keene, Michael, and L. Bensel-Meyers. "The Establishment of Rhetoric: Developing a Sense of Community." *JAC* 8 (1988): 41–49.

Argues that the best relationship among composition specialties is mutually enlightening community. Composition, including writing across the curriculum, belongs in English departments.

121. Kellogg, Ronald T. "Attentional Overload and Writing Performance: Effects of Rough Draft and Outline Strategies." *JEPL* 14 (April 1988): 355–365.

Experiments show that both mental and written outlines but not rough drafts improve writing quality and decrease attentional overload.

122. Kellogg, Ronald T. "Knowledge and Strategy in Writing." Paper presented at the Annual Meeting of the Psychonomic Society, Seattle, November 1987. ERIC ED 293 155. 27 pages

Supports the hypothesis that knowledge of language and the use of a prewriting strategy independently affect writing quality and efficiency.

123. Kelly, Leonard P. "Relative Automaticity without Mastery: The Grammatical Decision Making of Deaf Students." *WC* 5 (July 1988): 325–351.

Suggests that deaf students devote "substantially less attention to grammatical decision making during composition."

124. Kelly, Leonard P., and Thomas W. Nolan. "Using the Three-Sigma Limit to Identify Significantly Long Pauses during Composing." Paper presented at the AERA Convention, Washington, D.C., April 1987. ERIC ED 288 339. 12 pages

Observes 10 deaf and five hearing college students as they compose. Finds the pause rate measure adequate to identify interruptions.

125. Kerby, Anthony P. "The Adequacy of Self-Narration: A Hermeneutical Approach." *P&L* 12 (October 1988): 232–244.

Analyzes interrelationships between a sense of self, experiences, and narratives that embody them. Finds that we give life a meaning that surpasses a mere recounting of events.

126. Kertzer, J. M. "Rhetorical Questions: Consensus, Authority, Enigma." *Lang & S* 20 (Summer 1987): 242–256.

Analyzes how rhetorical questions change the conditions imposed by ordinary questions, influencing the consensus between speaker and responder, the authority of the responder, and contextual limitations.

127. King, Andrew. "The Most Significant Passage in I. A. Richards for the Theory and Practice of Rhetoric." *RSQ* 18 (Fall 1988): 159–162.

Sees the rhetoric's obsession with the text as object and with the theory of interanimation as flawed offshoots of Richards's theory that language has a formative function.

128. Kintsch, Walter. "The Role of Knowledge in Discourse Comprehension: A Construction-Integration Model." *PsyR* 95 (1988): 163–182.

Argues for a model of initial processing in reading that is bottom-up rather than expectation-driven or top-down.

129. Kirsch, Gesa. "Audience Awareness and Authority: A Study of Experienced Writers Composing for Contrasting Audiences." *DAI* 49 (December 1988): 1394A.

Reports that writers analyze audience more frequently when writing for freshmen. They evaluate their goals more frequently when writing for faculty members.

130. Kirsch, Gesa. "Students' Interpretations of Writing Tasks: A Case Study." *JBW* 7 (Fall 1988): 81–90.

Provides evidence that "successful interpretation of writing tasks . . . demands writers' authority, confidence, and knowledge of rhetorical choices."

131. Kleine, Michael. "The Rhetoric of *I Am an Alcoholic* : Three Perspectives." *RSQ* 17 (Spring 1987): 151–165.

Examines a single rhetorical act, "I am an alcoholic," from the perspectives of the new rhetoric, speech-act theory, and social construction.

132. Kneupper, Charles W. "The Referential-Emotive Distinction: A Significant Passage for Understanding I. A. Richards." *RSQ* 18 (Fall 1988): 173–179.

    Discusses Richards's classification of emotive language as separate from referential language, a precursor to Kenneth Burke's concept of language as motive.

133. Knoblauch, C. H. "Rhetorical Constructions: Dialogue and Commitment." *CE* 50 (February 1988): 125–140.

    Applies Freire's concept of *praxis* to four rhetorical statements: ontological, objectivist, expressionist, and sociological. Explores how these statements have validated and transformed instruction.

134. Knutson, Peter Reinhardt. " 'You Take Serious What's Said in Play!' Systematic Distortion of Communication on a Fishing Boat." *DAI* 48 (June 1988): 3144A.

    Contends that, even in social contexts structured by a command relationship, the claims of reciprocity presupposed in making a communicative act cannot be avoided.

135. Krayer, Karl J. "Whither Applied Interpersonal Communication Research?: A Practical Perspective for Practicing Practitioners." *SSCJ* 53 (Summer 1988): 339–343.

    Calls for examining the direction and presentation of research to benefit consumers, scholars, and practitioners.

136. Lauer, Janice, and J. William Asher. *Composition Research: Empirical Designs.* New York: Oxford University Press, 1988. 302 pages

    Explains eight empirical research designs, illustrating each with two or three composition studies and clarifying the technical issues researchers must address.

137. Logue, Cal M., and Thurmon Garner. "Shift in Rhetorical Status of Blacks after Freedom." *SCJ* 54 (Fall 1988): 1–39.

    Analyzes relationships among the credibility of individuals and groups, their status, and resulting strategies in written and spoken language.

138. Long, Debra, and Arthur Graesser. "Wit and Humor in Discourse Processing." *DPr* 11 (January–March 1988): 35–60.

    Speech-act theory can clarify the semantic basis of humorous discourse. Understanding such discourse may require parallel processing strategies.

139. Manning, Alan D. "Literary Versus Technical Writing: Substitute Versus Standards for Reality." *JTWC* 18 (1988): 241–262.

    Argues that literary and technical writing can be distinguished by their perceived relationship to reality and by the type of detail that predominates.

140. Markel, Michael H. "The Writing Process Teaching the Writing Process Revising." *CE* 50 (September 1988): 509–510.

    Written as a freewriting, attempts to understand students' difficulties with revising.

141. Martin, Michele. "Communication and Social Forms: A Study of the Development of the Telephone System, 1876–1920." *DAI* 48 (May 1988): 2984A.

    Uses a Marxist perspective to analyze interactive means of communication such as the telephone.

142. McCleary, Bill. " 'Best Articles' for 1987 Represent Less Traditional Research Methods." *CompC* 1 (September 1988).

    Summarizes two award-winning articles, an ethnographic study by Robert Brooke and a clinical study by Paul Hunter and Nadine Pearce.

143. McNabb, Scott E. "Revision Processes of Four Skilled College Writers." *DAI* 48 (June 1988): 3042A.

    Finds that skilled writers revise by elaborating initial ideas, learn more from seeing the revisions of others, and appreciate positive teacher feedback.

144. McNamee, Sheila. "Accepting Research as Social Intervention: Implications of a Systemic Epistemology." *ComQ* 36 (Winter 1988): 50–68.

Calls for an assessment of communication research by recognizing that research is an interactive process subject to the same assumptions applied to other interactive systems.

145. McPhail, Mark Lawrence. "The Language of Racism: A Contemporary Rhetorical Analysis." *DAI* 48 (March 1988): 2194A.

Examines the relationship between rhetoric and racial interaction. Argues that the problems of racism are intimately connected to problems of language.

146. Meyer, Sam. "Prose by Any Other Name: A Context for Teaching the Rhetoric of Titles." *JAC* 8 (1988): 71–81.

Argues that titling is an integral part of composition. Analyzes four major types with many examples.

147. Mitchell, David B. "The Concepts of Text and Situation in the Reconstruction of Representational Discourse." *DAI* 48 (June 1988): 3127A.

Argues that knowledge is codified in representational texts. Examines how meaning is socially mediated and reconstructed.

148. Moore, Mark Paul. "Rhetoric and Paradox: Seeking Knowledge from the 'Container and Thing Contained.' " *RSQ* 18 (Summer 1988): 15–30.

Investigates the epistemic qualities of paradox when used in argument.

149. Murray, Margaret Thorell. "A Psychoanalytic Study of Narrativity: An Analysis of Academic Discourse in *College English* ." *DAI* 49 (August 1988): 214A.

Using rhetorical, structural, and archetypal analysis, this study examines lead essays appearing in *College English* during 12 years of Ohmann's editorship.

150. Neel, Jasper. *Plato, Derrida, and Writing.* Carbondale, Ill.: Southern Illinois University Press, 1988. 252 pages

Combines a sustained reflection on Plato's *Phaedrus* with a synthesis of Derrida's writing theory in the context of writing pedagogy.

151. Newell, Sara E., and Randall K. Stutman. "The Social Confrontation Episode." *ComM* 55 (September 1988): 266–285.

Focuses on confrontations over violations of social or relational expectations and their resolution through negotiation or management.

152. Ninio, Anat. "The Roots of Narrative: Discussing Recent Events with Very Young Children." *LangS* 10 (1988): 35–52.

Studies the utterances of 24 Hebrew-speaking mothers and their infants.

153. Norman, G. R. "Problem-Solving Skills, Solving Problems, and Problem-Based Learning." *MEd* 22 (July 1988): 279–286.

Reviews the empirical evidence supporting the three concepts given in the article's title. Explores the use of problem-based learning as an educational strategy.

154. North, Stephen M. "A Response to Daniel Voiku [*BADE* 86 (Spring 1987)]." *BADE* 89 (Spring 1988): 72–74.

Faults Voiku for his "vehemence" and simplistic treatment of "traditional" and "process" composition theories.

155. O'Hair, Dan. "Relational Communication in Applied Contexts: Current Status and Future Directions." *SSCJ* 53 (Summer 1988): 317–330.

Reviews definitions and examines applied and basic research.

156. O'Keefe, Barbara J. "The Logic of Message Design: Individual Differences in Reasoning about Communication." *ComM* 55 (March 1988): 80–103.

Presents a non-constructivist model to analyze alternative ways whereby individuals and communities might constitute communication processes.

157. O'Looney, John A. "The Role of Engagement in the Persuasive Writing of Twelfth-Grade Students." *DAI* 48 (May 1988): 2824A.

Findings indicate that a measure of ethical or intellectual development was a significant predictor of writing quality.

158. Palmeri, Anthony Joseph. "Walter J. Ong's Perspectives on Rhetorical Theory." *DAI* 49 (October 1988): 658A.

Reviews Ong's work and offers four reasons for his relevance to contemporary rhetoric.

159. Payne, David. *Coping with Failure: The Therapeutic Uses of Rhetoric*. Studies in Rhetoric and Communication. Columbia: University of South Carolina Press, 1988. 210 pages

Investigates the importance of failure in our ways of talking about and resolving problems through communication. Shows how failure and therapy are interwoven in our views of ourselves and the world and how rhetoric helps us overcome feelings of failure.

160. Perry, David K. "Implications of a Contextualist Approach to Media-Effects Research." *ComR* 15 (June 1988): 246–264.

Summarizes William McGuire's version of contextualism and discusses its implications for research practices.

161. Pettegrew, Loyd S. "The Importance of Context in Applied Communication Research." *SSCJ* 53 (Summer 1988): 331–338.

Advocates setting clear guidelines for reporting research and making rigorous distinctions in terminology surrounding communication phenomena, using typological analysis.

162. Phelps, Louise Wetherbee. *Composition as a Human Science: Contributions to the Self-Understanding of a Discipline*. New York: Oxford University Press, 1988. 272 pages

Attempts to define the contribution and place of composition studies within the larger intellectual and cultural community. Discusses the conceptual and ethical basis for a new discipline of written language and constructs an open framework for the field.

163. Pixton, William H. "The Triangle and the Stance: Toward a Rhetoric of Novice Writers." *RSQ* 17 (Summer 1987): 263–279.

Modifies the communications triangle by listing subordinate elements that reflect "the various operations needed for the production of a satisfactory text."

164. Pomerantz, Anita. "Offering a Candidate Answer: An Information-Seeking Strategy." *ComM* 55 (December 1988): 360–373.

Traces how people analyze situations and how their analyses help them select strategies to elicit information.

165. Pounds, Wayne. "The Context of No Context: A Burkean Critique of Rogerian Argument." *RSQ* 17 (Winter 1987): 45–59.

Uses Burkean concepts of transformation, identification, representation, and symbolic action to critique Rogerian idealism, which "posits the human subject without objective history, without a world."

166. Pryor, Robert Herbert. "Reading Ideology in Discourse: A History, Theory, and Case Study." *DAI* 49 (December 1988): 1312A.

Reviews the history of ideology as a concept in social science and modern rhetorical criticism. Then develops a materialist-semiotic reading of ideology in three texts.

167. Purvell, Kathleen Ann. "Children's Storytelling." *DAI* 48 (February 1988): 2465A.

Studies how children tell stories about families to examine whether instructions and the child's characteristics affect storytelling.

168. Purves, Alan C. "Commentary." *RTE* 22 (February 1988): 104–108.

Generally applauds Hillocks's *Research on Written Composition* for its careful analysis and critique of "comparative studies," but critiques American writing research for narrow, overly simplistic, and culturally biased assumptions.

169. Purves, Alan C. *Writing across Languages and Cultures: Issues in Contrastive Rhetoric*. Written Communication Annual, vol. 2. Edited by Charles R. Cooper and Sidney Greenbaum. Newbury Park, Calif.: Sage, 1988. 304 pages

    A collection of 11 essays treating differences in cultural expectations for those learning to write in a foreign language as well as those evaluating such writing. Essays are grouped into four sections: theoretical considerations, national differences in writing styles, the transfer of rhetorical patterns in second language learning, and notes toward a theory of contrastive rhetoric.

170. Raschke, Deborah. "Creating 'A World Elsewhere'—The Self Resisting Society: A Cultural Perspective." Paper presented at the CCCC Convention, St. Louis, March 1988. ERIC ED 296 346. 16 pages

    Suggests that composition teachers should study their pedagogy to understand the realities they propose.

171. Reboul, Olivier. "Can There Be Nonrhetorical Argumentation?" *P&R* 21 (Summer 1988): 220–233.

    Examines the definition and uses of *rhetoric* and *argumentation*, concluding that nonrhetorical argumentation is impossible.

172. Reed, Janine. "Who's Expressing in 'Expressive Writing'?" Paper presented at the CCCC Convention, St. Louis, March 1988. ERIC ED 292 127. 13 pages

    Advises teachers to reflect on the concept of self presented in current composition textbooks. Theorists as different as Maslow, Freud, and James have influenced the concept.

173. Reinard, John C. "The Empirical Study of the Persuasive Effects of Evidence: The Status after 50 Years of Research." *HCR* 15 (Fall 1988): 3–59.

    A review of research on how evidence influences persuasive argument. Focuses on the type of evidence, its source, the message, and the receiver.

174. Renz, Mary Ann, and John Greg. "Flaws in the Decision-Making Process: Assessment of Risk in the Decision to Launch Flight 51-L." *CSSJ* 39 (Spring 1988): 67–75.

    Focuses on the format of risk analysis, the phrasing of decision questions, and shifts in the burden of proof.

175. Rivers, William E. "Problems in Composition: A Vygotskian Perspective." *DAI* 49 (October 1988): 808A.

    A study based on the idea that writing is primarily a means of knowing and only secondarily a means of communicating.

176. Roemer, Marjorie Godlin. "Marjorie Godlin Roemer Responds [to Krauss, *CE* 49 (December 1987)]." *CE* 50 (September 1988): 582–583.

    Concedes that she and Krauss read Freire differently, choosing her own view of Freire's liberatory pedagogy, which seeks dialogue through disagreement.

177. Rosenblatt, Louise. *Writing and Reading: The Transactional Theory*. Technical Report, no. 416. Cambridge, Mass.: Bolt, Beranek, and Newman, 1988. ERIC ED 292 062. 20 pages

    Justifies a transactional view of the interrelationships between reading and writing processes.

178. Rowan, Katherine E. "A Contemporary Theory of Explanatory Writing." *WC* 5 (January 1988): 23–56.

    Offers a new definition of explanatory writing, classifying it as a type of informative discourse and explaining the value of this definition for research and pedagogy.

179. Satterfield, Leon. " 'Myself Must I Remake': An Existentialist Philosophy of Composition." *JAC* 8 (1988): 82–87.

> Argues that writing generates new thinking and thus new selves. Meaning is made, not discovered, and the writer's voice need not authentically mirror a "real" self.

180. Schilb, John. "Ideology and Composition Scholarship." *JAC* 8 (1988): 22–29.

> Examines one article published in *Research in the Teaching of English*. Illustrates how to identify in research the ideological presuppositions that lead to dodging political questions.

181. Schwegler, Robert A. "Composition Studies: Applied Research and Stephen M. North's *The Making of Knowledge in Composition: Portrait of an Emerging Field*." *JTW* 7 (Spring-Summer 1988): 113–121.

> Views North's set of methodological communities as moving away from the primacy of practice in composition studies. Reviews each of the communities.

182. Schwegler, Robert A. "Conflicting Methods in Composition Research." *CE* 50 (April 1988): 444–453.

> Discusses the debate between experimental and naturalistic research as represented by the works of George Hillocks, Jr., and Ben W. McClelland and Timothy R. Donovan.

183. Shanahan, Timothy, and Richard G. Lomax. "A Developmental Comparison of Three Theoretical Models of the Reading-Writing Relationship." *RTE* 22 (May 1988): 196–212.

> An interactive model of reading and writing better explains data from 69 beginning readers and 137 proficient readers than two other models that are one-directional.

184. Sipiora, Phillip. "Rearticulating the Rhetorical Tradition: The Influence of *A Theory of Discourse*." *JAC* 8 (1988): 123–136.

> Regards Kinneavy's *A Theory of Discourse* as the most significant contribution to contemporary rhetoric. Provides grounds for examining the relation of rhetoric, composition, and liberal arts.

185. Sirc, Geoffrey M. "Composing Processes in Writing: A Critical Review of Paradigms in Theory and Research." *DAI* 49 (September 1988): 451A.

> Studies current composition theory to determine the validity for the claims that process theorists make. Combines critical theory with case study research.

186. Sirc, Geoffrey M., and Lillian Bridwell-Bowles. "A Computer Tool for Analyzing the Composing Process." *CollM* 6 (May 1988): 155–160.

> Discusses the ability of the University of Minnesota's Recording WordStar program to aid research on composing by recording the keystrokes of students engaged in composing tasks.

187. Slater, Marsha S. "Collaboration as Community: Outcome of Conducting Research on One's Colleagues." Paper presented at the CCCC Convention, St. Louis, March 1988. ERIC ED 294 212. 8 pages

> Studies the effects on writing teachers of studying other teachers of writing.

188. Smith, Louise Z., ed. *Audits of Meaning: A Festschrift in Honor of Ann E. Berthoff*. Portsmouth, N.H.: Boynton/Cook, 1988. 280 pages

> Twenty-three essays and poems extend and comment on Berthoff's work in interpretation and hermeneutics, research on teaching, and the ideology and politics of composition studies.

189. Smith, Ted J., III. "Diversity and Order in Communication Theory: The Uses of Philosophical Analysis." *ComQ* 36 (Winter 1988): 28–40.

> Proposes the metatheoretical stance of skeptical pluralism ordering and integrating knowledge of communication. Discusses four fundamentally different conceptions of communication and science.

190. Smitherman-Donaldson, Geneva, and Teun A. Van Dijk, eds. *Discourse and Discrimination*. Detroit: Wayne State University Press, 1988. 269 pages

A collection of 10 essays that explore discrimination, prejudice, and racism in the discourse of dominant group members, institutions, and media.

191. Staley, Constance Courtney, and Jerry L. Cohen. "Communicator Style and Social Style Similarities and Differences between the Sexes." *ComQ* 36 (Summer 1988): 192–202.

Finds no significant difference between males' and females' self-reported perceptions of communicator style.

192. Stark, Heather. "What Do Paragraph Markings Do?" *DPr* 11 (July–September 1988): 275–303.

Readers showed considerable, though not perfect, agreement about the boundaries between paragraphs in unindented texts. However, paragraph boundaries may not improve reading speed.

193. Stiff, James B., James Price Dillard, Lilnabeth Somera, Hyun Kim, and Carra Sleight. "Empathy, Communication, and Prosocial Behavior." *ComM* 55 (June 1988): 198–213.

Addresses the causal sequencing of some components of empathy and relates the process to communicative responsiveness.

194. Stotsky, Sandra. "Commentary." *RTE* 22 (February 1988): 89–99.

Reviews Hillocks's *Research on Written Composition*. Applauds its perspective, reviews of research, and distinctions between observations and findings. Regrets that it is not more comprehensive.

195. Targowski, Andrew S., and Joel P. Bowman. "The Layer-Based, Pragmatic Model of the Communication Process." *JBC* 25 (Winter 1988): 5–24.

Proposes a multilayered and faceted communication model in which the idea of "information steering" is central. Current

models inaccurately portray communication as static.

196. Tebo-Messina, Margaret. "Collaborative Learning in the College Writing Workshop: Two Case Studies of Peer Group Development." *DAI* 48 (February 1988): 1974A.

Examines how writing groups work. Draws on composition research and theory dealing with group dynamics and on a nonparticipant observational study.

197. Thomas, Susan. "Reported Speech in English: Form and Function in a Testimonial Setting." *DAI* 49 (August 1988): 247A.

Examines the recontextualization of reported speech, whereby an utterance is refitted to another context.

198. Thompson, Nancy, ed. *Teacher Research*. Florence, S.C.: South Carolina Council of Teachers of English (distributed by NCTE), 1988. 87 pages

Eleven essays discuss the methods and benefits of ethnographic research conducted while teaching. Originally published as *Carolina English Teacher* (Special Issue 1988).

199. Thralls, Charlotte, Nancy Roundy Blyler, and Helen Rothschild Ewald. "Real Readers, Implied Readers, and Professional Writers: Suggested Research." *JBC* 25 (Spring 1988): 47–65.

A pilot protocol study of 10 business writers revealed complex simultaneous imaging both of audience types through endophoric and exophoric references and of genre constraints on implied readers.

200. Ting-Toomey, Stella. "Rhetorical Sensitivity Style in Three Cultures: France, Japan, and the United States." *CSSJ* 39 (Spring 1988): 28–36.

A statistical analysis of diversity and interactional richness across cultures.

201. Todd, Alexandra Dundas, and Sue Fisher, eds. *Gender and Discourse: The Power of*

Talk. Advances in Discourse Processes, vol. 30. Norwood, N.J.: Ablex, 1988. 304 pages

Twelve essays examine, from different theoretical perspectives, women's uses of language in social interactions. Treats doctor-patient communication, the language of children at play, storytelling in families, institutional discourse in medicine and law, and ideological discourse in music, radio, and literature.

202. Tomlinson, Barbara. "Tuning, Tying, and Training Texts: Metaphors for Revision." *WC* 5 (January 1988): 58–81.

Discusses metaphors used by professional writers when they describe their own writing processes. Argues that these metaphors affect our perception of revision.

203. Tracy, Karen. "A Discourse Analysis of Four Discourse Studies." *DPr* 11 (April–June 1988): 243–259.

Studies published in four different journals varied in their justifications for the research, in the methods of investigation, and in the function of citations.

204. Tuman, Myron C. "Whose Text Is It Anyway? Intentions and the Rules of Play." *RSQ* 17 (Spring 1987): 121–133.

Contrasts the games or performance model of writing with a model based largely on rhetoric and psychology. Uses a cloze procedure to argue that "texts are public documents and the access to them are not the exclusive proprietary rights of their writers."

205. Turetzky, Philip. "Metaphor and Paraphrase." *P&R* 21 (Summer 1988): 205–219.

Examines "reductionist" and "nonreductionist" views of metaphor. Concludes that the latter offers greater potential for developing a theory of metaphor.

206. Tutzauer, Frank, and Michael E. Roloff. "Communication Processes Leading to Integrative Agreements: Three Paths to Joint Benefits." *ComR* 15 (August 1988): 360–380.

An empirical study of communication and conflict. Communication processes both predicted integrative outcomes and mediated the influence of aspirations on integrative outcomes.

207. Villaume, William A. "Identity and Similarity Chains in the Conversation of High-Involved and Low-Involved Speakers: Evidence of Integrated Discourse Strategies." *WJSC* 52 (Summer 1988): 185–202.

Examines the strategic coordination of local and global textual resources of dyads with three different patterns of interaction.

208. Voiku, Daniel J. "Reply to Stephen M. North's Response [*BADE* 89 (Spring 1988)]." *BADE* 89 (Spring 1988): 74.

Argues that North's response ignores Voiku's thesis.

209. Waller, Robert. "The Typographic Contribution to Language: Towards a Model of Typographic Genres and Their Underlying Structures." *DAI* 49 (September 1988): 493A.

Explains typographic genres in terms of reader-writer relations.

210. Weiser, Irwin. "The Relationship between Theory and Practice." *JTW* 7 (Spring-Summer 1988): 1–8.

Speculative and descriptive theories need not generate instructional activities. Applied to pedagogy, they may, however, "go beyond a theorist's intention."

211. Wildeman, James. "Defining Audiences Negatively: One Way That Writers Keep Readers from Their Texts." Paper presented at the CCCC Convention, St. Louis, March 1988. ERIC ED 293 152. 6 pages

Links the inaccessibility of such texts as government and legal documents to the writer's assuming too much knowledge on the reader's part.

212. Wiley, Marle L. "The Contexts of Composing: A Dynamic Scene with Movable Centers." Paper presented at the CCCC Conven-

tion, St. Louis, March 1988. ERIC ED 296 335. 16 pages

Argues that when the description of composing changes, how we view composing also changes.

213. Williams, Charles E. "Fantasy Theme Analysis: Theory Versus Practice." *RSQ* 17 (Winter 1987): 11–20.

Discusses the theory on which fantasy theme analysis is based and explains how critics may conduct such an analysis.

214. Witteman, Hal. "Interpersonal Problem Solving: Problem Conceptualization and Communication Use." *ComM* 55 (December 1988): 336–359.

Examines the relationship between the mental representation of problem situations and the communication used to manage the situation.

215. Woal, Michael, and Marcia Lynn Corn. "Text as Image." Paper presented at the SCA Meeting, Boston, November 1987. ERIC ED 294 250. 26 pages

Discusses how print is regaining pictorial qualities in the electronic age.

216. Woods, Donald R. "Novice Versus Expert Research." *JCST* 18 (December–January 1988): 193–195.

Discusses characteristics marking unsuccessful and successful problem solvers, exploring the implications of these characteristics for classroom teaching.

217. Woods, Donald R. "Novice Versus Expert Research Suggests Ideas for Implementation." *JCST* 18 (September–October 1988): 77–79, 66–67.

Discusses novice and expert approaches to the process of problem-solving. Treats the approach taken, attitudes, reasoning skills, and means of entering into a solution.

218. Woods, Donald R. "Novice Versus Expert Research Suggests Ideas for Implementation II." *JCST* 18 (November 1988): 138–141.

Discusses some characteristics of unsuccessful and successful problem solvers, treating exploration, translational activities, planning, executing, reviewing, and checking solutions.

219. Woods, Donald R. "PS [Problem-Solving] Research: Ideas on Creating the Internal Representation and Identifying Knowledge Structure." *JCST* 17 (February 1988): 317–321.

Summarizies Norman Frederiksen's review of problem-solving research and outlines heuristics for research and teaching that focus on problem solving.

220. Worsham, Lynn. "The Question Concerning Invention: Hermeneutics and the Genesis of Writing." *Pre/Text* 8 (Fall–Winter 1987): 197–244.

Argues for the conflation of invention and technology, exploring Heidegger's critique of technology and its implications for writing.

221. Yum, June Ock. "The Impact of Confucianism on Interpersonal Relationships and Communication Patterns in East Asia." *ComM* 55 (December 1988): 374–388.

Explores communication patterns as a fundamental social process, influenced by philosophical foundations and value systems in any society.

See also 232, 398, 410, 632, 881, 924, 980, 1009, 1139

2.2 RHETORICAL HISTORY

222. Abbott, Don Paul. "The Doctrine of Double Form: Benedetto Croce on Rhetoric and Poetics." *P&R* 21 (First Quarter 1988): 1–18.

A historical examination of Croce's theories. Compares Croce and Vico.

223. Adams, Katherine H., and John L. Adams. "The Paradox Within: Origins of the Current-Traditional Paradigm." *RSQ* 17 (Fall 1987): 421–431.

Traces the origins of the current-traditional paradigm by focusing on A. S. Hill, Barrett Wendell, and Fred Newton Scott, whose textbooks codified the tradition but whose teaching and research increasingly began to counter it.

224. Alexandrakis, Dimitris. "The Education of Children from Birth to Age 14 in Classical Athens, 500–300 B.C." *DAI* 49 (August 1988): 210A.

Provides an overview and analysis of the Athenian philosophy of education, describing various curricula and pedagogical methods.

225. Alford, Elisabeth M. "Thucydides and the Plague in Athens: The Roots of Scientific Writing." *WC* 5 (April 1988): 131–153.

Argues that two passages from *History of the Peloponnesian War* illustrate how scientific writing began and how this writing is related to epideictic rhetoric.

226. Altman, Karen Elizabeth. "Modernity, Gender, and Consumption: Public Discourses on Woman and the Home." *DAI* 49 (October 1988): 656A.

Analyzes 1920s institutions with conflicting interests to build a critical theory of "the generative power of public discourse."

227. Andrews, Robert R. "Peter of Auvergne's Commentary on Aristotle's *Categories :* Edition, Translation, and Analysis." *DAI* 49 (August 1988): 267A.

Based on an edition from the manuscripts and supplemented by a translation. Includes information about similar commentaries.

228. Batschelet, Margaret W. "Plain Style and Scientific Style: The Influence of the Puritan Plain Style Sermon on Early American Science Writers." *JTWC* 18 (1988): 287–295.

Early American science writers derived from Puritan sermons an organizational pattern, a format, the use of simple language, and a concern for the needs of their audience.

229. Beggs, Don. "Sons of the Dragon's Teeth: Value and Violence in Plato's Dialogues." *DAI* 49 (December 1988): 1475A.

Argues that Socrates's actions and ideas are much more criticized by Plato than has been recognized. Includes readings of the *Gorgias, Ion,* and *Phaedrus.*

230. Benson, Thomas W., and Michael H. Prosser, eds. *Readings in Classical Rhetoric.* Davis, Calif.: Hermagoras Press, 1988. 341 pages

Presents translations of selected Greek and Roman texts that define rhetoric, its value and scope, and its five departments. Includes a chronology of classical rhetoric and a bibliography.

231. Berlin, James A. "Revisionary History: The Dialectical Method." *Pre/Text* 8 (Spring-Summer 1987): 47–61.

Proposes using Foucault's historical work to critique current histories of rhetoric and offers Marxism as an alternative model for writing rhetorical history.

232. Berthoff, Ann E. "From *Mencius on the Mind* to *Coleridge on Imagination .*" *RSQ* 18 (Spring 1988): 163–166.

Discusses two books by I. A. Richards and how they reflect his understanding of C. S. Peirce's and Coleridge's concepts of interpretation and imagination.

233. Biester, James. "Samuel Johnson on Letters." *Rhetorica* 6 (Spring 1988): 145–166.

Presents a brief history of changing *ars dictaminis* from Cicero to Johnson. Argues that Johnson opposed the plain and sincere style in favor of *ethos* and *pathos* in letters.

234. Black, Deborah L. "The Logical Dimensions of Rhetorical Poetics: Aspects of Nondemonstrative Reasoning in Medieval Arabic Philosophy." *DAI* 48 (June 1988): 3125A.

Examines the writings of medieval Arabic philosophers and finds that they exhibit sophisticated logic and epistemology and unexpected discourse range.

235. Boitano, James J. "Educating Citizens for Democracy: Aristotle, John Locke, and Jean-Jacques Rousseau on Civic Education." *DAI* 48 (June 1988): 3187A.

Concludes that Aristotle's approach should be regarded as the most convincing political foundation for the needs of American civic education.

236. Boswell, Grant. "The Disfunction of Rhetoric: Invention, Imaginative Excess, and the Origin of the Modes of Discourse." *RSQ* 18 (Spring-Summer 1988): 239–250.

Argues that historical forces in the late Renaissance resulted in a suspicion of traditional rhetoric, which led to modern rhetorical and literary theories.

237. Brinton, Alan. "Cicero's Use of Historical Examples in Moral Argument." *P&R* 21 (Summer 1988): 169–184.

Concludes that Cicero's historical examples are more persuasive than Plato's theoretical analysis.

238. Brockmann, R. John. "Does Clio Have a Place in Technical Writing? Considering Patents in a History of Technical Communication." *JTWC* 18 (1988): 297–304.

Suggests that patent documents can serve as artifacts for studying the history of technical writing in America.

239. Browne, Stephen H. "Aesthetics and the Heteronomy of Rhetorical Judgment." *RSQ* 18 (Fall 1988): 141–152.

Examines Edmund Burke's *Enquiry into the Sublime and Beautiful* as the embodiment of classical and modern conceptions of knowledge and the discursive arts.

240. Browne, Stephen H. "The Gothic Voice in Eighteenth-Century Oratory." *ComQ* 36 (Summer 1988): 227–236.

Examines an oration by Edmund Burke and judges gothic voice to be a significant way to deploy general aesthetic sensibilities for rhetorical ends.

241. Camargo, Martin. "Toward a Comprehensive Art of Written Discourse: Geoffrey Vinsauf and the *Ars Dictaminis*." *Rhetorica* 6 (Spring 1988): 167–194.

Discusses Vinsauf's *Documentum* as a union of the arts of poetry and letters. Offers a brief history of the *ars dictaminis* in relation to poetry and rhetoric.

242. Campbell, George. *The Philosophy of Rhetoric*. Edited by Lloyd F. Bitzer. Landmarks in Rhetoric and Public Address. Carbondale, Ill.: Southern Illinois University Press, 1988. 504 pages

A new edition of Campbell's rhetoric with a revised and expanded critical introduction. Campbell's work engages themes prevailing during the Scottish Enlightenment: empiricism, the association of ideas, and explanations of natural phenomena by reference to principles and processes of human nature.

243. Carter, Michael. "The Role of Invention in Belletristic Rhetoric: A Study of the Lectures of Adam Smith." *RSQ* 18 (Summer 1988): 3–13.

Focuses on Smith as a transitional figure between traditional and modern rhetoric. Describes Smith's view of the forms of discourse, arrangement, and style.

244. Carter, Michael. "*Stasis* and *Kairos:* Principles of Social Construction in Classical Rhetoric." *RR* 7 (Fall 1988): 97–112.

Parallels between *stasis* and *kairos* and epistemic and social construction theories suggest that classical rhetoric is a source of "powerful insights" into contemporary theory.

245. Chance, Thomas Hugh. "Euthydemian Studies: Analysis of Plato's *Euthydemus*." *DAI* 48 (February 1988): 2056A.

Analyzes a neglected work and argues for its value in understanding Platonic dialectic, falsehood, contradiction, and eristic activity.

246. Cohen, Herman, Edward P. J. Corbett, S. Michael Halloran, Charles W. Kneupper, Eric Skopec, and Barbara Warnick. "The Most Significant Passage in Hugh Blair's *Lectures on Rhetoric and Belles Lettres*." *RSQ* 17 (Summer 1987): 281–304.

Six scholars explain the significance of passages from Blair's Lectures 1, 10, 25, 32, and 34.

247. Conley, Thomas. "Plato's *Phaedrus*." *WI* 8 (Fall 1988): 23–28.

Presents a reading of the *Phaedrus,* emphasizing style and organization over "worldview." Claims that such a reading shows how to use the *Phaedrus* in composition classes.

248. Connelly, Betty J. "Ethical Pleasure: Aristotle's Two Treatments of Pleasure in the *Nicomachean Ethics*." *DAI* 49 (August 1988): 268A.

Through contextual analysis, illustrates that Aristotle's two different treatments of pleasure are harmonious.

249. Consigny, Scott. "Transparency and Displacement: Aristotle's Concept of Rhetorical Clarity." *RSQ* 17 (Fall 1987): 413–419.

Attempts to resolve apparent contradictions between construing clarity as a criterion of undistorted style and as a deception resulting from artifice. Suggests that Aristotle's *Rhetoric* offers two distinct notions of *saphes*.

250. Conway, Kathryn M. "Gertrude Buck: Rhetorician." Paper presented at the CCCC Convention, St. Louis, March 1988. ERIC ED 296 348. 9 pages

Examines the rhetorical theories of Gertrude Buck in three articles written between 1900 and 1901.

251. Corler, Woldemar. "From Athens to Tusculum: Gleaning the Background of Cicero's *De Oratore*." *Rhetorica* 6 (Summer 1988): 215–235.

Discusses *De Oratore*'s relationship to the *Phaedrus* and *De Legibus,* the appropriate-

ness of the Tuscan estate to the reception of truth, and Book Three as Crassus's swan song.

252. Court, Franklin E. "The Social and Historical Significance of the First English Literature Professorship in England." *PMLA* 103 (October 1988): 783–807.

Argues that the professorship was established, not to impose social control, but to promote political reform through the public awareness that is generated by "useful reading."

253. Covino, William A. *The Art of Wondering: A Revisionist Return to the History of Rhetoric*. Portsmouth, N.H.: Boynton/Cook, 1988. 152 pages

Argues that the rhetoric of Plato, Aristotle, and Cicero mistakenly has been reduced to formal rules and pedagogic advice. Their work provides the basis of a rhetoric of inquiry and ambiguity that is continued by Montaigne, Vico, and DeQuincey, and in the twentieth century, by Burke, Geertz, Feyerabend, and Derrida.

254. DeCiccio, Albert C. "Social Constructionism and Collaborative Learning: The Implications for Rhetoric and Composition." *DAI* 48 (January 1988): 1679A.

Traces the origin and development of collaborative approaches to teaching writing in the late nineteenth and early twentieth centuries. Also discusses recent developments in theory and practice.

255. DeLong, Mark R. "*Res et Verbum:* Rhetorical Unities of Act and Word." *DAI* 49 (December 1988): 1447A.

Investigates sixteenth-century thought through rhetoric. Concludes that rhetoric is a formative influence in the development of ideological power.

256. Deslauriers, Marguerite L. "Aristotle on Definition." *DAI* 48 (May 1988): 2894A.

Argues that the requirements of Aristotle's theory of definition raise metaphysical issues that cannot be resolved within the terms of a logical theory.

257. Donovan, Brian R. "Saying and Knowing: A Study in Early Greek Concepts of Rhetoric." *DAI* 48 (November 1988): 1166A.

Traces the development of epistemic rhetoric from its early Greek precedents. Finds that for early rhetoricians rhetoric was universal.

258. Enos, Richard Leo. "Douglas W. Ehninger's 'The Promise of Rhetoric': A Ten-Year Review." *RSQ* 18 (Fall 1988): 191–200.

Reprints Ehninger's address to the 1978 Doctoral Honors Seminar at Ann Arbor, Michigan.

259. Fantham, Elaine. " *Varietas* and *Satietas: De Oratore* 3.96–103 and the Limits of *Ornatus*." *Rhetorica* 6 (Summer 1988): 275–290.

Probes Cicero's meaning of *varietas* as a cure for excessive ornament, showing that he followed Theophrastus's advocacy of restraint and theory of ornament.

260. Fortenbaugh, William W. " *Benevolentiam Conciliare* and *Animos Permovere* : Some Remarks on Cicero's *De Oratore* 2.178–216." *Rhetorica* 6 (Summer 1988): 259–273.

Argues that Cicero's account of winning good will, based on tradition and current practice, blurs the distinction between *ethos* and *pathos* and excludes the impartial auditor.

261. Garver, Eugene. "Aristotle's *Rhetoric* on Unintentionally Hitting the Principles of the Sciences." *Rhetorica* 6 (Autumn 1988): 381–393.

Explains Aristotle's original account of moving from rhetoric to scientific argument. "Hitting on a principle" is unintentional, transgressive, and applicable to *idia,* not common topics.

262. Gilman, Sander L., and Carole Blair, eds. *Friedrich Nietzsche on Rhetoric and Language.* New York: Oxford University Press, 1988. 320 pages

Presents the entire German text of Nietzsche's lectures on rhetoric and language and his notes for them. Includes critical notes and facing page translations in English.

263. Gonzalez, Hernando. "The Evolution of Communication as a Field." *ComR* 15 (June 1988): 302–308.

A review essay defending communication research against John Durham Peters's criticisms of its evolution, relevance, and progress toward becoming a discipline.

264. Gould, Christopher. " 'Science' and the 'Grammar Wars' of the 1930s." *RSQ* 18 (Fall 1988): 121–131.

A historical study focusing on the changing definitions of science in relation to "illiteracy crises."

265. Grygiel, Terry Edward Michael. "Aristotle, Function, and Intentionality." *DAI* 49 (August 1988): 244A.

Chisholm's theories about the psychological nature of sentences can be traced back to Aristotle's treatment of sensing in *De Anima.*

266. Halloran, S. Michael. "John Witherspoon on Eloquence." *RSQ* 17 (Spring 1987): 177–192.

Presents a precis of Witherspoon's 16 *Lectures on Eloquence.*

267. Halloran, S. Michael. "Rhetoric and the English Department." *RSQ* 17 (Winter 1987): 3–10.

Discusses the position of new rhetoric within English departments, tracing nineteenth-century influences that shifted the academy's concern from the art of public discourse to the study of literary texts.

268. Hayes, Christopher G. "Defining Composition: Evidence from the Citations, Years 1971–1972." Paper presented at the CCCC Convention, St. Louis, March 1988. ERIC ED 294 235. 20 pages

Examines articles on composition to explore how knowledge about composition evolves.

269. Hildebrandt, Herbert W. "Some Influences of Greek and Roman Rhetoric on Early Letter Writing." *JBC* 25 (Summer 1988): 7–27.

Medieval letter-writing manuals in Italian, German, and English show the direct influence of classical rhetoric, borrowing terms and concepts for invention, arrangement, and style.

270. Hughes, Joseph John. "Comedic Borrowing in Selected Orations of Cicero." *DAI* 48 (January 1988): 1759A.

Examines how Cicero combined the attributes of orator, humanist, and wit, realizing ancient theories about the applicability of humor to oratory.

271. Hunt, Everett Lee. "General Specialists: Fifty Years Later." *RSQ* 17 (Spring 1987): 167–176.

Reprints Hunt's keynote address, given at the Bowling Green State University Conference on Rhetoric and the Modern World in July 1965. Reflects on the first 50 years of the speech profession.

272. Innes, Doreen. "Cicero on Tropes." *Rhetorica* 6 (Summer 1988): 307–325.

Studies Cicero's theory of tropes, especially his largely Roman examples, which blend the traditional and the new. Tropes examined include archaisms, neologisms, and metaphors.

273. Jarratt, Susan C. "Toward a Sophistic Historiography." *Pre/Text* 8 (Spring–Summer 1987): 9–26.

Looks to sophistic historical representation for the element of a revised historiography for rhetoric.

274. Johnson, Nan. "Rhetoric and *Belles Lettres* in the Canadian Academy: An Historical Analysis." *CE* 50 (December 1988): 861–873.

Uses students' notes, course titles, and course descriptions to trace the influence of Campbell, Whately, Blair, Bain, and Genung on the academy from the nineteenth century into the current decade.

275. Kinneavy, James. "The Exile of Rhetoric from the Liberal Arts." *JAC* 8 (1988): 105–112.

Argues that the eighteenth-century exile of rhetoric from the arts and sciences persists. As a result, contemporary education is isolated from the populace and the ethical stance of scholar-educator is diminished.

276. Kittay, Jeffery. "Utterance Unmoored: The Changing Interpretation of the Act of Writing in the European Middle Ages." *LSoc* 17 (June 1988): 209–230.

Traces in one historical context the changing status of writing from a transcription of an oral act to a written utterance preserved and valorized for itself.

277. Labor, Alfred B. "An Evaluation of the Moral-Analogical Arguments of Socrates." *DAI* 48 (February 1988): 2078A.

Explores Socrates's use of analogical arguments in philosophical discourse. Discovers that their strength is also their weakness.

278. Legomsky, Diane Susan. "Plato's *Ion* and Socratic Education." *DAI* 48 (April 1988): 2620A.

Analyzes the *Ion* as a methodological exposition of Socratic philosophy, a network of epistemological, pedagogical, and ethical religious principles.

279. McCleary, Bill. "Student Lecture Notes from Nineteenth-Century Scottish Rhetoric Courses Providing Insights on Then and Now for TCU's Winifred Horner." *CompC* 1 (May 1988): 1–2.

Reports on Horner's annotated bibliography of manuscript notes.

280. McDonald, James C. "Imitation of Models in the History of Rhetoric: Classical, Belletris-

tic, and Current-Traditional." *DAI* 48 (April 1988): 2613A.

Compares the use of imitation in classical rhetoric, which emphasized *kairos* or situational context, with current-traditional rhetoric, which focuses on structure and style.

281. McGann, Patrick. "Women and the Dichotomy of Literacy: Public-Private Discourse." Paper presented at the CCCC Convention, St. Louis, March 1988. ERIC ED 294 200. 15 pages

Views women's literacy within American culture from the Colonial Period to the present.

282. McKerrow, Raymie E. "The Ethical Implications of a Whatelian Rhetoric." *RSQ* 17 (Summer 1987): 321–327.

A champion of the practical intellect, Whately believed that audiences must be given information sufficient to form judgments, but the rhetor's primary focus is on what reason and evidence suggest as the truth about an issue.

283. McKerrow, Raymie E. "Whately's Philosophy of Language." *SSCJ* 53 (Spring 1988): 211–226.

Focuses on the relationships among language, thought, reality, and meaning to counteract the claim that the treatment of style in *Rhetoric* is devoid of theoretical underpinnings.

284. Miller, Carolyn R. "Aristotle's 'Special Topics' in Rhetorical Practice and Pedagogy." *RSQ* 17 (Winter 1987): 61–70.

Briefly traces the history of topical theory, arguing that the special topics, which served to connect human reasoning to the particularities of practical situations, became "academic" when rhetoric became an academic subject.

285. Moline, Jon M. "Plato on Persuasion and Credibility." *P&R* 21 (Fall 1988): 260–278.

Examines Plato's definition of rhetorical credibility.

286. Montague, Holly W. "Style and Strategy in Forensic Speeches: Cicero's Caesarian Perspective." *DAI* 48 (May 1988): 2864A.

Discusses the relationship of judicial and political issues as the basis of a stylistic and rhetorical anomaly in Cicero's *Pro Ligario*.

287. Moran, Michael. "Adam Smith and the Rhetoric of Style." Paper presented at the CCCC Convention, St. Louis, March 1988. ERIC ED 293 149. 12 pages

Argues that Smith based his theory of style on the communication triangle and thus is more classical than supposed.

288. Moss, Jean Dietz. "Aristotle's Four Courses: Forgotten *Topos* of Renaissance Rhetoric." *RSQ* 17 (Winter 1987): 71–88.

Examines Aristotle's conception of causality, discusses examples of the *topos* of cause in Italian rhetorics of the Renaissance, and suggests why interest in the *topos* declined in the late sixteenth century.

289. Mulderig, Gerald P. "Composition Teaching in America, 1930–1950: Reconsidering Our Recent Past." *RSQ* 17 (Summer 1987): 305–319.

Although heavy teaching loads prevailed during the period 1930–1950, many composition teachers resisted drills in grammar and mechanics and proposed alternatives that anticipate current approaches to teaching writing.

290. Murphy, James J. "The Politics of Historiography." *RR* 7 (Fall 1988): 5–49.

Edits transcripts of eight panelists' statements, discussions, and reflections during the 1988 CCCC Convention to examine the political, social, and philosophical implications of writing histories of rhetoric.

291. Murray, James S. "Disputation, Deception, and Dialectic: Plato on the True Rhetoric." *P&R* 21 (Fall 1988): 279–289.

Argues that Plato's *Phaedrus* constructs a rhetorical structure based on dialectical processes.

292. Nicholson, Dale A. "The Enlightenment, Anti-Enlightenment, and Edmund Burke: A Re-Examination." *DAI* 49 (August 1988): 325A.

Until the twentieth century, Burke was viewed as a liberal utilitarian not far removed from the values of the Enlightenment. This study analyzes his ambiguous position.

293. Pankratz, John R. "New Englanders, the Written Word, and the Errand into Ohio, 1788–1830." *DAI* 49 (February 1989): 2368A.

Analyzes the extension of the written and printed word in the settlement of Ohio.

294. Quandahl, Ellen. "What Is Plato? Inference and Allusion in Plato's *Sophist.*" *RR* 7 (Spring 1989): 338–348.

Reads this dialogue as undercutting the traditional view of Plato as being opposed to "sophistic relativism." It demonstrates instead "the power of contextual and contigent."

295. Quiroz, Sharon R. "Rhetoric and the Conduct of Public Business: A Critical Reading of Works in Rhetoric and Political Economy by Adam Smith, Richard Whately, and Herbert Spencer." *DAI* 49 (October 1988): 828A.

Argues that Smith, Whately, and Spencer assigned importance to modifying existing theories of rhetoric to make language signal the assumption of political community.

296. Rigney, Ann. "Studies in the Rhetoric of Historical Representation: Four Nineteenth-Century Histories of the French Revolution." *DAI* 48 (June 1988): 3106A.

Examines the literary study of the French Revolution, exploring how meaning is produced in four representative histories.

297. Rosner, Mary. "The Two Faces of Cicero: Trollope's *Life* in the Nineteenth Century." *RSQ* 18 (Spring-Summer 1988): 251–258.

Discusses how Trollope tries to accommodate his complex vision of Cicero to a unified portrayal.

298. Rossetti, Livio. "The Rhetoric of Zeno's Paradoxes." *P&R* 21 (Second Quarter 1988): 146–152.

Advances a theory of paradoxical statements. Identifies Gorgianic, Socratic, and Platonic strategies.

299. Schenkeveld, Dirk M. "*Judicia Vulgi:* Cicero, *De Oratore* 3.195ff and *Brutus* 183ff." *Rhetorica* 6 (Summer 1988): 291–305.

Argues that, from *De Oratore* onwards, Cicero advocates the intuitive judgments of lay audiences, equal to those of experts, on prose rhythms and total performance.

300. Schilb, John. "Differences, Displacements, and Disruptions: Toward Revisionary Histories of Rhetoric." *Pre/Text* 8 (Spring–Summer 1987): 29–44.

Argues for the role of deconstruction and social criticism in a revisionary history of rhetoric suited to composition studies. Illustrates with Paul de Man's work.

301. Schilb, John. "The Historiography of Rhetoric: Conflicts and Their Implications." *WI* 8 (Fall 1988): 15–22.

Critiques Donald Stewart's "The Continuing Relevance of Plato's *Phaedrus*" (*Essays on Classical Rhetoric and Modern Discourse,* 1984), arguing that rhetorical history can be used in composition classrooms to explore conflict rather than promote closure.

302. Schutrumpf, Eckart. "Platonic Elements in the Structure of Cicero, *De Oratore* Book I." *Rhetorica* 6 (Summer 1988): 237–258.

Examines Platonic influences in the encomium on the power of eloquence, the dispute over the scope of rhetoric, the need for the knowledge of justice, and the relationship between philosophy and rhetoric.

303. Shenk, Robert. "The Ancient Rhetorical *Suasoria* Versus the Modern Technical Case." *RR* 7 (Fall 1988): 113–127.

Philosophical similarities and differences between the modern case study and classical imitation exercises suggest that we move toward a "more integrated and coherent curriculum."

304. Shuger, Debora K. *Sacred Rhetoric: The Christian Grand Style in the English Renaissance*. Princeton, N.J.: Princeton University Press, 1988. 336 pages

Argues for the growth of a Christian aesthetic out of the classical grand style, tracing its development from Isocrates to the sacred rhetorics of the Renaissance.

305. Sinclair, Patrick. "Pitiless Diagnoses and Deadly Appendages: The Rhetorical and Historiographical Background to Tacitus's *Sententiae* in *Annales* 1–6." *DAI* 48 (February 1988): 2057A.

Analyzes Tacitus's *sententia* from the perspective of ancient rhetoric and historiography, especially the work of Cicero and Quintillian.

306. Smith, Robert W. "The Most Significant Rhetorical Work in French Is L'Abbe Joseph Cyprian Nadal's *Dictionnaire d'Eloquence Sacree*." *RSQ* 17 (Winter 1987): 21–32.

Explains the significance of the French Jesuit priest's encyclopedic work and brings together Nadal's views on invention, disposition, style, memory, and delivery, dispersed under various alphabetical entries.

307. Solomon, Julie Robin. "Between Magic and Travel: Francis Bacon and the Theaters of Human Knowing." *DAI* 48 (February 1988): 2070A.

Examines the origins and contexts which led Bacon to construct a scientific language.

308. Struever, Nancy S. "Shakespeare and Rhetoric." *Rhetorica* 6 (Spring 1988): 137–144.

Argues that Shakespeare's rhetorical competence, like Stoppard's, was an aural mastery of intonation and rhythm, used to examine ethical issues and to subvert academic rhetoric.

309. Tristram, Robert J. "Vico on the Production and Assessment of Knowledge." *PPR* 48 (March 1988): 355–388.

Vico believed that there was a dialectical and historical logic in the relationship among the faculties, operations, and arts.

310. Vickers, Brian. "The Atrophy of Modern Rhetoric, Vico to de Man." *Rhetorica* 6 (Winter 1988): 21–56.

Argues that rhetoric has declined in modern times due to its fragmentation and misapplication. The reduction of tropes by Vico, Jakobson, and de Man has been particularly influential.

311. Vickers, Brian. *In Defence of Rhetoric*. New York: Oxford University Press, 1987. 500 pages

Traces the history of rhetoric from the classical era to the present. Includes a discussion of the role of rhetoric in the critical theories of Paul de Man and Roman Jakobson.

312. Vitanza, Victor J. " 'Notes' towards Historiographies of Rhetorics; or, Rhetorics of the Histories of Rhetorics: Traditional, Revisionary, and Sub/Versive." *Pre/Text* 8 (Spring–Summer 1987): 63–125.

Sketches "actual and possible" historiographies of rhetorics. Includes a critique of Stephen North's sense of writing history.

313. Ward, John O. "Magic and Rhetoric from Antiquity to the Renaissance: Some Ruminations." *Rhetorica* 6 (Winter 1988): 57–118.

Discusses the distinction between rhetoric as *dunamis* and *techne* in medieval and Renaissance culture. Concludes that the struggle was between maintaining institutional status and asserting the self.

314. Weber, Donald. *Rhetoric and History in Revolutionary New England*. New York: Oxford University Press, 1988. 224 pages

Uses methods of literary analysis, psychohistory, and social history to study the complex world of revolution and reaction.

315. Weidhorn, Manfred. *Churchill's Rhetoric and Political Discourse*. Exxon Education Foundation Series on Rhetoric and Political Discourse, vol. 17. Lanham, Md.: University Press of America, 1987. 135 pages

   A study of Churchill's verbal craft and style in writing. Seven chapters discuss the writer, the speaker, the word, the name, the image, the witticism, and the phrase.

316. Welch, Kathleen E. "Keywords from Classical Rhetoric: The Example of *Physis*." *RSQ* 17 (Spring 1987): 193–204.

   Traces the fluctuating meanings of *physis* as "nature," "essence," and "process." Argues against reducing keywords in classical rhetoric to static concepts.

317. Welch, Kathleen E. "The Platonic Paradox: Plato's Rhetoric in Contemporary Rhetoric and Composition Studies." *WC* 5 (January 1988): 3–21.

   Argues that Plato's rhetoric is central to contemporary interpretations of classical rhetoric because it gives philosophical rhetoric increased prominence over technical rhetoric.

318. Wilkerson, K. E. "Carneades at Rome: A Problem of Sceptical Rhetoric." *P&R* 21 (Second Quarter 1988): 132–144.

   Examines antithetical speeches that reflect a "sceptical epistemology" and reviews tenets of academic scepticism.

319. Williamson, L. Keith. "The Origins of Rhetoric: Corax and Tisias Reconsidered." Paper presented at the SCA, Boston, November 1987. ERIC ED 295 226. 32 pages

   Reconsiders the significance of Corax and Tisias in the development of rhetoric by investigating their cultural contents.

320. Wolff, Janice M. " *Phaedrus* and the First Person." Paper presented at the CCCC Convention, St. Louis, March 1988. ERIC ED 294 204. 15 pages

   Suggests that much can be learned about how Plato wrote by studying his dialogues, particularly for their point of view.

321. Woodman, A. J. *Rhetoric in Classical Historiography: Four Studies*. Portland, Oreg.: Areopagitica Press, 1988. 236 pages

   Discusses the problems of writing history by analyzing the writings of Tacitus, Cicero, Sallust, and Livy. Argues that classical historiography employs the concepts associated with, and relies upon the expectations generated by, a rhetorical genre.

See also 3, 10, 14, 148, 150, 328, 331, 338, 345, 411, 520, 598, 601, 638, 764, 789, 991, 1026, 1239, 1303, 1439

2.3 POLITICAL, RELIGIOUS, AND JUDICIAL RHETORIC

322. Ashley, Kevin D. "Modelling Legal Argument: Reasoning with Cases and Hypotheticals." *DAI* 49 (November 1988): 1799B.

   Shows that Hypo, a computer program, effectively models legal argument. Suggests other computer applications based on cases and precedents.

323. Beraradi, Gayle Kathleen. "Jurgen Habermas's Conception of the Public Sphere." *DAI* 48 (February 1988): 2152A.

   Investigates Habermas's development of the public sphere concept in relation to communicative rationality.

324. Bielfeldt, Dennis D. "Luther, Logic, and Language Games: An Inquiry into the Semantics of Theological Language in the Writings of Martin Luther." *DAI* 48 (April 1988): 2655A.

   Examines Luther's theological language and proposes a theological interaction metaphor model to explain his meaning.

325. Bode, Robert Allen. "Mohandas Karamchand Gandhi's Rhetorical Theory: Implications for Communications Ethics." *DAI* 48 (May 1988): 2761A.

   Identifies Gandhi's primary thematic concerns as nonviolent action, interpersonal relationships, openness, and flexibility.

Derives a 12-part ethical system based on these tenets.

326. Bostdorff, Denise Marie. "The Contemporary Presidency and the Rhetoric of Promoted Crisis." *DAI* 49 (September 1988): 378A.

Uses dramatism and generic principles to analyze the crisis rhetoric of Presidents Kennedy, Johnson, Nixon, Ford, Carter, and Reagan.

327. Boyd, Richard Edward. "The Rhetorical Transformation of Soviet-American War Rhetoric in the U.N. Security Council." *DAI* 49 (July 1988): 12A.

Examines Soviet and American rhetoric used to justify or denounce military actions. Concludes that both nations ground their discourse on national and U.N. values.

328. Browne, Stephen H. "Edmund Burke in the Humanist Tradition: Case Studies in Rhetoric and Rhetorical Judgment." *DAI* 49 (September 1988): 378A.

Links Burke's political principles and public discourse, focusing on aesthetic, political, and individual principles as evidenced in three close textual readings.

329. Browne, Stephen H. "Edmund Burke's *Letter to a Noble Lord* : A Textual Study in Political Philosophy and Rhetorical Action." *ComM* 55 (September 1988): 215–229.

Exemplifies how theoretical precepts may be activated through a collaboration between philosophy and rhetoric.

330. Brummett, Barry. "Using Apocalyptic Discourse to Exploit Audience Commitments through 'Transfer.' " *SCJ* 54 (Fall 1988): 58–73.

Analyzes how religious discourse motivates actions and attitudes toward secular issues by appealing to sacred texts.

331. Burke, Martin J. "The Conundrum of Class: Public Discourse on the Social Order in America." *DAI* 49 (November 1988): 1253A.

Focuses on how Americans have described and interpreted the structure and dynamics of society in public discourse from 1760 to 1880.

332. Callahan, Linda Florence. "A Fantasy-Theme Analysis of the Political Rhetoric of the Reverend Jesse Louis Jackson, the First 'Serious' Black Candidate for the Office of the President of the U.S." *DAI* 48 (March 1988): 2192A.

Identifies and explicates Jackson's rhetorical strategies and draws implications for the study of other black politicians.

333. Campbell, J. Louis, III. " 'All Men Are Created Equal': Waiting for Godot in the Culture of Inequality." *ComM* 55 (June 1988): 143–161.

Examines three major problems in ideological rhetoric: criteria, masking, and accountability.

334. Castelli, Elizabeth A. "Mimesis as a Discourse of Power in Paul's Letters." *DAI* 48 (April 1988): 2651A.

Claims that mimesis functions as a power strategy in Paul's letters. Examines the ways such discourse relates to society.

335. Chapell, Bryan S. "The Effective Use and Development of Life-Situation Illustrations in Contemporary Preaching: Analysis and Application of Interpersonal Hermeneutics for a Rhetorical Model of Homiletical Communication." *DAI* 49 (September 1988): 379A.

Analyzes modern preaching, using phenomenological methodology, narrative theory, and Ponty's "lived body" theory.

336. Clark, Jeanne Ellen. "Prophetic Rhetoric and the Sanctuary Movement." *DAI* 49 (November 1988): 997A.

Explores the sanctuary movement's use of Hebrew prophetic rhetoric to increase national support for its aims.

337. Cohn, Carol. "Nuclear Discourse in a Community of Defense Intellectuals: The Effects of Techno-Strategic Language and Ra-

tionality, and Their Role in American Political Culture." *DAI* 49 (February 1989): 2374A.

Examines the discourse of nuclear defense intellectuals.

338. Dickson, Wilma A. "The Rhetoric of Religious Polemic: A Literary Study of the Church Order Debate in the Reign of Queen Elizabeth I." *DAI* 49 (August 1988): 274A.

Examines the methods of disputation as practiced in the universities during the reign of Elizabeth I, finding that new polemical forms emerged at this time.

339. Duke, Rodney K. "The Rhetorical Analysis of the Books of Chronicles: The Persuasive Appeal of the Chronicler." *DAI* 49 (December 1988): 1481A.

Rhetorically examines both the structure and the mode of persuasion in the Chronicler's retelling of the story of Israel.

340. Gustainis, J. Justin, and Dan F. Hahn. "While the Whole World Watched: Rhetorical Failures of Anti-War Protest." *ComQ* 36 (Summer 1988): 203–216.

Suggests that because of various rhetorical errors, Vietnam protesters alienated their Middle American audience and may have contributed to lengthening the war.

341. "Japanese Doublespeak." *QRD* 15 (October 1988): 10.

Cites examples of doublespeak in Japan and efforts there to eliminate misleading language from parliamentary debate.

342. Keeney, Donald Earl. "Paul's Opponents in Acts in Light of Gentile Descriptions of Jews." *DAI* 49 (August 1988): 279A.

A rhetorical analysis of how Gentiles described and characterized Jews in relation to their setting in the early Roman Empire.

343. Kelley, Colleen E. "The Public Rhetoric of Mikhail Gorbachev and the Promise of Peace." *WJSC* 52 (Fall 1988): 321–334.

Uses Burke's pentad to examine rhetorical choices.

344. King, Janis Lynn. "A Rhetorical Study of a State Divided: Missouri during the Civil War." *DAI* 48 (April 1988): 2488A.

A rhetorical analysis of the arguments advanced by unionists and secessionists. Uses the rhetorical models of Toulmin and Bitzer.

345. Kinneavy, James L. *Greek Rhetorical Origins of Christian Faith: An Inquiry.* New York: Oxford University Press, 1987. 186 pages

Demonstrates through a study of *pistis* or "proof" that "many of the major features of the concept of persuasion, as embodied in Greek rhetoric of the Hellenistic period, are semantically quite close to the Christian notion of faith." Contends that a majority of New Testament texts mentioning *pistis* as faith can be read with a rhetorical interpretation.

346. Kowalski, Judith A. "Of Water and Spirit: Narrative Structure and Theological Development in the Gospel of John." *DAI* 48 (March 1988): 2364A.

Analyzes the structure of the Gospel of John, focusing on the motif of water as it affects narrative temporality and mode.

347. Lewis, David. "An Argument for the Lucan Authorship of Hebrews." *DAI* 49 (December 1988): 1492A.

Uses text linguistics, stylistics, and lexical similarities to argue that Luke authored Hebrews.

348. Lippard, Paula V. "The Rhetoric of Silence: The Society of Friends' Unprogrammed Meeting for Worship." *ComQ* 36 (Spring 1988): 145–156.

The philosophical bases of Quaker worship are seen to contribute to a participatory form of rhetoric where silence is the primary means of group identification.

349. Luchsinger, John F. "A Rhetorical Critical Study of the Homiletical Theory of Frederick Buechner." *DAI* 49 (August 1988): 279A.

Examines Buechner's three forms of preaching, using a two-phased rhetorical model. Finds that for Buechner preaching is "telling the truth."

350. Makus, Anne L. "Ideology Critique and the Rhetoric of Diversity: Implications of Stuart Hall's Critical Paradigm of Ideology for Contemporary Rhetorical Theory and Criticism." *DAI* 49 (October 1988): 658A.

Examines Hall's theories on the tendency of ideology to limit public discourse by analyzing the rhetoric surrounding the Strategic Defense Initiative.

351. McDonald, Becky Ann. "Falwell and Fantasy: The Rhetoric of a Religious and Political Movement." *DAI* 48 (March 1988): 2194A.

Examines the rhetorical strategies of the Moral Majority and their effect on the movement's success or failure.

352. Meyer, Donald G. "The Use of Rhetorical Technique by Luke in the Book of Acts." *DAI* 49 (November 1988): 1134A.

Concludes that Luke rhetorically packaged the events of Christ's life so that the message would have a convincing impact.

353. Miller, Keith D. "Epistemology of a Drum Major: Martin Luther King, Jr., and the Black Folk Pulpit." *RSQ* 18 (Spring-Summer 1988): 225–236.

Explores slave theology and epistemology as used in the rhetoric of the black folk pulpit. Analyzes "The Drum Major Instinct."

354. Miller, Nancy K. *Subject to Change: Reading Feminist Writing.* Gender and Culture. Edited by Carolyn Heilbrun and Nancy K. Miller. Irvington-on-Hudson, N.Y.: Columbia University Press, 1988. 320 pages

Examines French theories of discourse and American feminist politics to establish a critical framework for discussing women and writing.

355. Mohsen, Raed A. "The Communicative, Persuasive, and Agitational Aspects of Revo-

lutionary Terrorism." *DAI* 48 (May 1988): 2763A.

Analyzes four interviews with terrorist informants. Concludes that acts of terrorism are "definable messages" and thus appropriate objects for rhetorical examination.

356. "Nazi Speech." *QRD* 15 (October 1988): 10.

Cites examples of doublespeak used in the Nazi regime.

357. Panetta, Edward Mark. "Rhetorical Responses to the Unemployment Crisis in the Monongahela Valley." *DAI* 49 (December 1988): 1312A.

A study of three community support groups reveals different rhetorical responses to the unemployment crisis, each rhetorical type being a component of a "socio-political movement."

358. Pearson, Michael Vincent. "Audience Adaptation and Argument in John Paul II's American Speeches, October 1979: A Textual Analysis." *DAI* 49 (November 1988): 998A.

Analyzes the rhetorical problems, audiences, and arguments of Pope John Paul II's speeches, concluding that 10 speeches can be regarded as one extended discourse to the general American public.

359. Penn, C. Ray. " 'When God Is Manly, All Men Are God-Like': A Rhetorical Analysis of the Protestant Christian Feminist Movement." *DAI* 48 (February 1988): 1930A.

Applies a model of the rhetoric of social movements to the study of Christian feminism. Concludes that Protestantism is shifting its view of language.

360. Peterson, Tarla Rai. "The Rhetorical Construction of Institutional Authority in a Senate Subcommittee Hearing on Wilderness Legislation." *WJSC* 52 (Fall 1988): 259–276.

Argues that all structures are vulnerable to strategic alteration through effective participation.

361. Pomeroy, Ralph S. " 'To Push the World': Orwell and the Rhetoric of Pamphleteering." *RSQ* 17 (Fall 1987): 365–412.

Discusses Orwell's interest in writing and collecting pamphlets. Constructs a rhetoric of pamphleteering from Orwell's works.

362. Posner, Richard A. "Interpreting Law, Interpreting Literature I." *Raritan* 7 (Spring 1988): 1–31.

Discusses different models of language and rhetoric informing critical approaches to language, law, and literature.

363. Posner, Richard A. "Interpreting Law, Interpreting Literature II." *Raritan* 8 (Summer 1988): 59–78.

Argues that differences between the rhetorics of literature and law preclude interpreting laws by using the precepts of literary criticism.

364. Saks, Eva. "Representing Miscegenation Law." *Raritan* 8 (Fall 1988): 39–69.

Traces the development of post-Civil War miscegenation discourse as it affected the rhetoric of legal decisions.

365. Sanford, Stephanie. "The Nature of Discourse in the Courtroom: The Complete Rape Trial." *DAI* 48 (March 1988): 2460A.

Studies courtroom participants' reliance on multiple sources of information to manage interaction. Focuses on cohesion devices.

366. Sellnow, Timothy Lester. "A Rhetorical Analysis of Hubert H. Humphrey's Public Image in the Print Media, 1948–1978." *DAI* 49 (October 1988): 659A.

Uses Burke's methods of cluster-agon analysis and dramatism to determine how media shaped and manipulated Humphrey's political image.

367. Smith, Donald Charles. "Korean Airlines 007: Official and Alternative Realities, Their Linguistic Strategies, and Rhetorical Implications." *DAI* 48 (March 1988): 2195A.

Explores the interdependent relationships of government, media, and the public in stories generated by the downing of an airliner.

368. Smith, Larry David, and James L. Golden. "Electronic Storytelling in Electoral Politics: An Anecdotal Analysis of Television Advertising in the Helms-Hunt Senate Race." *SSCJ* 53 (Spring 1988): 244–258.

Comparing the soap opera anecdote to one-shot storytelling suggests that thematic continuity is a fundamental ingredient for effectiveness.

369. Smith, Stephen A., and Cherri D. Roden. "CBS, *The New York Times,* and Reconstructed Political Reality." *SSCJ* 53 (Winter 1988): 140–158.

Examines bias in news and editorial positions in the 1984 national election.

370. Spencer, J. William. "The Role of Text in the Processing of People in Organizations." *DPr* 11 (January–March 1988): 61–78.

Presentencing reports filed by probation officers reflect the background knowledge officers have of the court system.

371. Stoner, Mark Reed. "The Free Speech Movement: A Case Study in the Rhetoric of Social Intervention." *DAI* 49 (August 1988): 167A.

Analyzes the 1964 movement at the University of California—Berkeley by examining the rhetorical activities of students and administrators. Attempts to clarify the relationship between power and "rhetorical visions."

372. "Tracking the Polls." *QRD* 14 (April 1988): 9.

Comparing presidential primary polls to election results, finds polls inaccurate.

373. Turner, Jack D. "A Rhetorical Analysis of Liberation Theology." *DAI* 48 (March 1988): 2360A.

Analyzes the rhetoric of liberation theology and finds such theology openly rhetorical.

374. Underberg, Larry Ralph. "An Analysis of the Rhetoric of the International Society for Krishna Consciousness: An Implicit Theory Perspective." *DAI* 49 (October 1988): 660A.

Analyzes four areas of importance to the movement to show how people follow the movement's implicit theory of discourse.

375. Wallace, James Andrew. "Imaginal Preaching: The Centrality of the Image in the Preaching Event from the Perspective of Archetypal Psychology." *DAI* 48 (February 1988): 1931A.

Uses archetypal psychology to focus on how biblical imagery functions in preaching.

376. Walton, Michael. "Inoculation in Political Campaign Communication." *DAI* 48 (March 1988): 2195A.

Finds that messages attacking issues are more persuasive than character attacks. Applies McGuire's theory, showing that messages can be designed to diffuse attacks.

377. Warren, Timothy S. "Rhetorical Strategies for Biblical Hermeneutics." *DAI* 49 (August 1988): 167A.

Examines the relationship between rhetoric and hermeneutics by constructing a four-stage model of argumentation appropriate for evaluating the "reasonableness and rationality" of biblical interpretations.

378. Webster, Linda Jean. "A Rhetorical Analysis of Selected Republican Speeches in the 1856 Presidential Election Campaign." *DAI* 9 (March 1989): 2195A.

Examines individual speeches made by members of the Republican party during its first organized Presidential campaign.

379. Winkler, Carol Kay. "Argumentative *Topoi* in Presidential Responses to Hostage Situations: Truman to Reagan." *DAI* 48 (February 1988): 1932A.

Examines recurring rhetorical strategies used by five presidents with increasing frequency in addressing hostage situations.

380. Wolfe, Christopher Sterling, and Michael J. Cody. "Perspectives on Legal Interviewing and Counseling." *SSCJ* 53 (Summer 1988): 360–384.

Reviews psychological, dialogic, and utilitarian perspectives. Offers guidelines for research.

381. Wuthnow, Robert. "Religious Discourse as Public Rhetoric." *ComR* 15 (June 1988): 318–338.

A review essay discussing the public understanding of religious discourse. Examines the centrifugal and centripetal orientations of liberal and conservative churches.

See also 211, 286, 315, 497, 525, 721, 762, 913, 961, 970, 982

2.4 COMPUTER AND LITERACY STUDIES

382. Allen, Robert F. "The Stylo-Statistical Method of Literary Analysis." *CHum* 22 (1988): 1–10.

Describes computer programs and methodologies for stylo-statistical analysis, which determines significant deviations from normal word or structure frequencies.

383. Arnove, Robert F., and Harvey J. Graff, eds. *National Literacy Campaigns: Historical and Comparative Perspectives*. New York: Plenum, 1987. 332 pages

A collection of essays offering a theoretical introduction and an overview of large-scale literacy campaigns. Case studies describe historical examples in Germany, Scotland, Sweden, Russia, and the U.S. as well as current efforts in Cuba, Nicaragua, China, India, Tanzania, and UNESCO's Experimental World Literacy Campaign.

384. Baldwin, Elizabeth F. "Linguistics and Ideology in the 'English-Only' Movement." *DAI* 49 (January 1989): 1988A.

Examines attempts to legislate English as the official language of the U.S.

385. Barnard, David, Ron Hayter, Maria Kara-baba, George Logan, and John McFadden. "SGML-Based Markup for Literary Texts: Two Problems and Some Solutions." *CHum* 22 (1988): 265–276.

Defends SGML as the best standard for encoding texts, despite its apparent inflexibility and burdensome keyboarding. Argues that the problems are surmountable.

386. Bizzell, Patricia. "Arguing about Literacy." *CE* 50 (February 1988): 141–153.

Explores and rejects the premises on which humanist and cultural literacy theories are based. Argues for a rhetorical perspective on literacy.

387. Bizzell, Patricia. "Patricia Bizzell Responds [to Ong, *CE* 50 (February 1988)]." *CE* 50 (October 1988): 701–702.

Clarifies her view on Ong's theories of orality and literacy and asserts that she attacks the misuse of his theories, not the theories themselves.

388. Bleich, David. *The Double Perspective: Language, Literacy, and Social Relations,* New York: Oxford University Press, 1988. 400 pages

Examines the relationship between language and literacy and the societal experiences that help shape it. Interrelated essays explore the process of language development, conceptions of knowledge offered by feminist epistemologists, social conceptions of language and knowledge, and current views on the social character of the classroom and academic communities.

389. Brancheau, James Clayton. "The Diffusion of Information Technology: Testing and Extending Innovation Diffusion Theory in the Context of End-User Computing." *DAI* 49 (September 1988): 549A.

Concludes that information systems groups acted too late and offered too little support to affect the diffusion of financing and accounting software.

390. Casement, William. "Bloom and the Great Books." *JGE* 39 (1987): 1–9.

Critiques Bloom for his statements on the learning capacities of average students, arguing that all students may benefit from a Great Books curriculum.

391. Ceesay, Marianna Sarr. "Literacy Issues in National Development." *DAI* 48 (March 1988): 2251A.

Shows that successful literacy campaigns in the Third World depend on popular participation, government commitment, socio-economic structures that reward literacy, and other initiatives.

392. Collier, Mary Jane. "A Comparison of Conversations among and between Domestic Culture Groups: How Intra-and Inter-Cultural Competencies Vary." *ComQ* 36 (Spring 1988): 122–144.

Identifies intercultural conversational competencies for Mexican Americans, black Americans, and white Americans, focusing on rules and outcomes perceived in intercultural interactions.

393. Combs, Mary Carol, and Lynne M. Lynch. "English Plus." *EngT* 4 (October 1988): 36–42.

Reports on the debate over whether English should be made the official language of the U.S.

394. Daniell, Beth. "Literacy, Politics, and Resistance: Moffett's Study of Censorship." *JTW* 7 (Fall-Winter 1988): 237–246.

As in Moffett's experience, people may resist literacy because of the world view embodied. Language is needed to discuss the interconnectedness of the cognitive, emotional, political, and spiritual.

395. Daniell, Beth. "Rereading Ong: Literacy and Social Change." Paper presented at the CCCC Convention, St. Louis, March 1988. ERIC ED 294 216. 14 pages

Reevaluates Ong's theories of literacy in light of Luria's work.

396. Davis, Kevin. "Literacy in the Classroom: The Difference between 'Writing' and 'Writing Down.'" *JTW* 7 (Fall-Winter 1988): 181–186.

Literacy is "the ability to make productive use of language to understand" ourselves and our world. Offers five ways to encourage students to be literate.

397. Gee, James Paul. "Discourse Systems and Aspirin Bottles: On Literacy." *JEd* 170 (1988): 27–40.

Argues that language use involves three connected systems. Gives a definition of literacy by discussing discourse systems.

398. Gibbons, Reginald. "Writing at the Computer." *Raritan* 7 (Spring 1988): 122–150.

Discusses the physical and philosophical impact of the word processor on reading and writing processes.

399. Gordon, W. Terrence. "Undoing Babel: C. K. Ogden's Basic English." *ETC* 45 (Winter 1988): 337–340.

Summarizes historical attempts to simplify English. Sees computer applications for basic English.

400. Grow, Gerald. "Computers and the Writing Process: Interactive Outlining." *CollM* 6 (November 1988): 368–374.

Traces the development of technology for outlining on microcomputers, from word-processing programs through outlining software to programs that integrate outlining with word processing.

401. Haas, Christina. "What Research with Computers Can Tell Us about the Uses of Reading in Writing." Paper presented at the CCCC Convention, Atlanta, March 1987. ERIC ED 284 252. 28 pages

Reports on a longitudinal study of students composing on computers. Finds benefits in evaluating hard copy, especially for long or knowledge-forming tasks.

402. Hanson-Smith, Elizabeth. "Computer Dialect Study: The Findern Anthology." *CollL* 15 (Winter 1988): 47–56.

Describes how the computer facilitated a spelling and dialect study of the Findern anthology. Discusses possibilities for similar research on other texts.

403. Hawisher, Gail. "Research in Computers and Writing: Findings and Implications." Paper presented at the AERA, New Orleans, April 1988. ERIC ED 293 140. 40 pages

Finds a lack of rigor and hasty conclusions in a number of research studies. Recommends several guidelines for improvement.

404. Helgerson, Linda W. "CD-ROM and Scholarly Research in the Humanities." *CHum* 22 (1988): 111–116.

Describes projects to convert and store literary texts on CD-ROM. Focuses on classical literature.

405. Hernadi, Paul. "Doing, Making, Meaning: Toward a Theory of Verbal Practice." *PMLA* 10 (October 1988): 749–758.

Whether situated in speech, writing, or thought, discourse is simultaneously doing, making, and meaning to constitute our conceptions of self, society, and nature.

406. Hollis, Karyn. "Literacy Theory, Context, and Feminist Response." Paper presented at the CCCC Convention, Atlanta, March 1987. ERIC ED 292 098. 25 pages

To promote truly critical literacy, an alternative dialectic theory that mediates "literacy determinant" and "context-determinant" is needed.

407. Holzman, Michael. "A Post-Freirean Model for Adult Literacy Programs." *CE* 50 (February 1988): 177–189.

Compares Laubach's and Freire's methods. Sees a current consensus as endorsing both phases of Freire's model, which uses community members as animators and central decision makers.

408. Horowitz, Roselind, and S. Jay Samuels, eds. *Comprehending Oral and Written Language*. San Diego: Academic Press, 1987. 411 pages

Thirteen essays explore theoretical and research questions associated with the relationships among oral and written language, listening and reading, and speaking and writing.

409. Johnson, Nicholas. "The Semantics of Computer Communications." *ETC* 45 (Fall 1988): 250–255.

Analyzes the language and uses of electronic mail. Shows how print terminology can hamper the effective use of computer media.

410. Juel, Connie. "Learning to Read and Write: A Longitudinal Study of 54 Children from First through Fourth Grades." *JEdP* 80 (1988): 437–447.

Focuses on literacy development in children. Finds that children who were poor readers and writers at the end of first grade were poor readers and writers at the end of fourth grade.

411. Kellendorf, Craig. "Ancient, Renaissance, and Modern: The Human in the Humanities." *JGE* 39 (1987): 133–151.

Summarizes the work of several classical and Renaissance humanists, applying their ideas to the current debate on humanities curricula and cultural literacy.

412. Kintgen, Eugene R., Barry M. Kroll, and Mike Rose, eds. *Perspectives on Literacy*. Carbondale, Ill.: Southern Illinois University Press, 1988. 464 pages

Twenty-eight essays arranged in four sections: psychological and economic consequences of literacy, the development of literacy in the West, the teaching of literacy, and literacy outside the classroom. Treats literacy as a complex area of inquiry in which all aspects are interrelated. Includes bibliography.

413. Koohang, Alex A. "A Study of Attitudes toward Computers: Anxiety, Confidence, Liking, and Perception of Usefulness." *DAI* 49 (September 1988): 486A.

Studies the attitudes of 81 undergraduate students enrolled in different computer-based education courses at Southern Illinois University.

414. *Literacy: Your Community and the Workplace*. Washington, D.C.: American Association of Community and Junior Colleges, 1988.

A videotape exploring issues related to adult illiteracy and the efforts initiated by community, technical, and junior colleges to combat the problem. VHS format only.

415. Marcus, Stephen. "Reading, Writing, and Hypertext." *CollL* 15 (Winter 1988): 9–18.

Students create "hypertext environments" by arranging the parts of a text on a computer screen as the parts come to mind or are generated on the screen.

416. Murray, Denise E. "The Context of Oral and Written Language: A Framework for Mode and Medium Switching." *LSoc* 17 (September 1988): 351–373.

Uses a case study of communication through computers to develop a framework for understanding oral and written language as essentially integrated in social practice.

417. Myers, Miles. *The Present Literacy Crisis and the Public Interest*. Bloomington, Ind.: ERIC/RCS, 1986. ERIC ED 288 183. 18 pages

Discusses the support for education needed to implement new interactionist approaches to the transmission of literacy.

418. Neilsen, Lorraine Ann. "Literacy for Living: What Literacy Means in the Lives of Three Adults." *DAI* 49 (December 1988): 1395A.

Suggests that the concept of literacy cannot be separated from the personality, history, goals, life issues, and problems of the people involved.

419. Olson, David R. "Interpreting Texts and Interpreting Nature: The Effects of Literacy on Hermeneutics and Epistemology." *VLang* 20 (Summer 1986): 302–317.

Argues that the ability to distinguish between what is given and what is inferred or interpreted is decisive to the development of a literate mode of thought.

420. Olson, David R. "Mind and Media: The Epistemic Functions of Literacy." *JC* 38 (Summer 1988): 27–36.

Shifting from orality to literacy to visual media (film, television, and computers) requires the development of new cognitive strategies for understanding and remembering ideas.

421. Olson, David R. "Mythologizing Literacy." *EQ* 21 (1988): 115–126.

Advocates solving social problems constructively rather than blaming them on illiteracy.

422. Pattison, Robert. "The Stupidity Crisis." *BADE* 89 (Spring 1988): 3–10.

Rebuts the premises of Bloom and Hirsch, arguing that they invented a "stupidity crisis."

423. Penrose, John M., and Lawrence M. Seiford. "Microcomputer Users' Preferences for Software Documentation: An Analysis." *JTWC* 18 (1988): 355–566.

Presents results of a survey. While users agree that manuals are necessary, there is "room for improvement in terms of content, organization, and presentation."

424. Phillips, Gerald M., and Bradley R. Erlwein. "Composition on the Computer: Simple Systems and Artificial Intelligence." *ComQ* 36 (Fall 1988): 243–261.

Examines whether computers can duplicate composing. Uses a protypical expert system to determine whether a computer can generate speeches.

425. Raymond, James C. "Desire and the Teaching of Writing." *Focuses* 1 (Spring 1988): 29–39.

Offers "several more or less independent meditations on the subject of literacy."

426. Sadler, Lynn Veach. "An Overview of the CAC Movement." *CAC* 3 (Summer 1988): 22–29.

Reviews the first two waves of the computer-assisted composition movement. Identifies benefits of heuristics-based software and text-analysis programs.

427. Scholes, Robert. "Robert Scholes Responds [to Kamath and Ruston, *CE* 50 (March 1988)]." *CE* 50 (October 1988): 702–703.

Defends his views of Bloom and Hirsch, but urges civility in discussing their works.

428. Scholes, Robert. "Three Views of Education: Nostalgia, History, and Voodoo." *CE* 50 (March 1988): 323–332.

Evaluates Allan Bloom's *The Closing of the American Mind*, Gerald Graff's *Professing Literature*, and E. D. Hirsch's *Cultural Literacy*, finding them "ineffectual," "consequential," and "simplistic," respectively.

429. Scott, Patrick. "A Few Words More about E. D. Hirsch and *Cultural Literacy*." *CE* 50 (March 1988): 333–338.

Supports Hirsch's central thesis that reading requires cultural education. Sees the profession's negative response to the book as intellectually shortsighted and politically inept.

430. Selfe, Cynthia L., and Billie J. Wahlstrom. "Computers and Writing: Casting a Broader Net with Theory and Research." *CHum* 22 (1988): 57–66.

Argues that we must explore the computer's effects on pedagogy, the history of computing, and the implications for theory and interdisciplinary study.

431. Shirk, Henrietta Nickels. "Technical Writing's Roots in Computer Science: The Evolution from Technician to Technical Writer." *JTWC* 18 (1988): 305–323.

"Summarizes some historical trends in computer software technology, their contributions to the field of technical writing, and their implications for the current communicator."

432. Sledd, Andrew. "Readin' Not Riotin': The Politics of Literacy." *CE* 50 (September 1988): 495–508.

Argues that the current literacy crisis is a hoax. Suggests tailoring standards of literacy to students' interests, prior experiences, and future needs.

433. Smith, Frank. *Joining the Literacy Club: Further Essays into Education*. Portsmouth, N.H.: Heinemann, 1988. 154 pages

Eight essays by Smith explore the social and educational dynamics by which students become literate.

434. Swearingen, C. Jan. "Bloomsday for Literacy: How Reactionaries and Relativists Alike Undermine Literacy While Seeming to Promote It." *FEN* 17 (Fall 1988): 2–5.

Reviews positions taken by the left and the right to mystify language and interpretation rather than produce a pedagogy of clarity for students.

435. Trachsel, Mary Caroline Brayton. "The History of College Entrance Examinations in English: A Record of Academic Assumptions about Literacy." *DAI* 49 (September 1988): 489A.

A historical study that uses college entrance examinations in English to explain how the American academy institutionally has defined literacy.

436. Urla, Jacqueline. "Being Basque, Speaking Basque: The Politics of Language and Identity in the Basque Country." *DAI* 48 (March 1988): 2376A.

Examines conditions under which language differences begin to be seen as a problem to be solved through language planning.

437. U.S. Conference of Mayors. *Adult Literacy: A Policy Statement and Resource Guide for Cities*. Washington, D.C.: U.S. Conference of Mayors, June 1986. ERIC ED 287 023. 26 pages

Expands a policy resolution approved in 1985, noting the magnitude of adult illiteracy and suggesting guidelines for literacy initiatives.

438. Valentine, Carol Ann, and Nancy Hoar, eds. *Women and Communicative Power: Theory, Research, and Practice*. Annandale, Va.: SCA, 1988. 160 pages

Ten scholars explore women's communicative power from several perspectives. Discusses politeness, sex roles, and conversation, women managers and development programs, gender and culture, communication strategies, and the feminization of power.

439. Warren, Douglas James. "A Critical Study of Communication in Land Use Hearings." *DAI* 49 (October 1988): 974A.

Explores the communicative competence of participants in land use hearings. Discusses the ability to influence decisions of variance committees and participants' expressions of dissatisfaction with the hearing process.

440. Westland, James C. "Semantic Networks: A Stochastic Model of Their Performance in Information Retrieval." *DAI* 48 (May 1988): 2921A.

Compares two classes of document-based information retrieval strategies: Boolean and "concept" extended.

See also 108, 264, 281, 1161, 1183, 1266, 1272, 1423

2.5 ADVERTISING, PUBLIC RELATIONS, AND BUSINESS

441. Abernathy, Avery M. "Determinants of Audience Exposure to Radio Advertising." *DAI* 49 (January 1989): 1886A.

Hypothesizes that people's loyalties to a radio station, their attitudes toward radio advertising, and the ease of avoiding commercials impact exposure to radio advertising.

442. "Advertising and Popular Magazines." *QRD* 15 (October 1988): 9.

Cites an 18 April 1988 issue of *Advertising Age* as a resource for studying print advertising and its influence on what we read in popular magazines.

443. Anderson, W. Steve, and Michael Kleine. "Excellent Writing: Educating the Whole Corporation." *JBTC* 2 (January 1988): 49–62.

Explains how writing problems derive from managers' misconceptions about writers and writing, not from an employee's lack of motivation or ability. Advocates using educator-consultants to stress a process view and corporation-wide collaboration.

444. Benson, James A. "Crisis Revisited: An Analysis of Strategies Used by Tylenol in the Second Tampering Episode." *CSSJ* 39 (Spring 1988): 49–66.

Discusses strategies for crisis management in business organizations.

445. Berger, Karen. "The Effect of Report, Inference, and Judgment Messages in the Absence and Presence of a Source on Attitudes and Beliefs." *DAI* 49 (November 1988): 1205A.

Studies a semantic trichotomy under three source conditions using messages about three products: a pain reliever, a bar soap, and a toothpaste.

446. Bettencourt, Michael. "The Language of Military Recruitment." *QRD* 15 (October 1988): 6–7.

Analyzes the language of military recruitment as an example of doublespeak based on the language of business.

447. Brown, Jane Ledwell. "A Survey of Writing Practices in Management." *EQ* 21 (1988): 7–18.

Surveys writing practices in four Montreal corporations and argues for further study of business writing environments.

448. Choe, Man Kee. "Organizational Performance and Communication Contents in Annual Reports." *DAI* 48 (March 1988): 2385A.

Presents longitudinal and cross-sectional analyses of how U.S. oil corporations manage their images in letters to shareholders.

449. Chung, Kun Young. "Firm Size, Industry Accounting Norms, and the Information Content of Accounting Change Announcements." *DAI* 49 (December 1988): 1508A.

Contrary to the size-related differential information hypothesis, this study finds an inverse relationship between firm size and the information content of accounting change announcements.

450. Cornwell, Tammy Bettina. "Comprehension and Miscomprehension of Selected Print Advertisements: Focus on the Hispanic Consumer." *DAI* 49 (December 1988): 1519A.

Attempts to determine the amount of miscomprehension resulting from advertisements that contain subjective opinions, superlatives, exaggerations, and no specific facts.

451. Crable, Richard E., and Melissa M. Faulkner. "The Issue Development Graph: A Tool for Research and Analysis." *CSSJ* 39 (Summer 1988): 110–120.

Reviews research on issue management, describes criteria for analysis, and discusses implications for business organizations.

452. Darley, William K. "The Roles of Message Content, Product Risk, and Communication Modality in Determining Consumer Response to Advertising." *DAI* 49 (October 1988): 883A.

Examines the cognitive and affective effects of modality, product type, and claim type.

453. De Land, H. Brent. "Managerial Understanding of Public Relations in Illinois Community Action Agencies." *DAI* 48 (March 1988): 2385A.

Finds a lack of interest in and knowledge about public relations among executives in Illinois community action agencies.

454. Dill, William Noel. "Tests of Information Evaluation in a Competitive Environment." *DAI* 48 (April 1988): 2668A.

Uses a competitive two-person setting to examine decision strategies individuals employed to evaluate subjective information.

455. Dionisopoulos, George N., and Richard E. Crable. "Definitional Hegemony as a Public Relations Strategy: The Rhetoric of the Nuclear Power Industry after Three Mile Island." *CSSJ* 39 (Summer 1988): 134–145.

Examines the architectonic function of public relations in the management of issues.

456. Dougan, William Lee. "Using Information Theory in the Study of Group Decision Making." *DAI* 48 (March 1988): 2386A.

Uses mathematical techniques from information theory to study how management makes decisions in organizations.

457. Finch, James Earl. "The Role of Involvement and Source Credibility as Determinants of Vehicle-Source Effects in Persuasive Communication." *DAI* 48 (February 1988): 2107A.

Examines the nature of involvement and the credibility of message- and vehicle-source in determining the acceptance of written messages.

458. Fisher, Debra Comer. "Organizational Newcomers' Acquisition of Information from Peers." *DAI* 48 (April 1988): 2672A.

Fourth-month employees in a service organization were interviewed to determine if their peers were significant sources of information about the organization.

459. Galbraith, Sharon M. "A Study of Cognitive Processing of Pragmatic Implications: Ads Versus Non-Ads." *DAI* 48 (June 1988): 3156A.

Finds no difference in processing and remembering pragmatically implied claims in advertisements when compared with other types of messages.

460. Halpern, Jeanne W. "Getting in Deep: Using Qualitative Research in Business and Technical Communication." *JBTC* 2 (September 1988): 22–43.

Identifies current needs for research. Explains ethnographic study, its recursive methods, and professional benefits.

461. Haswell, Richard H. "Toward Competent Writing in the Workplace." *JTWC* 18 (1988): 161–173.

Compares undergraduates and employees writing on the same topic. Finds differences in length, vocabulary, organization, specificity, sentence formation, and surface error.

462. Hazelton, Vincent, Jr., and Larry W. Long. "Concepts for Public Relations Education, Research, and Practice: A Communication Point of View." *CSSJ* 39 (Summer 1988): 77–87.

Uses general systems theory to describe the interdisciplinary nature of the public relations process.

463. Heath, Robert L. "The Rhetoric of Issue Advertising: A Rationale, a Case Study, a Critical Perspective—and More." *CSSJ* 39 (Summer 1988): 99–109.

Applies archetypes as guidelines to develop critical and ethical standards useful in evaluating corporate operations and communication behavior.

464. Heneghan, Beverly Bates. "The Composing Processes of Computer Documentation Writers." *DAI* 48 (April 1988): 2562A.

Interviews directors, analyzes minutes of meetings, and surveys 15 writers in an international telecommunications corporation. Includes a discussion of drafts, revision, and training.

465. Heroux, Lise A. "Buyer-Seller Interaction: A Script Theoretic Approach." *DAI* 49 (August 1988): 297A.

Investigates the theory that buyers and sellers who are repeatedly exposed to sales interactions develop scripts to guide behavior and influence outcomes.

466. "The High Cost of Television Advertising." *QRD* 14 (April 1988): 10.

Cites the 4 January 1988 issue of *Advertising Age* as a resource for studying the cost of advertising.

467. Higie, Robin A. "The Receiver's Enduring Involvement and Situational Involvement: Effects on Processing and Persuasion." *DAI* 49 (November 1988): 1206A.

Concludes that enduring involvement had a significant effect on message recall and attitudes toward content. In this experiment, computers served as a source of contact.

468. Hirota, Janice M. "Cultural Mediums: The Work World of 'Creatives' in American Advertising Agencies." *DAI* 49 (January 1989): 1864A.

Examines the occupational community of art directors and copywriters in American advertising agencies.

469. Jaffe, Francoise G. "Metaphors and Memory: A Study in Persuasion." *DAI* 49 (February 1989): 2311A.

Provides a theoretical framework for successfully using metaphors in advertising.

470. Johnston, Patricia A. "Edward Steichen's Advertising Photography: The Visual Strategies of Persuasion." *DAI* 49 (September 1988): 531A.

Photography replaced drawing in the 1920s because potential consumers responded to photography's inherent "truth."

471. Kim, Tong Hun. "The Value of Communication in a Multiple Agent Framework." *DAI* 49 (October 1988): 870A.

Derives the necessary and sufficient conditions that give communication value in terms of expected utility.

472. Knouse, Stephen B. "The Letter of Recommendation: Writer Familiarity with the Recommendee." *MCQ* 2 (August 1988): 46–62.

Proposes attribution theory as a means of understanding the reader's perceptions of the letter of recommendation.

473. "The Leading Advertisers." *QRD* 14 (January 1988): 9–10.

Describes the 24 September 1987 issue of *Advertising Age* as a valuable resource for researching, teaching, or studying advertising.

474. Lin, Jimming Tzu-Ming. "The Impact of Computer-Mediated Communication Systems on Interpersonal Relations and Task Performance." *DAI* 48 (March 1988): 2388A.

Compares the impact of face-to-face and computer-mediated communication on two facets of interpersonal interaction: interpersonal situations and task performance.

475. McCollum, Marion Ewing. "Subcultures and Stories: Reflections of a Multicultural Reality in Organizations." *DAI* 48 (April 1988): 2741A.

Critically examines the premise that organizations are culturally monolithic. Questions the concept of "organizational story."

476. Miceli, Thomas J. "Contractual Responses to Information Costs: A Positive Analysis of the Real Estate Market." *DAI* 49 (February 1988): 2345A.

Analyzes the role of contracts in resolving problems of imperfect information in exchange relationships.

477. Mick, David Glenn. "Levels of Comprehension in Consumers' Processing of Print

Advertising Language." *DAI* 49 (October 1988): 884A.

Tests nine hypotheses about the effects of three levels of comprehension on brand attitude polarization, on brand attitude accessibility, and on delayed message recall.

478. Mirel, Barbara E. "Text and Context: The Special Case of In-House Documentation." *DAI* 48 (January 1988): 1758A.

Uses documentation development and organizational theory to study in-house manuals as instructional guides and as a stabilizing communication in a changing technology.

479. Morrison, Deborah Kauffroth. "Approaches to Clio, 1964–1980: A Study of Social Communication in Clio Award-Winning Television Advertising." *DAI* 49 (December 1988): 1521A.

Reviews award-winning advertisements for symbolic and social communication, examining them from three perspectives: as communication, as cultural process, and as creative art.

480. "Most Hated Ads." *QRD* 15 (October 1988): 11.

Cites the 18 July 1988 issue of *Advertising Age* as a resource for studying the effectiveness of television commericals.

481. Motameni, Reza. "Advertising Competition in U.S. Cigarette Industry, 1949–1980." *DAI* 48 (May 1988): 2927A.

Studies the nature of advertising competition among brands of cigarettes in an advertising-intensive industry.

482. Mueller, Barbara. "Multinational Advertising: An Examination of Standardization and Specialization in Commercial Messages." *DAI* 49 (October 1988): 885A.

Examines the degree to which standardized or specialized approaches to advertising are employed in international campaigns. Discusses the factors influencing which approach advertisers choose.

483. Murphy, Margaret. "The Functions of Humor in the Workplace." *DAI* 48 (April 1988): 2675A.

Tests four specific functions of humor: building consensus, resolving conflict, exercising control, and channeling intergroup and intra-group competition.

484. Papa, Michael J., and Karen Tracy. "Communicative Indices of Employee Performance with New Technology." *ComR* 15 (October 1988): 524–544.

Individuals who are communicatively competent, effective listeners, and able to interact with others are likely to be productive using a new computer system.

485. Patrick, Michael Strausbaugh. "A Theory-Based Methodology for Determining the Organization of Product Concepts in Memory." *DAI* 49 (November 1988): 1208A.

Applies the Proximities Analysis of Multi-Trial Free Recall to direct research with consumers.

486. Pepper, Gerald Lee. "A Procedure for Assessing and Contrasting the Metaphorical and Literal Perceptions of Leadership within a Society." *DAI* 48 (February 1988): 1930A.

Presents a method for examining constructions of meaning by analyzing metaphors within an organization.

487. Petelle, John L., Gerald Z. Slaughter, and Jerry D. Jorgensen. "New Explorations in Organizational Relationships: An Expectancy Model of Human Symbolic Activity." *SSCJ* 53 (Spring 1988): 293–306.

Addresses the dimensions of congruent expectancies and symbolic exchanges between supervisors and subordinates.

488. Peterson, Tarla Rai. "The Meek Shall Inherit the Mountains: Dramatistic Criticism of Grand Teton National Park's Interpretive Program." *CSSJ* 39 (Summer 1988): 121–133.

Applies Burke's theory of rhetoric to disclose organizational myths that affect public relations efforts.

489. Pribble, Paula Tompkins. "A Critical Study of Rhetoric in Employee Orientation Programs: Becoming an Employee." *DAI* 48 (February 1988): 1930A.

Investigates the persuasive process used by a business to socialize new employees.

490. Price, Vincent. "On the Public Aspects of Opinion: Linking Levels of Analysis in Public Opinion Research." *ComR* 15 (December 1988): 659–679.

Discusses the importance in public opinion research of linking cognitive and mass communication approaches. Suggests using social identification theories to link the approaches.

491. "Puffing the Product." *QRD* 14 (January 1988): 10.

Defines the concept of "puffing" in advertising and provides examples of its use.

492. Sanft, Henrianne. "Children's Processing of Advertising: Mediating Variables and Measurement Issues." *DAI* 48 (April 1988): 2680A.

Examines multiple measures and variables that may mediate the effects of advertising in children.

493. "The Second 100 Leading Advertisers." *QRD* 14 (April 1988): 10.

Cites the 23 November 1987 issue of *Advertising Age* as a source for researching, teaching, or studying advertising.

494. Serini, Shirley. "Towards an Understanding of the Social-Cultural Aspects of Special Events." *CSSJ* 39 (Summer 1988): 146–157.

Applying the Chicago School's process of symbolic interaction, broadens the concept of a special event as a function in public relations.

495. Smolinski, Harold Carl. "An Examination of Media Information Preceding Potential Firm Financial Distress: The Case of Debt Rerating to CAA and Below." *DAI* 48 (March 1988): 2382A.

Uses standard event methodology to discover whether downgrading bonds conveys new information to the market.

496. Souther, James W. "Effective Management: The Key to Quality Communication." *JTWC* 18 (1988): 1–9.

Suggests how managers can improve the quality of writing in business and government.

497. "Special Effects and Political Commercials." *QRD* 14 (July 1988): 11–12.

Discusses postproduction techniques and their effects, implying that these treatments are a form of visual doublespeak.

498. Speck, Paul S. "On Humor and Humor in Advertising." *DAI* 49 (September 1988): 557A.

Explores the differential benefits and risks associated with five humorous message types.

499. Stohl, Cynthia, and W. Timothy Coombs. "Cooperation or Cooptation: An Analysis of Quality Circle Training Manuals." *MCQ* 2 (August 1988): 63–89.

A content analysis of over 500 messages in quality circle manuals indicates that the messages overwhelmingly represent the concerns, values, and perspectives of management.

500. Stohl, Cynthia, and Kenneth Jennings. "Volunteerism and Voice in Quality Circles." *WJSC* 52 (Summer 1988): 238–251.

Explores the interactions between workers' expectations and job satisfaction.

501. Stout, Daniel A., Jr., and Russell H. Mouritsen. "Prosocial Behavior in Advertising Aimed at Children: A Content Analysis." *SSCJ* 53 (Winter 1988): 159–174.

Examines ethical issues of persuasion, consumerism, and socialization.

502. "Teenagers and Advertising." *QRD* 14 (April 1988): 10.

Summarizes an article reporting on teenagers' negative responses to television commercials. Concludes that students need to study the language of advertising.

503. Tjosvold, Dean, and Leonard T. McNeely. "Innovation through Communication in an Educational Bureaucracy." *ComR* 15 (October 1988): 568–581.

Individuals who cooperate in achieving interdependent goals contribute to innovation in organizations, while those who are competitive or independent do not.

504. Tolar, Debra Olson. "A Measure of General Persuasibility." *DAI* 48 (June 1988): 3010A.

Finds that an individual's gender, though not age or educational level, correlates with general susceptibility to persuasive communications.

505. Tonn, Mari Boor. "The Rhetorical Personae of Mary Harris 'Mother' Jones: Industrial Labor's Maternal Prophet." *DAI* 49 (December 1988): 1313A.

Describes problems that Jones faced as a female labor agitator and the rhetorical strategies she used, whereby she developed dual roles as "mother" and "prophet."

506. Van Esch, Linda Ann. "An Experimental Investigation of Mixed-Media Advertising Effects." *DAI* 48 (April 1988): 2681A.

Tests the hypothesis that mixed-media advertising is more effective than simple repetition.

507. Vianello, Robert. "The Rhetoric of the 'Spot': The Textual Analysis of the American Television Commercial." *DAI* 49 (December 1988): 1304A.

Studies how meaning is generated in television commercials by means of three rhetorical postures: the rhetorics of truth, personality, and everyday life.

508. Vickery, Michael Ray. "The Rhetoric of Commercial Nuclear Power: A Study of Technique." *DAI* 49 (December 1988): 1313A.

Argues that, through the "rhetoric of technique," the technological society justifies social applications of technological instruments, helping to maintain a preferred vision of reality.

509. Vinikas, Vincent A. "Market Forces and Human Values: National Advertising and American Mores, 1920–1940." *DAI* 48 (May 1988): 2965A.

Seeks to integrate the methodologies of social and business history. Explores the cultural content of advertisements while assessing their impact on the demand for goods.

510. Wallace, Bill D. "A Synthesis, Operationalization, and Test of the Functional Theories of Persuasion." *DAI* 49 (November 1988): 999A.

Tests the theoretical assumptions of Smith, Bruner, White, Katz, and Kelman, showing limited support for them.

511. White, Kim Denise. "Influence of the Target, Agent, and Message Type on Compliance Resistance Strategies in Organizations: The Development of a Competence Resistance Taxonomy." *DAI* 48 (February 1988): 1932A.

Examines the nature of persuasion in organizational settings.

512. Wicke, Jennifer A. *Advertising Fictions: Literature , Advertisement , and Social Reading.* Irvington-on-Hudson, N.Y.: Columbia University Press, 1988. 224 pages

Examines the development of advertising and the growth of the narrative novel as a popular social institution.

See also 368, 439, 534, 842, 1457

2.6 LITERATURE, FILM

513. Ahmad, Shafiuddin. "Performing the Other: Rhetoric, Genre, and George Ryga's Drama." *DAI* 49 (November 1988): 100A.

Argues that George Ryga's plays use language to build an ideological and rhetorical stance to affect social change.

514. Allen, Carolyn. "Louise Rosenblatt and Theories of Reader-Response." *Reader* 20 (Fall 1988): 32–39.

Reviews Rosenblatt's career and thought.

515. Almeida, Michael J. "Reasoning about the Temporal Structure of Narratives." *DAI* 48 (April 1988): 3022B.

Examines temporal relations within narratives to determine how a parser-derived model accounts for the discourse.

516. Angenot, Marc, and Darko Suniv. "A Response to Professor Fekete's 'Five Theses' [*SFS* 15 (November 1988)]." *SFS* 15 (November 1988): 324–333.

Attempts to "make out a real mandate for science fiction" that goes beyond Fakete's "relativism" and "nihilism."

517. Barreca, Regina. "Metaphor into Narrative: Being Very Careful with Words." *WS* 15 (October 1988): 243–256.

Discusses the literalization of metaphor in the comedies of women writers, in which cliches become literal and turn into event.

518. Barzilai, Shuli. "Unmaking the Words That Make Us: Doris Lessing's 'How I Finally Lost My Heart.'" *Style* 22 (Winter 1988): 595–612.

Describes Lessing's subversion of language as a means of expressing discontent with dominant social conventions. Examines women's relationship to prevailing rhetoric.

519. Barzilai, Shuli. "Virginia Woolf's Pursuit of Truth: 'Monday or Tuesday,' 'Moments of Being,' and 'The Lady in the Looking-Glass.'" *JNT* 18 (Fall 1988): 199–210.

Woolf presents her search for truth stylistically by using a variety of perceiving minds all focusing on one object.

520. Bell, George E. "Aristotle and Barnum: A Study of the Rhetorical Backgrounds, Subjects, and Practice of H. L. Mencken's 'Monday Articles,' 1920–1929." *DAI* 49 (September 1988): 504A.

Concludes that Mencken's formal and informal education placed him in the classical rhetorical tradition.

521. Benston, Alice. "Framing and Being Framed by Art: Theatricality and Voyeurism in Balthus." *Style* 22 (Summer 1988): 341–360.

Argues that Balthus purposely manipulates the reader's subjective reactions, creating the effect of modern theater.

522. Berger, Albert I. "Theories of History and Social Order in *Astounding Science Fiction*, 1934–1955." *SFS* 15 (March 1988): 12–33.

Finds that stories published in *Astounding Science Fiction* from 1934 to 1955 evolve towards misanthropy, elitism, and authoritarianism.

523. Berthoff, Ann E. "Democratic Practice, Pragmatic Vistas." *Reader* 20 (Fall 1988): 40–47.

Identifies Rosenblatt as a significant pragmatic and democratic voice.

524. Blewett, Mary Edge. " 'The Silver Key': The Familiar Letter in Nineteenth-Century American Literature." *DAI* 48 (March 1988): 2336A.

Shows how the letters of Adams, Howells, and James are as interesting and literary as eighteenth-century classics and nineteenth-century canonical works.

525. Blount, Marcellus. "Broken Tongues: Figures of Voice in Afro-American Poetry." *DAI* 48 (April 1988): 2661A.

Describes the use of Afro-American sermons in providing a consistent "figure of voice" for Afro-American poets.

526. Bock, Carol A. "Storytelling and the Multiple Audiences of *Shirley*." *JNT* 18 (Fall 1988): 226–242.

Answers critics of Charlotte Brontë's use of intrusive narrators. Raises thematic questions by examining complex intra-textual and extra-textual relationships between author and audience.

527. Boehm, Beth A. "A Rhetoric of Metafiction." *DAI* 48 (January 1988): 1765A.

Examines the rhetorical processes in metafiction, a label for texts that self-consciously flaunt their own processes of construction.

528. Bonheim, Helmut. "Narrative Technique in Emily Dickinson's 'My Life Had Stood a Loaded Gun.' " *JNT* 18 (Fall 1988): 258–268.

Uses narrative theory and stylistic analysis to show how Dickinson's poem can be read as a narrative, thereby revealing its hidden meanings.

529. Brayndick, Michael Sidney. "Joseph Cornell and the Dialectics of Human Time." *DAI* 48 (April 1988): 2619A.

Discusses Cornell's creative process, his approaches, and responses to him. Gives excerpts from readings, resource materials, and diaries.

530. Bromell, Nicholas K. "By the Sweat of Our Brows: Literature and Labor in Antebellum American Culture." *DAI* 48 (May 1988): 2913A.

Argues that Emerson, Thoreau, Melville, and Stowe uncovered hidden psychological dimensions of human and literary work.

531. Byrne, Margaret M. "A Working Theory of Film Genre." *DAI* 49 (October 1988): 642A.

Defines film as synthetic art and explores multiple uses of the genre: as a naming tool, as a process of film-theory building, and as a means for useful categorization.

532. Carlton-Ford, Cynthia Clara. "Conversation, Gender, and Power: Dialogue in the Nineteenth-Century Novel." *DAI* 48 (March 1988): 2341A.

Examines social relationships and power struggles in the dialogue of characters in *Pride and Prejudice, Jane Eyre, David Copperfield,* and *The Egoist.*

533. Casagrande, Peter J. "Biography and Creativity: 'Mysterious Mutation.' " *SNNTS* 20 (Summer 1988): 206–222.

Finds that four recent biographies of novelists lack a reliable hypothesis of literary creativity.

534. Chapman, Raymond. "We Gonna Rite Wot We Wanna: The Appeal of Misspelling." *EngT* 4 (April 1988): 39–42.

Describes the uses of deliberate misspellings to show dialect in literary texts and to produce special effects in advertising.

535. Clausen, Christopher. "Moral Inversion and Critical Argument." *GR* 42 (Spring 1988): 9–22.

Argues that moral criticism is almost unavoidable in critical thinking and in the interpretation of literature.

536. Cohen, Michael. "The Sport of American-Bashing in Modern English Authors." *SNNTS* 20 (Fall 1988): 316–322.

Explores chauvinistic caricatures of Americans in twentieth-century British fiction by Forster, Wodehouse, Waugh, and Amis.

537. Collins, Christopher. "Groundless Figures: Reader Response to Verbal Imagery." *CEAC* 51 (Fall 1988): 11–29.

Distinguishes productive from reproductive imagination in the act of reading, concluding that literary imagery is more visionary than visual.

538. Cooper, Richard R. "The Languages of Philosophy, Religion, and Art in the Writings of Iris Murdock." *DAI* 48 (April 1988): 2653A.

Applies to Murdock's writings a theoretical model for conceptualizing relationships. Discovers a tension between and among her poles of thought.

539. Corder, Jim. "When (Do I/Shall I/May I/ Must I/Is It Appropriate for Me to) (Say No to/Deny/Resist/Repudiate/Attack/Alter) Any (Poem/Poet/Other/Piece of the World) for My Sake?" *RSQ* 18 (Summer 1988): 49–68.

Discusses the role of criticism in argument.

540. Coyle, Michael Gordon. " 'The Poetry Breaks Off': Generic Combination in the *Cantos* of Ezra Pound." *DAI* 49 (August 1988): 253A.

Studies Pound's editing and combining historical texts to create the heterogeneous text of the *Cantos*.

541. Culler, Jonathan. "It's Time to Set the Record Straight about Paul de Man and His Wartime Articles for a Pro-Fascist Newspaper." *CHE* 34 (13 July 1988): B1.

The young Paul de Man wrote fascist articles for approval by authorities in occupied Belgium. He should be judged for his scholarly writing, not his youthful indiscretions.

542. Daleski, H. M. "Imagining Revolution: The Eye of History and of Fiction." *JNT* 18 (Winter 1988): 61–72.

Considers stylistic similarities and differences between historians and novelists by comparing Carlyle's *The French Revolution* and Dickens's *A Tale of Two Cities*.

543. Davies, Stephen. "True Interpretations." *P&L* 12 (October 1988): 290–297.

Addresses the issue of why contrary but equally acceptable interpretations of the same literary text exist. They are equally plausible insofar as they are equally true.

544. de Beaugrande, Robert. "In Search of Feminist Discourse: The 'Difficult' Case of Luce Irigaray." *CE* 50 (March 1988): 253–272.

Illustrates Irigaray's tactics of quotation, mimicry, paraphrase, displacement, dispersion, metaphoricity, and logic breaking as ways for experimental discourse to challenge pre-established systems.

545. Desmet, Christy. "Rhetorical Selves: Shakespeare's Problem Characters and Their Critics." *DAI* 49 (March 1988): 2342A.

Focuses on metaphor and hyperbole as keys to Shakespeare's epideictics and his evolution of characters, not as "essential selves," but as controlled by plot.

546. Dorsey, Peter Andrew. "The Rhetoric of Conversion in Early Twentieth-Century American Autobiography." *DAI* 49 (August 1988): 253A.

Proposes conversion as a metaphorical system and examines how the search for illumination, traditionally a search for social role, creates estrangement.

547. Draine, Betsy. "Academic Feminists Must Make Sure Their Commitments Are Not Self-Serving." *CHE* 34 (10 August 1988): A40.

Believes that several feminist novelists have criticized their white, middle class, female readers for promoting the cause solely to advance their own parochial views.

548. Duyfhuizen, Bernard. "Textual Harassment of Marvell's Coy Mistress: The Institutionalization of Masculine Criticism." *CE* 50 (April 1988): 411–423.

Accuses published guides to literary analysis, especially *A Handbook of Critical Approaches to Literature,* of transmitting a clear cultural bias that excludes women.

549. Emmerson, Richard Kenneth. "Apocalypse Now and Then." *MLQ* 46 (December 1985): 429–439.

Notes new scholarly interest in the significance of apocalypticism for literature and art.

550. Engel, William Edward. "Emblems and *Sententiae* in Seventeenth-Century Prose: Mystical and Literary Design in Robert Burton and Thomas Browne." *DAI* 48 (March 1988): 2193A.

Reconstructs the assumptions of figurative and literal expression in literature from Shakespeare's time to Milton's.

551. Esrock, Ellen Jordan. "Visual Imaging and Reader Response." *CEAC* 51 (Fall 1988): 30–38.

Discusses how the narrator's language can trigger or block the reader's visual imaging, creating empathy or distance.

552. Evans, Arthur B. "Science Fiction Versus Scientific Fiction in France: From Jules Verne to J.-H. Rosny Aine." *SFS* 15 (March 1988): 1–11.

Draws theoretical distinctions between science fiction and scientific fiction by investigating "narratological phenomena" that differentiate the two genres.

553. Fekete, John. "The Stimulation of Simulations: Five Theses on Science Fiction and Marxism." *SFS* 15 (November 1988): 312–323.

Considers Marxism a specific form of science fiction that happens to mistake itself for "the real" rather than serving as a "benchmark" for evaluating science fiction.

554. Ferris, Ina. "The Historical Novel and the Problem of Beginning: The Model of Scott." *JNT* 18 (Winter 1988): 73–82.

The beginnings of Scott's novels, which are either "steppings in" or linear narratives, help differentiate historical novels from historiography.

555. Fogelin, Robert J. *Figuratively Speaking.* New Haven: Yale University Press, 1988. 128 pages

Examines figures of speech that concern meaning—irony, hyperbole, understatement, similes, metaphors, and others—to show how they work and why they are appealing. Contends that figures derive power from the reader's participation in the text.

556. Frank, Luanne T. "Criticism and the Meaning of Writing." *Pre/Text* 8 (Fall-Winter 1987): 185–194.

Dramatizes possible relations between criticism and writing. Suggests how contem-porary models of criticism view their writing.

557. Frantisek, W. Galen. *Historic Structures: The Prague School Project , 1928–1946.* University of Texas Press Slavic Series, no. 7. Austin, Tex.: University of Texas Press, 1988. 268 pages

Discusses the evolution within the Prague Linguistic Circle of theories that concern literature's changes in time and the place of literature in society. Demonstrates that the structuralist approach is not unhistorical as some critics have charged.

558. Garrett-Petts, W. F. "Exploring an Interpretive Community: Reader Response to Prairie Literature." *CE* 50 (December 1988): 920–926.

Explores the constraints of the contemporary critical paradigm and the beginnings of a paradigm shift.

559. Gillespie, Michael Joseph. "Translation, Reading, and Literary Theory." *DAI* 48 (March 1988): 2331A.

Elevates translation theory by connecting it with four literary theorists: Jauss, Bloom, Iser, and Fish.

560. Goatly, Andrew. "Interrelations of Metaphors in Golding's Novels: A Framework for the Study of Metaphoric Intensity." *Lang S* 20 (Spring 1987): 125–144.

Develops and illustrates a linguistic system for analyzing how metaphors interact to interlock and extend meanings in literary works. Based on Richards and Leech.

561. Goff, Barbara Elizabeth. "Speech and Silence in Euripides's *Hippolytas*." *DAI* 48 (March 1988): 2329A.

Explores how the opposition of speech and silence relates to other aspects of *Hippolytas*. Suggests how contemporary critical concerns may apply to an ancient text.

562. Gordon, David J. "Character and Self in Autobiography." *JNT* 18 (Spring 1988): 105–119.

Describes the inescapable tension between authorial reflexivity and fictional self or narrator. The work must be read as fiction and as on-going discourse.

563. Gordon, Linda A. "The Martinville Steeplechase: Charting the Course." *Style* 22 (Fall 1988): 402–409.

The two versions of the Martinville Steeplechase scene in *Swann's Way* show a changing narrative perspective over time. They present reality's variability and the impossibility of "accurate" portrayal.

564. Green, Debra L. "The Divided I/Eye: Problems of Subjectivity in the Novels and Films of Marguerite Duras." *DAI* 49 (December 1988): 1447A.

Analyzes Duras's novels and films, applying contemporary theories of language drawn from linguistics, narratology, psychoanalysis, and film theory.

565. Greene, Sharon Elaine. "The Body Politic: Women, Language, and Revolution in Three Contemporary Novels." *DAI* 49 (December 1988): 1599A.

Uses narratives by Naipaul, Didion, and Atwood to test the theories of *ecriture feminine* as well as Peter Brooks's narrative theory.

566. Greenhut, Deborah S. *Feminine Rhetorical Culture: Tudor Adaptations of Ovid's Heroides*. American University Studies, English Language and Literature, vol. 59. New York: Peter Lang, 1988. 213 pages

Focuses on nominally feminine speech in the works of Ovid, George Turberville, and Michael Drayton, examining the literary problems faced by male writers who attempt to develop speech for female characters.

567. Harris, Jeane. "The Emergence of a Feminizing *Ethos* in Adrienne Rich's Poetry." *RSQ* 18 (Fall 1988): 133–140.

Claims that Rich's *ethos* is "good," giving her poetry authority.

568. Heller, Scott. "Scholars Defend Their Efforts to Promote Literature by Women and Blacks, Decry Attack by Bennett." *CHE* 34 (17 February 1988): A1, A16.

Scholars argue with William Bennett's claim that classic literary texts are in danger of being replaced by minority-written works.

569. Heller, Scott. "Scholars Grapple with Literary Critic's Early Writings for Pro-Nazi Periodical." *CHE* 34 (11 May 1988): A1, A6.

Critic Paul de Man's anti-Semitic essays provoke debate on the political aspects of deconstruction.

570. Hershey, Lewis. "The Performance of Literature as Argument." *SSCJ* 53 (Spring 1988): 259–278.

Reviews the interdependence of rhetoric and poetic language, narrative and argument, in the generating of critical discourse from performance-based knowledge.

571. Howard, June. "Feminist Differings: Recent Surveys of Feminist Theory and Criticism." *FS* 14 (Spring 1988): 167–190.

Finds in five recent studies of feminist criticism diverse attempts to make explicit and practical the politically radical implications of critical theory.

572. Kaplan, Louis Perry. "Laszlo Moholy-Nagy: Biographical Writings." *DAI* 49 (October 1988): 644A.

Demonstrates how Moholy-Nagy's writings are concerned with problematics of signature. Uses critical methodologies of biography, aesthetic analysis, and deconstruction.

573. Kastely, James L. "Toward a Politically Responsible Ethical Criticism: Narrative in *The Political Unconscious* and *For Whom the Bell Tolls*." *Style* 22 (Winter 1988): 535–558.

Compares Marxist criticism to ethical criticism. Argues that Hemingway's novel exemplifies the narrative's conflict and defines the tension between ethical and political obligations.

574. Kearns, Judith E. "Poet and Lover: Rhetorical Stance in the Elizabethan Sonnet Sequence." *DAI* 48 (June 1988): 3116A.

By analyzing three elements of Sidney's and Spenser's rhetorical stance, claims that *Astrophel and Stella* is superior to *Amoretti*.

575. Kernan, Keith, Sharon Sabsay, and Neil Shinn. "Discourse Features as Criteria in Judging the Intellectual Ability of Speakers." *DPr* 11 (April–June 1988): 203–220.

Judges listened to narrations of events in a film and frequently cited six criteria for their judgments: detail, coherence, story construction, storytelling, performance, and metacomments.

576. Kitch, Sally L. "Gender and Language: Dialect, Silence, and the Disruption of Discourse." *WS* 14 (July 1987): 65–78.

Studies language as a subject of women's fiction as well as a tool for female expression and repression.

577. Kolodny, Annette. "Respectability Is Eroding the Revolutionary Potential of Feminist Criticism." *CHE* 34 (4 May 1988): A52.

Feminism's rise to respectability has attracted white males with a limited background in traditional materials, while female feminists appear as tokens.

578. Lane, Nancy. "From Saint-Hilaire to Martinville and Beyond: Self, Desire, and Writing in *Remembrance of Things Past*." *Style* 22 (Fall 1988): 391–401.

Spires, steeples, and towers are metaphors for the tension between the experiencing, empirical self and the transcendental self, which emerges through writing.

579. Lebowitz, Naomi. "Defenses of Vengeance: Rousseau's Legacy to the Novel." *MLQ* 46 (September 1985): 250–275.

Examines Rousseau's structural and stylistic strategies for executing and exonerating vengeance as his chief legacy to nineteenth-and twentieth-century French novelists.

580. Lee, Josephine D. "Language and Action in the Plays of Wilde, Shaw, and Stoppard." *DAI* 48 (March 1988): 2345A.

Discusses the relationship between linguistic style and action in three British playwrights.

581. Lensink, Judy Nolte. "Expanding the Boundaries of Criticism: The Diary as Female Autobiography." *WS* 14 (July 1987): 39–53.

Argues that diaries are quintessentially female literature, close to "inner culture" in their language of detail, unconstructed narrative form, and immediate content.

582. Lin, Mao-Chu. "Identity and Chinese-American Experience: A Study of Chinatown American Literature since World War II." *DAI* 48 (April 1988): 2662A.

Examines 14 Chinese-American writers' literary responses to American racial attitudes and policies.

583. Linkin, Harriet Kramer. "Narrative Technique in 'An Occurrence at Owl Creek Bridge.' " *JNT* 18 (Spring 1988): 137–152.

Bierce's linguistic strategies, primarily the shifting narrative consciousness, dislocates the reader's perception of the text. Retrospective visions from subtle authorial hints provide eventual understanding.

584. Malkin, Jeanette Rosenzweig. "Verbal Violence in Modern Drama: A Study of Language as Aggression." *DAI* 49 (November 1988): 1001A.

Argues that post-World War II dramatists view language as an aggressor. It molds reality, undermines critical thought, and destroys human autonomy and individuality.

585. Malmgren, Carl D. "Towards a Definition of Science Fantasy." *SFS* 15 (November 1988): 259–281.

Defines science fantasy as an "unstable" subgenre that combines features of both science fiction and fantasy. Identifies four types of science fantasy.

586. Martin, Reginald. "The New Black Aesthetic Critics and Their Exclusion from American 'Mainstream' Criticism." *CE* 50 (April 1988): 373–382.

Argues that the standard critical corpus should recognize the new black aesthetic as a codification of a particular school of American literary criticism.

587. Martin, Reginald. "New Ideas for Old: New Black Aesthetics." *CEAC* 50 (Winter 1987): 90–104.

Shows the range of articulation by black writers and critics of the "black aesthetic," which grew to adopt socially progressive, Marxist, and feminist principles.

588. Martinez, Zulma Nelly. "From a Mimetic to a Holographic Paradigm in Fiction: Toward a Definition of Feminist Writing." *WS* 14 (February 1988): 225–245.

Asserts that the character of the contemporary novel is essentially feminine: participatory, dynamic, re-creative, and undefined by specific closure, like the life process itself.

589. McCormick, Kathleen. " 'First Steps' in 'Wandering Rocks': Students' Differences, Literary Transactions, and Pleasures." *Reader* 20 (Fall 1988): 48–67.

Supplements Rosenblatt with Barthes to examine students' responses.

590. Merideth, Eunice Mae. "Stylistic Gender Patterns in Fiction: A Curricular Concern." *DAI* 48 (January 1988): 1644A.

Presents a method of identifying gender patterns in fiction, rhetorical patterns of style assigned by gender, by using several rhetorical variables embedded in language.

591. Meyer, Sam. "Color and Cogency in Titles of John D. MacDonald's Travis McGee Series." *RSQ* 18 (Spring-Summer 1988): 259–260.

Discusses the schemes used to exact the novel's titles.

592. Mitchell, Arlene Harris. "A Study of the Literary Understanding of *The Adventures of Huckleberry Finn* and the Attitudes of Students toward the Characterizations and Language Used in the Novel." *DAI* 48 (April 1988): 2562A.

Studies 71 students through quantitative tests and journals. Seeks answers to questions and hypotheses concerning racial bias in attitudes toward the novel.

593. Mitchell, W. J. T. "Tableau and Taboo: The Resistance to Vision in Literary Discourse." *CEAC* 51 (Fall 1988): 4–10.

Presents two contradictory responses of readers—the desire to visualize literary meaning and the resistance to visualization—as the necessary condition of reading.

594. Moore, George Lee. "Nietzsche's Concept of Poetry." *DAI* 49 (August 1988): 270A.

Analyzes Nietzsche's concept of poetry as making, arguing that poetry is at the heart of his understanding of philosophy.

595. Morrissey, Robert. "Breaking In (Flaubert in Parentheses)." *SubStance* 56 (1988): 49–62.

Examines the multiplicity of voices and discourse patterns in Flaubert's texts.

596. Muller, Marcel. "The Rhetoric of Pseudo-Nature; or, Tropes and Dialectic in Proust's Novel." *Style* 22 (Fall 1988): 382–390.

Argues that Proust uses all of the master tropes to develop his categories of idealistic dialectic in *Remembrance of Things Past*.

597. Nelson, Laura Lyn. "American Conceptions of the Relationship between Poetic and Rhetoric, 1920–1970, and Their Influence on Oral Interpretation." *DAI* 48 (April 1988): 2490A.

Examines four major critical schools that view poetic and rhetoric differently, as mutually exclusive or as interdependent modes of discourse.

598. Offenhauer, Priscilla. "Search for a Social Science of Literature: The First Decade of Sartre's Cultural and Literary Theory." *DAI* 49 (December 1988): 1554A.

Reviews Sartre's consideration of the ontological and epistemological foundations of theory. Discusses his interactional view of meaning, in which the text is not independent of the reader.

599. O'Regan, Daphne E. "Rhetoric, Comedy, and the Violence of Language in Aristophanes's *Clouds*." *DAI* 48 (June 1988): 3103A.

Identifies *logos* as the empowering concept that restores Aristophanes's art of comedy.

600. Paul, Angus. "Rising Interest in Analysis of American Nonfiction Is Exemplified by Work on Agee, Crane, Parkman, and Others." *CHE* 34 (13 January 1988): A4-A5, A10.

Recent MLA Convention speakers revealed a growing interest in the study of nonfiction narratives, especially works describing the urban and rural poor.

601. Payne, Paula Harms. "Aristotle's *Rhetoric:* Matter and Manner in Sidney's Sonnet Sequence *Astrophel and Stella* and in His *Defense of Poesie*." *DAI* 49 (August 1988): 260A.

Analyzes Sidney's poetry and prose, focusing on matter, manner, *gnosis, praxis,* and other Aristotelian concepts that chart a new direction in English poetry.

602. Pennock, Janice L. "Rhetorical Strategies in the Plays of Fulke Greville." *DAI* 48 (June 1988): 3117A.

Assesses how rhetorical means of argumentation are applied in Greville's closet plays, *Mustapha* and *Alaham.*

603. Pfaelzer, Jean. "The Changing of the Avant Garde: The Feminist Utopia." *SFS* 15 (November 1988): 282–294.

Argues that feminist discourse theorists and utopian authors both deconstruct material space but to different ends. The former subvert old perceptual orders; the latter, inequality and inevitability.

604. Ponder, Melinda Mowry. "The Role of Eighteenth-Century Anglo-Scottish Theorists in Hawthorne's Aesthetic Education and Literary Creation of the Early Tales." *DAI* 49 (August 1989): 255A.

Examines Hawthorne's use of the theorists Addison, Burke, Kames, and Alison, who place the writer's imagination at the center of the text.

605. Prince, Gerald. "The Disnarrated." *Style* 22 (Spring 1988): 1–8.

Argues that the disnarrated, consisting of passages explaining what does not take place, can serve as a heuristic for characterizing literary movements.

606. Purves, Alan C. "The Aesthetic Mind of Louise Rosenblatt." *Reader* 20 (Fall 1988): 68–76.

Considers Rosenblatt's aesthetic stance and bemoans our cultural bias toward the efferent.

607. Randall, Neil. "Determining Literariness in Interactive Fiction." *CHum* 22 (1988): 183–191.

Argues that interactive fiction is literary in a formalist sense of making the strange familiar and the familiar strange.

608. Roberts, Eddene. "Plot: A Structuralist Approach to Modern Fiction." *DAI* 48 (February 1988): 2060A.

Surveys historical definitions and approaches to plot, arguing that Chatman's methodology is effective and relevant for analyzing specific works.

609. Robinson, Marsha Studebaker. "Shakespeare and the Rhetoric of History." *DAI* 48 (February 1988): 2069A.

Examines rhetorical and literary strategies in several dramas, exploring their relation to the historical representations that characterize the texts of Shakespeare's time.

610. Rosenblatt, Louise M. "Writing and Reading: The Transactional Theory." *Reader* 20 (Fall 1988): 7–31.

A discussion of Rosenblatt's theoretical approach to interrelationships between reading and writing.

611. Sankovitch, Tilde A. *French Women Writers and the Book: Myths of Access and Desire.* Syracuse, N.Y.: Syracuse University Press, 1988. 176 pages

Deals with the attempts by a number of writers from the medieval period to the present to invent their own authority of origin, their own empowering myths.

612. Schwarz, Daniel. "Humanistic Formalism: A Theoretical Defense." *JNT* 18 (Winter 1988): 1–17.

Proposes a revised "humanistic formalism," which accepts concepts of mimesis and "enriching" interpretation but also accepts some elements of new historicism and deconstruction.

613. Shapiro, Michael, and Marianne Shapiro. *Figuration in Verbal Art.* Princeton, N.J.: Princeton University Press, 1988. 300 pages

Applies a unified theoretical framework to argue that the process of figuration is basic to theories of cognition and meaning. Draws on rhetoric, linguistics, literary history, and other fields to show relations between the tropological nature of language as a system and the tropological nature of style as a means for organizing perception.

614. Shaw, Peter. "Feminist Literary Criticism: A Report from the Academy." *ASch* 57 (Autumn 1988): 495–513.

Examines the debate among feminist critics concerning gender differences in writing. Attempts to assess feminist criticism from the perspective of someone "outside the movement."

615. Shifrer, Anne. "The Humilities of Language in Twentieth-Century Poetry." *DAI* 48 (March 1988): 2335A.

Shows how modern poets deal with or refute the myth of language's inadequacy, frailty, exhaustion, alienation, and imprisonment.

616. Shilling, Daniel D. "Rhetorical Strategy in Samuel Johnson's 'Rambler' Essays." *DAI* 49 (October 1988): 829A.

Discusses Johnson's use of rhetorical strategies to create readers with the sensibilities of Mr. Rambler.

617. Smith, Carol H. "The Literary Politics of Gender." *CE* 50 (March 1988): 318–322.

A review essay showing the importance of feminist scholarship in defining new issues in literary studies and in addressing more broadly social and political concerns.

618. Spacks, Patricia Meyer. "Forgotten Genres." *MLS* 18 (Winter 1988): 47–57.

Argues that letters should be part of the literary canon even though we are not comfortable theorizing about them.

619. Stringfellow, Frank H. "Verbal Irony in Literature: A Psycholinguistic Investigation." *DAI* 48 (June 1988): 3106A.

Concludes that verbal irony in literature can be assessed more successfully through a psychoanalytic approach than a linguistic-rhetorical one.

620. Sultana, Niloufar. "The Translation of Literary Texts: A Paradox in Theory." *Lang S* 20 (Summer 1987): 269–284.

Examines the assumptions that literary texts are untranslatable. Concludes that translatability varies with the extent of the narrative core and with increasing distance between the worlds of experience and the text.

621. Tatsumi, Takayuki. "Disfiguration of Genres: A Reading in the Rhetoric of Edgar Allan Poe." *DAI* 48 (March 1988): 2339A.

Explores how Poe displaces, disconnects, or landscapes the rhetoric of literary conventions, especially genre.

622. Thomson, Douglass H. "Rhetoric Meets Philosophy: The Place of Description in Literary Criticism." *P&R* 21 (Second Quarter 1988): 77–102.

Reviews description's rhetorical and literary status. Argues against mimetic theories and for symbolic interpretations that transcend semiosis, narrative theory, and psychology.

623. Tiner, Elza C. "*Inventio , Dispositio,* and *Elocutio* in the York Trials." *DAI* 48 (June 1988): 3108A.

Analyzes the six trial plays rhetorically, illustrating the importance of their effect on the audience.

624. Toll, Katharine. "The Rhetoric of Irreconciliation: A Reading of *Aeneid* VII and VIII." *DAI* 48 (June 1988): 3103A.

Examines the concept of Italian national identity, claiming that the poem creates national unity through a shared history.

625. Tompkins, Jane. "Fighting Words: Unlearning to Write the Critical Essay." *GR* 42 (Fall 1988): 585–590.

Argues that violence is as prevalent in literary criticism as it is in popular culture. The "moment of murderousness" should compel writers to stop and reflect as they write critically.

626. Tyman, Jonathan Paul. "Film in Science, Education, Propaganda: Examples of Its Use in America, 1940–1950." *DAI* 49 (November 1988): 1181A.

Examines the limits and uses of film in discovering new scientific knowledge and in propagating ideas. Focuses on Ford Motor Company films.

627. van Alphen, Ernst. "Reading Visually." *Style* 22 (Summer 1988): 219–229.

Brakman's novel *The Goddamned Party* represents a resolution to the problem of word versus image because the main character makes visual images "dynamic."

628. Van Luxemburg, Jan. "Ana's Pedestal: A Counterreading of *La Regenta*." *Style* 22 (Winter 1988): 559–575.

Undermines traditional thematic readings of the text by examining rhetorical constructions and the "excess" of the text. Builds on Roland Barthes, Terry Eagleton, and deconstruction.

629. Ward, David Malcolm. "Of Innocence and History: An Essay on Pier Paolo Pasolini." *DAI* 49 (December 1988): 1473A.

Examines in Pasolini's poetry and plays the clash between the desire to represent and the distrust of language and literary institutions.

630. Wasserman, Julian N., and Lois Roney, eds. *Sign, Sentence, Discourse: Language in Medieval Thought and Literature*. Syracuse, N.Y.: Syracuse University Press, 1988. 352 pages

Fourteen essays explore the problem of language in medieval literature and provide specific applications of linguistic theory to such works. Issues explored include the relationship between language and identity, the indeterminacy of texts, and the internal dialogue by which a society is reshaped by language.

631. Weixlmann, Joe. "Dealing with the Demands of an Expanding Literary Canon." *CE* 50 (March 1988): 273–283.

Advocates canon reformation by adding noncanonical authors and by using flexible teaching methods that acknowledge the racist, sexist, classist, traditionalist, and elitist shortcomings of canonical texts.

632. White, Hayden. "The Rhetoric of Interpretation." *PT* 9 (Spring 1988): 253–274.

Interpretation differs from description and explanation by pre-figuring referents to constitute them as possible objects of cognition. The rhetoric of interpretation is more figurative than logical.

633. Wiemer, Annegret J. "Foreign L(anguish), Mother Tongue: Concepts of Language in Contemporary Feminist Science Fiction." *WS* 14 (December 1987): 163–173.

Illustrates new features of *parole feministe:* naming as a quest for selfhood, punning on patriarchal language, and psychic forms of speech.

634. Yowell, Donna Lynne. "Human Speech and Bestial Silence: *De Vulgari Eloquentia* in *Inferno* 31–34." *DAI* 48 (March 1988): 2334A.

Posits that the language of beasts, men, and angels in the *Eloquentia* reappear as ideas about the nature and function of language in the *Inferno*.

635. Zeitz, Lisa Margaret. "The Physico-Theological Tradition in Eighteenth-Century Prose Literature in English." *DAI* 48 (February 1988): 2017A.

Examines the use of "design arguments" in various prose forms, their popularity and range of use, and the aims and effects achieved in individual texts.

See also 72, 84, 150, 233, 252, 297, 308, 311, 752, 775, 812, 995, 1029, 1035, 1191, 1206

2.7   READING

636. Adames, Jose Antonio. "A Study of the Reading Process of Selected English as a Second Language College Students." *DAI* 49 (July 1988): 51A.

Tests how "background knowledge, text structure, and tasks" affect reading comprehension. Results indicate that background knowledge was significant.

637. Atkinson, Rhonda H. "Factors Affecting Developmental College Readers' Ability to Mobilize and Use Prior Knowledge." *DAI* 48 (June 1988): 3083A.

Examines the ability to comprehend and recall expository texts by manipulating traditional factors to activate schemata and prior knowledge.

638. Bartine, David. *Early English Reading Theory: Origins of Current Debate*. Studies in Rhetoric and Communication. Columbia,

S.C.: University of South Carolina Press, 1988. 210 pages

Documents the eighteenth-and nineteenth-century struggle to shape a discipline of reading. Identifies debates central to the struggle, shows how participants borrowed from disciplines such as rhetoric and grammar, and traces the influence of rhetoric on reading theory.

639. Bartlett, Bertrice. "Negatives, Narrative, and the Reader." *Lang & S* 20 (Winter 1987): 41–62.

Examines how literary writers use negatives to control readers' experiences of the text, involving them directly in its meanings. Discusses specific techniques and effects.

640. Bloom, Charles P. "The Role of Schemata in Memory for Text." *DPr* 11 (July–September 1988): 319–335.

Different encoding perspectives led to either holistic representation or more restricted representation in immediate recall procedures. Different patterns emerged in delayed recall procedures.

641. Blutner, Reinhard, and Rosemarie Sommer. "Sentence Processing and Lexical Access: The Influence of the Focus-Identifying Task." *JML* 27 (August 1988): 359–367.

Examines the relation of a sentence's semantic focus to a reader's recognition of ambiguous words in the sentence.

642. Bristow, Page Simpson, and Lauren Leslie. "Indicators of Reading Difficulty: Discrimination between Instructional-and Frustration-Range Performance of Functionally Illiterate Adults." *RRQ* 23 (Spring 1988): 200–218.

A study of 81 functionally illiterate adults. For placement, reading rate should be included. Training in fluency should be added to instructional programs.

643. Cacciari, Cristina, and Patrizia Tabossi. "The Comprehension of Idioms." *JML* 27 (December 1988): 668–683.

Reports on three experiments examining literal and idiomatic interpretations of phrases, which affect subsequent lexical decisions.

644. Carson, Jean, Hans Christopher Micko, and Manfred Thuring. "Conjunctions and the Recall of Composite Sentences." *JML* 27 (June 1988): 309–323.

Finds that *because* elicits greater recall than *and* or *but*.

645. Cohick, Mikel William. "Academic Achievement and the Ability of Postsecondary Students to Read Assigned Material." *DAI* 48 (February 1988): 1996A.

Examines the relationship between reading ability and achievement in terms of success with course materials.

646. Coltheart, Veronika, Veronica Laxon, Mary Rickard, and Caroline Elton. "Phonological Recoding in Reading for Meaning by Adults and Children." *JEPL* 14 (July 1988): 387–397.

Reports on experiments clarifying whether assembled or addressed phonology produces error in children's and adults' reading for meaning.

647. Corder, Jim W. "Hunting for *Ethos* Where They Say It Can't Be Found." *RR* 7 (Spring 1989): 299–316.

Explores the implications of whether we find meaning in the text or in the reading strategies of an interpretive community.

648. Corrigan, Roberta. "Who Dun It? The Influence of Actor-Patient Animacy and Type of Verb in the Making of Causal Attributions." *JML* 27 (August 1988): 447–465.

Reports on three experiments in which students were asked to attribute causality to subjects or objects in given sentences.

649. Crismore, Avon, and William J. Vande Kopple. "Readers' Learning from Prose: The Effects of Hedges." *WC* 5 (April 1988): 184–202.

Results show that the experimental group learned most when hedges appeared in personal voice, in the second half of a passage, and in low intensity.

650. Dee-Lucas, Diana, and Jill H. Larkin. "Novice Rules for Assessing Importance in Scientific Texts." *JML* 27 (June 1988): 288–308.

Examines how readers unfamiliar with given scientific content determine the relative importance of different categories of information.

651. Dillman, Richard. "Reader Response to Thoreau's *Walden* : A Study of Undergraduate Reading Patterns." *Reader* 19 (Spring 1988): 21–36.

Identifies and explains response patterns observed in reading journals.

652. Dubois, Daniele, and Michel Denis. "Knowledge Organization and Instantiation of General Terms in Sentence Comprehension." *JEPL* 14 (October 1988): 604–611.

Studies how knowledge is represented in memory and how it is related to word meaning in sentence comprehension.

653. Duin, Ann Hill. "How People Read: Implications for Writers." *TWT* 15 (Fall 1988): 185–193.

Uses principles of psycholinguistics as a basis for effective document design.

654. Durgunoglu, Aydin Y. "Repetition, Semantic Priming, and Stimulus Quality: Implications for the Interactive-Compensatory Reading Model." *JEPL* 14 (October 1988): 590–603.

Studies the point in the reading process at which people turn to contextual clues.

655. Fincher-Kiefer, Rebecca, Timothy A. Post, Terry R. Greene, and James F. Voss. "On the Role of Prior Knowledge and Task Demands in the Processing of Text." *JML* 27 (August 1988): 416–428.

Examines mechanisms by which knowledge of a given subject matter domain aids in recalling the content of a prose passage.

656. Fletcher, Charles R., and Charles P. Bloom. "Causal Reasoning in the Comprehension of Simple Narrative Texts." *JML* 27 (June 1988): 235–244.

Proposes that short-term memory is the key to understanding causal connections in a narrative text.

657. Gordon, Christine J. "Contexts for Narrative Text Structure Use: What Do the Kids Say?" *EQ* 21 (1988): 148–163.

Analyzes student protocols to determine the contexts in which students use knowledge about narrative text structure.

658. Guagliardo, Dennis Anthony. "The Application of Cognitive and Metacognitive Strategies as Adjunct Aids to Text Processing." *DAI* 49 (July 1988): 66A.

Investigates the effect of cognitive and metacognitive strategies upon reading comprehension in a community college population.

659. Guthrie, John T. "Locating Information in Documents: Examination of a Cognitive Model." *RRQ* 23 (Spring 1988): 178–199.

A study of 26 undergraduates concludes that locating information in documents seems to be a unique cognitive process similar to analytical reasoning.

660. Haas, Christina, and Linda Flower. "Rhetorical Reading Strategies and the Construction of Meaning." *CCC* 39 (May 1988): 167–183.

Reports that, as they read, four experienced readers tried to understand the rhetorical situation of a text significantly more often than six student readers did.

661. Hegwer, Marie Louise. "Reading Related Problems of Illiterate Adults." *DAI* 48 (March 1988): 2296A.

Studies the relationships between illiteracy, individual perceptions of performance, and compensatory ways of dealing with reading problems.

662. Hull, Jonathan J. "A Computational Theory of Visual Word Recognition." *DAI* 49 (December 1988): 2262B.

Develops a three-stage computational theory of the visual recognition of words in a text. Demonstrates its superiority to segmenting programs.

663. Jackson, Nancy E., Gary W. Donaldson, and Lynne Cleland. "The Structure of Precocious Reading Ability." *JEdP* 80 (1988): 234–243.

Describes cognitive correlates of precocious reading achievement. The most critical locus of success or failure appears to be a child's ability to use relevant knowledge or reading ability.

664. Johns, Elizabeth E., and Leila G. Swanson. "The Generation Effect with Nonwords." *JEPL* 14 (January 1988): 180–190.

The generation effect, the enhanced memorability of words that people generate over those they read, is not influenced by meaning or the presence of nonwords.

665. Longman, Debbie Guice. "The Effects of Semantic Mapping Instruction on the Text-External Inferences of College Developmental Readers." *DAI* 48 (March 1988): 2253A.

Shows that prior knowledge aids readers but that semantic mapping does not activate prior knowledge in developmental readers.

666. Manske, Donna Harrison. "A Study of the Relationship of Preference Scores on the Meyers-Briggs Type Indicator and the Reading Comprehension of Adult Readers." *DAI* 49 (August 1988): 227A.

Analyzes the differences between sensing and intuitive adult readers as they determine main ideas and draw conclusions following silent reading.

667. Martin, Randi C., Michael S. Wogalter, and Janice G. Forlano. "Reading Comprehension in the Presence of Unattended Speech and Music." *JML* 27 (August 1988): 382–398.

> Examines the effects of phonological interference or background music on reading comprehension, drawing implications about phonological short-term memory.

668. McCormick, Thomas W. *Theories of Reading in Dialogue: An Interdisciplinary Study.* Lanham, Md.: University Press of America, 1988. 410 pages

> Notes a gap between psychologically oriented reading specialists and phenomenological studies in philosophy. Argues that phenomenology contributes positively toward the advancement of studies in reading.

669. McDonald, Deborah Rae. "Drawing Inferences from Expository Text." *DAI* 49 (December 1988): 2400B.

> Describes the ability of good and poor readers to draw inferences from material that is internally consistent or inconsistent.

670. McGlinn, James E. "Essential Education in the Reading Class." *JDEd* 12 (November 1988): 20–24.

> Recommends teaching reading in the context of the liberal arts as a means of acquiring both content and the essentials of education.

671. McNamara, Timothy P., and Alice F. Healy. "Semantic, Phonological, and Mediated Priming in Reading and Lexical Decisions." *JEPL* 14 (July 1988): 398–409.

> Reports on experiments investigating the relationships among phonemic, graphemic, and semantic relatedness and their influence on reading.

672. Moe, Laura A. "Constructing Understandings of Written Text: A Cultural Perspective." *DAI* 48 (January 1988): 1682A.

> Five readers retell and discuss a Tillie Olsen short story. The researcher analyzes these data by using ethnomethodology, linguistics, and literary theory.

673. Morriss, Robin K., and Keith Rayner. "Lexical Ambiguity and Fixation Times in Reading." *JML* 27 (August 1988): 429–446.

> Illustrates that the relative location of "disambiguating clauses" affects a reader's speed and proficiency in understanding ambiguous words.

674. Neill, W. Trammell, D. Vanessa Hilliard, and Elizabeth-Anne Cooper. "The Detection of Lexical Ambiguity: Evidence for Context-Sensitive Parallel Access." *JML* 27 (June 1988): 279–287.

> To determine the importance of context and primary/secondary definition in a reader's understanding of a word, students were asked to differentiate between homographs and nonhomographs.

675. Nell, Victor. *Lost in a Book: The Psychology of Reading for Pleasure.* Haven: Yale University Press, 1988. 352 pages

> Explores the social forces shaping pleasure reading and shows that skilled reading is a prerequisite for it. Advocates rejecting the belief that, as people become more sophisticated, they abandon "coarser" tastes. Discusses how pleasure reading can be used both to dull and heighten consciousness.

676. Norton, Janice Marie. "Lexical Ambiguity across the Adult Lifespan." *DAI* 48 (February 1988): 2477B.

> Examines the abilities of adults at different ages to assess lexically ambiguous sentences both in isolation and in context.

677. O'Brien, Edward J., Dolores M. Shank, Jerome L. Myers, and Keith Rayner. "Elaborative Inferences during Reading: Do They Occur On-Line?" *JEPL* 14 (July 1988): 410–420.

> Reports on experiments using gaze durations to measure how quickly people read repeated words when those words are presented in various contexts.

678. Ohlhausen, Marilyn M., and Cathy M. Roller. "The Operation of Text Structure and

Content Schemata in Isolation and in Interaction." *RRQ* 23 (Winter 1988): 70–88.

A study concluding that fifth-, seventh-, and ninth-graders as well as adults from a university employ prior knowledge, schooling, and text structure to comprehend reading.

679. Opdahl, Keith. "Imagination and Emotion: Toward a Theory of Representation." *Reader* 19 (Spring 1988): 1–20.

Argues that writers create verisimilitude by duplicating the process by which readers experience, remember, and imagine the world.

680. Patterson, Judith Morgan. "The Effects of Text Structure on Learning-Disabled College Students Comprehension and Recall of Expository Text." *DAI* 48 (January 1988): 1720A.

Examines written recall protocols of 36 normal and learning-disabled college students to determine differences in global organization and in the type of information recalled.

681. Perfetti, Charles A., Laura C. Bell, and Suzanne M. Delaney. "Automatic (Prelexical) Phonetic Activation in Silent Word Reading: Evidence from Backward Masking." *JML* 27 (February 1988): 59–70.

Explores the question, "Does visual access to a written word arouse the associated speech form of the word?"

682. Piepmeier, Karen Swanson. "Determining Readability by Computer Analysis Using the Fourier Transform to Calculate the Spatial Frequencies of Words." *DAI* 49 (September 1988): 471A.

Patterns formed by printed words yield an amplitude. These amplitudes were examined to determine readability.

683. Racheli, Ugo. "Contents of Working Memory in Discourse Comprehension." *DAI* 48 (February 1988): 2480B.

Investigates the real-time interaction of reading styles with the recall of verbatim and semantic data.

684. Recht, Donna, and Lauren Leslie. "Effect of Prior Knowledge on Good and Poor Readers Memory of Text." *JEdP* 80 (1988): 16–20.

Investigates how prior knowledge influences the amount of short-term nonverbal and verbal memory and long-term retention in good and poor readers. Results show a significant main effect for prior knowledge.

685. Reinking, David. "Computer-Mediated Text and Comprehension Differences: The Role of Reading Time, Reader Preference, and Estimate of Learning." *RRQ* 23 (Fall 1988): 484–498.

Replicates other studies. Finds that subjects' comprehension increased when reading computer-mediated texts that expanded or controlled students' options for acquiring information.

686. Sadoski, Mark, Ernest Goetz, and Suzanne Kangiser. "Imagination in Story Response: Relationships between Imagery, Affect, and Structural Importance." *RRQ* 23 (Summer 1988): 320–336.

Finds that 39 college students reading three short stories had consistent reactions that conformed with current literary and reading theories.

687. Sanocki, Thomas. "Font Regularity Constraints on the Process of Letter Recognition." *JEPH* 14 (August 1988): 472–480.

Finds that recognizing letters accurately is highest when all the letters are presented in the same type font.

688. Schwanenflugel, Paula J., Katherine Kipp Harnishfeger, and Randall W. Stowe. "Context Availability and Lexical Decisions for Abstract and Concrete Words." *JML* 27 (October 1988): 499–520.

Suggests that context is more important than the degree of concreteness in determining a reader's ability to make lexical decisions.

689. Slater, Wayne H. "Current Theory and Research on What Constitutes Readable Expository Text." *TWT* 15 (Fall 1988): 195–206.

Reviews findings on two features of expository prose that significantly influenced readers' comprehension of text: structure and interestingness.

690. Smith, Frank. *Understanding Reading: A Psycholinguistic Analysis of Reading and Learning to Read.* Hillsdale, N.J.: Erlbaum, 1988. 376 pages

A revised edition of a textbook on the psycholinguistics of reading.

691. Stevens, Robert J. "Effects of Strategy Training on the Identification of the Main Idea of Expository Passages." *JEdP* 80 (1988): 21–26.

Tested ways to teach remedial readers how to identify main ideas. Results suggest that comprehension and meta-cognitive strategies can improve the ability to identify main ideas.

692. Stevenson, Rosemary J. "Memory for Referential Statements in Texts." *JEPL* 14 (October 1988): 612–617.

Cautions that experiments to test verbatim memory should account for testing methods.

693. Stuart, Moray, and Max Coltheart. "Does Reading Develop in a Sequence of Stages?" *Cognition* 30 (1988): 139–181.

Evaluates three stage theories of reading acquisition and reports data on reading acquisition. Results suggest that phonological awareness and reading acquisition have a reciprocal causal relationship, not a unidirectional one.

694. Tabossi, Patrizia. "Accessing Lexical Ambiguity in Different Types of Sentential Contexts." *JML* 27 (June 1988): 324–340.

Argues for the importance of sentential context in a reader's ability to understand the meaning of ambiguous words.

695. Tabossi, Patrizia. "Effects of Context on the Immediate Interpretation of Unambiguous Nouns." *JEPL* 14 (January 1988): 153–162.

People recognize a word more quickly if the context primes an aspect of the word's meaning.

696. Taraban, Roman, and James L. McClelland. "Constituent Attachment and Thematical Role Assignment in Sentence Processing: Influence of Content-Based Expectations." *JML* 27 (December 1988): 597–632.

Discusses how syntax and content affect the interpretation of a sentence's constituents.

697. Treiman, Rebecca, and Andrea Zukowski. "Units in Reading and Spelling." *JML* 27 (August 1988): 466–477.

Looks at multiletter units readers use to process connections between print and speech. Draws implications for models of pronunciation and spelling.

698. Turner, Tom. "Art Thought and Everyday Thought." *JCS* 20 (March–April 1988): 173–179.

An essay review of a pamphlet detailing the "exploratory talk" of teenagers about a poem. Focuses on problems of literal and nonliteral meaning.

699. Van Orden, Guy C., James C. Johnston, and Benita L. Hale. "Word Identification in Reading Proceeds from Spelling to Sound to Meaning." *JEPL* 14 (July 1988): 371–386.

Demonstrates that phonology plays an important part in lexical coding.

700. Weaver, Constance. *Reading Process and Practice: From Socio-Psycholinguistics to Whole Language.* Rev. ed. Portsmouth, N.H.: Heinemann, 1988. 483 pages

Revised edition of *Psycholinguistics and Reading* (1980). An introduction to the psycholinguistic nature of the reading process, which is not passive but active. Readers predict, sample, and confirm or correct their hypotheses about written texts.

701. Wilkinson, Ian, James L. Waldrop, and Richard C. Anderson. "Silent Reading Reconsidered: Reinterpreting Reading Instruction and Its Effects." *AERJ* 25 (Spring 1988): 127–144.

> Reanalyzes data from a study by Leinhardt, Zigmond, and Cooley to challenge the claim that more silent reading should be used in instruction.

702. Wise, Barbara Woodward. "Word Segmentation in Computerized Reading Instruction." *DAI* 48 (February 1988): 2478B.

> Investigates whether beginning readers benefit differently from computerized instruction, depending on the type and size of the orthographic segment.

703. Yussen, Steven, Shik-Tseng Huang, Samuel Mathews, and Robert Evans. "The Robustness and Temporal Course of the Story Schema's Influence on Recall." *JEPL* 14 (January 1988): 173–179.

> Poorly organized stories inhibit recalling related ideas, specific features, and overall meaning.

704. Zimmy, Susan T. "Recognition Memory for Sentences from Discourse." *DAI* 48 (February 1988): 2482B.

> Investigates recognition memory for simple texts and finds that these texts are represented in memory on three levels.

See also 63, 76, 128, 177, 398, 410, 420, 537, 551, 593, 828, 859, 872, 1354

2.8 LINGUISTICS, GRAMMATICAL THEORY, AND SEMANTICS

705. Abbott, Gerry. "Mascaraed and Muumuued: The Spelling of Imported Words." *EngT* 4 (April 1988): 43–46.

> Discusses the advice given in dictionaries on spelling verbal inflections that have been added to exotic words.

706. Adair-Toteff, Stephanie. "Historical Perspectives on the Theory of Linguistic Relativity." *DAI* 48 (April 1988): 2613A.

> Examines the roles of Bacon, Locke, Vico, Hamann, Herder, and von Humboldt in viewing language as a controlling framework for creating and transmitting knowledge.

707. Afifi, Elhami Abdelzaher. "Linguistic Perspectives of Interlingual Translation." *DAI* 48 (April 1988): 2614A.

> Examines translation as a functional linguistic enterprise, proposes a comprehensive model of translation, and discusses issues for further research.

708. Alexander, James D. "The Erosion of English." *EngT* 4 (April 1988): 17–20.

> Discusses the reversal of phonic erosion in spoken English caused by newly literate peoples' belief that letters in written words should be pronounced.

709. Bainbridge, Roy I. "A Definite Clause Grammatical Inversion of Extended Montague Semantics." *DAI* 49 (September 1988): 819B.

> Presents a definite clause grammatical inversion designed both to stimulate and to assist in developing extended Montague grammar (TMG).

710. Baker, Nancy D., and Patricia M. Greenfield. "The Development of New and Old Information in Young Children's Early Language." *LangS* 10 (1988): 3–34.

> A longitudinal study of four children. Reveals the development of cognitive roots for presuppositions and assertions in one-word and two-word language stages.

711. Baron, Dennis. "The Ugly Grammarian." *EngT* 4 (October 1988): 9–12.

> Traces historically the perjoration of *grammar* and *grammarian*.

712. Beiner, Judith. "From Informal to Formal: Syntactic Variation in Written English." *DAI* 49 (December 1988): 1441A.

Uses sector analysis to determine that registers of written English differed in syntactic complexity.

713. Beshers, George M. "Regular Right Part Grammars and Maintained and Constructor Attributes in Language-Based Editors." *DAI* 48 (January 1988): 2024B.

Studies how and why language-specific editors are generated and enhanced through grammar and language adaptation.

714. Best, Catherine T., Gerald W. McRoberts, and Nomathemba M. Sithole. "Examination of Perceptual Reorganization for Nonnative Speech Contrasts: Zulu Click Discrimination by English-Speaking Adults and Infants." *JEPH* 14 (August 1988): 345–360.

Discusses kinds of sound discrimination that take place in infancy and how they aid language development.

715. Biber, Douglas, and Edward Finegan. "Adverbial Stance Types in English." *DPr* 11 (January–March 1988): 1–34.

Statistical analyses of a large corpus distinguished eight styles, identifiable on the basis of types of adverbials used.

716. Biq, Yung-O. "From Objectivity to Subjectivity: The Text-Building Function of *You* in Chinese." *SLang* 12 (1988): 99–122.

Argues that all uses of *you* are contextual variations of an underlying grammatical function.

717. Black, Alex. "The Syntax of Conversational Coherence." *DPr* 11 (October–December 1988): 433–455.

Analyses of four conversations indicate that the order of statements in a conversation tended to be the most globally coherent possible permutation of the statements.

718. Bouson, JoAnn Elizabeth. " 'Is You Jog?' The Interlanguage Verbal System of College ESL Students." *DAI* 49 (December 1988): 1391A.

Identifies features of the developing linguistic system of college ESL students.

719. Brownlee, Derek. "True, False, or Funny? Getting Your Way with Triple Logic." *ETC* 45 (Summer 1988): 128–131.

Analyzes relationships between truth, falsity, and humor as categories for evaluating information. Humor can highlight conflicts in perception, revealing multiple truths.

720. Bryony, Shannon. "Pronouns: Male, Female, and Undesignated." *ETC* 45 (Winter 1988): 334–336.

Suggests substituting *you* and third-person plural pronouns for third-person singular generic pronouns.

721. "Campaign '88 Doublespeak." *QRD* 14 (April 1988): 7.

Lists examples of campaign doublespeak and cites sources.

722. Chafe, Wallace. *What Good Is Punctuation?* CSW Occasional Paper, no. 2. Berkeley: CSW, 1987. ERIC ED 292 120. 10 pages

Articulates the ancient debate over the function of punctuation to signal prosody or grammar. Offers suggestions for teaching writing.

723. Chanawangsa, Somseen. "The Lexicology of Perception Verbs in English." *DAI* 48 (April 1988): 2614A.

Focusing on syntax, semantics, and pragmatics, assesses the status of the lexicon in the overall grammatical system of a language. Demonstrates possible applications to language-related activities.

724. Chang, Hisao M. "SWIS: See What I Say. A Speaker-Independent Word Recognition System by Phoneme-Oriented Mapping on a Phonetically Encoded Auditory-Perceptual Speech Map." *DAI* 48 (April 1988): 3023B.

Describes a prototype speaker-independent word recognition system and argues that such a phoneme-oriented system is generalizable.

725. Chen, Rey-Mei. "The Private Speech of a Chinese-English Bilingual Child: A Naturalis-

tic Longitudinal Study." *DAI* 49 (July 1988): 60A.

A Vygotskian analysis of "the functions, language choice, developmental changes, and cognitive and social contexts" of a developing bilingual speaker.

726. Chong, Hi-Ja. "A Study of the Function of Tense and Aspect in Korean Narrative Discourse." *DAI* 48 (April 1988): 2615A.

Demonstrates that Koreans distinguish five levels of information instead of the two—foreground and background—claimed in recent discourse studies.

727. Christophersen, Paul. " 'Native Speakers' and World English." *EngT* 4 (July 1988): 15–18.

Argues that linguists should replace the term *native* when referring to language proficiency.

728. Clacher, Arlene Denice. "An Exploratory Study of the Relationship between Three Dimensions of Locus of Control and Pidginization in Second Language Acquisition." *DAI* 48 (February 1988): 2054A.

Examines the acquisition of English language proficiency by Hispanic immigrants who are internally oriented, believing in personal ability, or externally oriented, believing in fate, luck, and chance.

729. Cockburn, Alexander. "One Author's CIA." *QRD* 14 (April 1988): 10–11.

Cites examples of doublespeak in Woodward's book, *Veil*.

730. Coe, Richard M. "Anglo-Canadian Rhetoric and Identity: A Preface." *CE* 50 (December 1988): 849–860.

Explores Canada's political, cultural, and economic history as a way of understanding differences between Canadian and American discourse and rhetoric.

731. Cordeiro, Patricia. "Children's Punctuation: An Analysis of Errors in Period Placement." *RTE* 22 (February 1988): 62–74.

Examines 22 first graders' and 13 third graders' understanding of period punctuation. Finds developmental differences in errors.

732. Crawford, Lyall. "Co-Interpreting Rejection." *ETC* 45 (Fall 1988): 258–261.

By consciously reinterpreting setbacks—using absurdity or expanding our perspective—we can transform initial disappointment into productive energy.

733. Crystal, David. "On Keeping One's Hedges in Order." *EngT* 4 (July 1988): 46–47.

Discusses the use of imprecise language and hedges in writing and speech.

734. Crystal, David. "What Was That Again?" *EngT* 4 (April 1988): 52–53.

Argues that repetition is a "neglected, undervalued feature" of speech and writing that deserves further study.

735. Cutler, Anne, and Dennis Norris. "The Role of Strong Syllables in Segmentation for Lexical Access." *JEPH* 14 (February 1988): 113–121.

Reports on experiments to determine what sort of nonsense syllables inhibit or do not mask words. Discusses implications for understanding lexical access.

736. Danielewicz, Jane Marie. "Developmental Differences between Spoken and Written Language." *DAI* 48 (March 1988): 2324A.

Explores how children depend on spoken language and phrase structure as they acquire written language and sentence structure.

737. Demel, Marjorie Jean Cornell. "The Relationship between Co-Referential Tie Comprehension and Overall Comprehension for Second Language Readers." *DAI* 49 (August 1988): 214A.

Analyzes metalinguistic awareness of concept designation as it relates to reading comprehension, specifically investigating errors in co-referential tie selection.

738. Dewberry, William David. "An Exploration of Linguistic Pragmatics Describing an Exemplary Model for Computer-Assisted Instruction in English as a Second Language with Pragmatics as Content." *DAI* 48 (April 1988): 2561A.

Reviews linguistic theory and the literature on applied pragmatics and ESL computer instruction. Examines program construction by focusing on computer language.

739. Dillon, George. "My Words of an Other." *CE* 50 (January 1988): 63–73.

Explores the use of quotation marks in light of Bakhtin's dialogics. Suggests that they indicate where the writer's language and an other's language intersect.

740. Doe, John. *Speak into the Mirror: A Story of Linguistic Anthropology.* Lanham Md.: University Press of America, 1988. 320 pages

Confronts political and economic problems of linguistic scholarship. Plays up disagreements in the field, attempting to discover the goals and objectives of different perspectives.

741. Dorgan, Ruth. "Third-Person Doublespeak." *QRD* 14 (April 1988): 11–12.

Cites examples of third-person doublespeak and explores its effect.

742. "Doublespeak Here and There." *QRD* 14 (January 1988): 5–8.

Notes examples of doublespeak in business, education, foreign countries, government, law, medicine, and the military.

743. "Doublespeak Here and There." *QRD* 14 (April 1988): 1–7.

Notes examples of doublespeak in business, education, foreign countries, government, medicine, and the military.

744. "Doublespeak Here and There." *QRD* 14 (July 1988): 1–10.

Notes examples of doublespeak in business, education, foreign countries, government, law, medicine, and the military.

745. "Doublespeak Here and There." *QRD* 15 (October 1988): 1–6.

Notes examples of doublespeak in business, education, foreign countries, government, medicine, and the military.

746. Edupuganty, Balanjaninath. "Two-Level Grammar: An Implementable Metalanguage for Consistent and Complementary Language Specifications." *DAI* 48 (February 1988): 2380B.

Proposes a two-level grammar as both a functional programming language and an elegant executable metalanguage.

747. Ehrenhaus, Peter. "Silence and Symbolic Expression." *ComM* 55 (March 1988): 41–57.

Regards silence from a phenomenological perspective that extends the domain of silence-as-object to silence-as-encounter.

748. Emmorey, Karen Denise. "Morphological Structure and Parsing in the Lexicon." *DAI* 48 (February 1988): 2054A.

Explores relationships between formal grammars and psychological parsing models.

749. Erlanger, Mary. "An Exploratory Study of the Genogram." *DAI* 48 (May 1988): 2989A.

Investigates variations in the quantity and type of information produced by a large number of individual genograms.

750. Errishi, Ali Saleh. "Prephysics." *DAI* 49 (August 1988): 269A.

Examines the quadrival nature of prephysics: measurement, languaging, historiography, theology, and the concept of a grammar of being.

751. Evans, Ron, Robin Venetozzi, Mike Bundrick, and Edna McWilliams. "The Effects of Sentence-Combining Instructions on Writing and on Standardized Test Scores." *JEdR* 82 (September–October 1988): 53–57.

Suggests that the most significant gains can be seen among those who initially scored lowest on tests of writing ability.

752. Fabb, Nigel, Derek Attridge, Alan Durant, and Colin MacCabe, eds. *The Linguistics of Writing: Arguments between Language and Literature*. New York: Methuen, 1988. 384 pages

> A collection of 18 essays developed for a 1986 conference in Glasgow. Scholars in the fields of literature and linguistics examine the interrelationship and joint future of linguistics and literary theory.

753. Farris, Catherine S. "Language and Sex Role Acquisition in a Taiwanese Kindergarten: A Semiotic Analysis." *DAI* 49 (February 1988): 2288A.

> Examines how gender as a meaning system is encoded in an urban Taiwanese speech community.

754. Felix, Sascha W. "Universal Grammar in Language Acquisition." *CJL* 33 (December 1988): 367–393.

> Argues that an intrinsic universal grammar determines both the rate and sequence of language acquisition in children.

755. Folarin, Antonia Yetunde. "Lexical Phonology of Yoruba Nouns and Verbs." *DAI* 48 (April 1988): 2615A.

> Differentiates between two types of compounding. Discusses semantic, phonological, syntactic, and morphological differences and similarities between compound and phrasal verbs and nouns.

756. Fry, Stephen. "Who Knows?: Purchasing Comprehension with Linguistic Currency." *ETC* 45 (Fall 1988): 256–257.

> The use of a word presumes a common understanding of its meaning, but because many words today lack that basis, jargon may be preferable to plain words.

757. Galindo, Delma Letticia. "Linguistic Influence and Variation on the English of Chicano Adolescents in Austin, Texas." *DAI* 48 (April 1988): 2616A.

> By combining quantitative and qualitative methods of analysis, accounts for both group and individual patterns of variation in 30 third-generation adolescents.

758. Gardiner, John M. "Generation and Priming Effects in Word-Fragment Completion." *JEPL* 14 (July 1988): 495–501.

> Reports on experiments investigating the relationships of memory, priming, generation, and recognition.

759. Gardiner, John M., Vernon H. Gregg, and James A. Hampton. "Word Frequency and Generation Effects." *JEPL* 14 (October 1988): 687–693.

> Word frequency does not define an essential boundary condition for generation effects.

760. Gibson, Walker. "On Defining Doublespeak." *QRD* 14 (April 1988): 8–9.

> Traces the origins of the term, expands its definition, and invites further debate.

761. Gilligan, Gary Martin. "A Cross-Linguistic Approach to the Pro-Drop Parameter." *DAI* 49 (August 1988): 244A.

> Uses Taraldsen, Rizzi, and others to bring cross-linguistic types to bear on the analysis of null subjects.

762. Goldstein, Diane E. "Sharing in the One: An Ethnography of Speaking in a Mystical Religious Community." *DAI* 49 (August 1988): 319A.

> Presents an ethnographic description of a speech community and its linguistic resources.

763. Gorrell, Paul Griffith. "Studies of Human Syntactic Processing: Ranked-Parallel Versus Serial Models." *DAI* 48 (April 1988): 2616A.

> Offers new experimental evidence of parser responses to structural ambiguity. Outlines a model of human sentence processing, seeking to reconcile results with recent findings.

764. Gray, Linda Christine. "Variations of Sentence Style in Informative Essays from the

1850s through the 1970s." *DAI* 48 (February 1988): 2007A.

Isolates aspects of writing style and then examines changes in them over time.

765. Greenberg, Joseph H. "The First-Person Inclusive Dual as an Ambiguous Category." *SLang* 12 (1988): 1–18.

Argues from synchronic and diachronic evidence that the first-person dual is an ambiguous linguistic category.

766. Hahn, Dan F., and Robert L. Ivie. "Sex as Rhetorical Invitation to War." *ETC* 45 (Spring 1988): 15–21.

Argues that, when public figures advocate war using sexual metaphors, their language reveals dangerous thinking by violating a realm traditionally controlled by females.

767. Hampton, James A. "Overextension of Conjunctive Concepts: Evidence for a Unitary Model of Concept Typicality and Class Inclusion." *JEPL* 14 (January 1988): 12–32.

Studies how people determine that a particular concept belongs to a conjunctive concept, why *blackboard* is "school furniture" but not "furniture."

768. Hare-Mustin, Rachel T., and Jeanne Marecek. "The Meaning of Difference: Gender Theory, Postmodernism, and Psychology." *AmP* 43 (June 1988): 455–464.

Examines gender theories via constructivism and deconstruction, with special emphasis on language and meaning making.

769. Harrington, Richard Alexander. "Metalinguistic Activities in Spoken and Written Communicative Events." *DAI* 49 (December 1988): 1393A.

Uses Jakobson and Hymes to apply a scheme of linguistic variables to seven case studies. Finds that teachers should use a social model for writing.

770. Harris, Lonnie Glenn. "The Relationship between Grammar and Phonology: A Comparative Analysis of Normal and Phonologically Impaired Children." *DAI* 48 (February 1988): 1929A.

Groups of normal and impaired children exhibited poorer phonological performance as linguistic complexity increased.

771. Harris, R. Allen. "Linguistics, Technical Writing, and Generalized Phrase Structure Grammar." *JTWC* 18 (1988): 227–240.

Briefly describes generalized phrase structure grammar and its applications to the technical writing classroom.

772. Harris, Zellig. *Language and Information*. Irvington-on-Hudson, N.Y.: Columbia University Press, 1988. 120 pages

Sets forth a formal theory of language structure and examines the results that follow from that theory.

773. Hayashi, Takuo. "Language Competence and Information Processing Strategy: A Comparison of First and Second Language Word Recognition." *DAI* 49 (July 1988): 84A.

"L2 listeners use top-down strategy more than L1 listeners when access to higher-level information is not prevented by their limited linguistic competence."

774. Hayes, Donald P. "Speaking and Writing: Distinct Patterns of Word Choice." *JML* 27 (October 1988): 572–585.

Examines patterns of word choice at different levels of lexical expertise, focusing on various language sources.

775. Henkel, Jacqueline. "A Comment on 'Deconstruction and Linguistic Analysis' [*CE* 49 (April 1987)]." *CE* 50 (April 1988): 454–457.

Comments that Schleifer's broad use of the term *linguistics* misrepresents both linguistics and deconstruction.

776. Hirshman, Elliot, and Robert A. Bjork. "The Generation Effect: Support for a Two-Factor Theory." *JEPL* 14 (July 1988): 484–494.

Reports on experiments suggesting that both memory and the relationship between the stimulus and response are responsible for the generation effect.

777. Hovy, Eduard H. "Generating Natural Language under Pragmatic Constraints." *DAI* 48 (April 1988): 3025B.

Investigates how the program Pauline produces varying outputs from a single set of linguistic inputs.

778. Ibrahim, Abdulla Ali. "Assaulting with Words: The Sociopoetics of the Rubatab Evil Eye Metaphors." *DAI* 49 (October 1988): 915A.

Examines the *sahin* (evil eye) performance in the context of Islamic models of speaking that promote silence, limit play, and abhor poetic metaphors.

779. Johanek, Michael. "Edspeak 1988." *QRD* 14 (January 1988): 9.

Points out new examples of doublespeak in education.

780. Johnson, Stephen B. "An Analyzer for the Information Content of Sentences." *DAI* 48 (May 1988): 3340B.

Describes a formal grammar that a sentence analyzer can use to decode sentences directly into informational relations.

781. Kachru, Braj B. "The Sacred Cows of English." *EngT* 4 (October 1988): 3–8.

Suggests attitude changes that will be necessary among native speakers of English as a result of its status as an international language.

782. Kadia, Kayiba. "The Effect of Formal Instruction on Monitored and on Spontaneous Naturalistic Interlanguage Performance: A Case Study." *TESOLQ* 22 (September 1988): 509–515.

Reports that, over nine weeks, formal instruction benefited monitored performance but did not affect unmonitored oral performance.

783. Kapili, Lily V. "Requeim for English?" *EngT* 4 (October 1988): 30–35.

Discusses the political, economic, sociocultural, and logistical problems involved in using American English in the Philippines.

784. Kaufman, Lionel M., Jr. "Tense Alternation by Native and Nonnative English Speakers in Narrative Discourse." *DAI* 49 (July 1988): 84A.

Investigates the use of present, past, and future tenses in relating a past event to situations of varying formality.

785. Kehl, D. G. "Doublespeak: Its Meaning and Its Menace." *QRD* 14 (January 1988): 8–9.

Analyzes seven functions and consequences of doublespeak, arriving at a definition of the term.

786. Kellas, George, F. Richard Ferraro, and Greg B. Simpson. "Lexical Ambiguity and the Timecourse of Attentional Allocation in Word Recognition." *JEPH* 14 (November 1988): 601–609.

Examines the attentional demands associated with word recognition. Finds that ambiguous words require the least attention.

787. Kelly, Michael H., and J. Kathryn Bock. "Stress in Time." *JEPH* 14 (August 1988): 389–403.

Explores the iambic, rhythmic bias in ordinary English speech and relates it to lexical stress patterns in English.

788. Kiefer, Ferenc. "Ability and Possibility: The Hungarian Verb *Tud,* To Be Able To. " *SLang* 12 (1988): 393–423.

Argues that in order to account for the meaning of *tud,* three types of knowledge must be distinguished: linguistic, conceptual, and encyclopedic.

789. Kilborne, William S., Jr. "History's Bad Rap." *ETC* 45 (Winter 1988): 307–310.

Considers implications of terms like *history,* where the term refers both to history-as-occurrence and to the abstracted histories historians produce.

790. Koreo, Kinosita. "Language Habits of the Japanese." *EngT* 4 (July 1988): 19–25.

Defines Japanese speech habits and discusses their evolution and potential causes for change.

791. Landau, Sidney I. "A Matter of Life and Death." *EngT* 4 (October 1988): 43–46.

Argues that the most common American dictionaries present misleading definitions of the word *abortion*.

792. Larson, Ben E. "An Investigation of Grammatical Differences in Writing as Found in Japanese and American Professional Letters." *DAI* 48 (April 1988): 2616A.

Analyzes which grammatical features in 44 professional letters affected Japanese and American judges' perceptions of politeness and directness.

793. Larson, Timothy J. "Semantics for Coordinated Substitution Grammars as Implemented in Prolog." *DAI* 48 (April 1988): 3026B.

Demonstrates that coordinated substitution grammars, as implemented in Prolog, appropriately represent syntax in natural language.

794. Lee, Ronald. "Moralizing and Ideologizing: An Analysis of Political Illocution." *WJSC* 52 (Fall 1988): 291–307.

Focuses on the rhetorical function of ideology on forms of normative discourse and on the critic's role.

795. Libben, Gary. "Morpheme Decomposition and the Mental Lexicon: Evidence from the Visual Recognition of Compounds." *DAI* 48 (April 1988): 2617A.

Presents three experiments and discusses the findings from a linguistic and psycholinguistic perspective.

796. Lutz, William. *QRD* 14 (January 1988): 1–5.

Announces the 1987 Orwell and Doublespeak awards, describing other nominees as well.

797. Macauley, Marcia I. "Oral and Written Speech in English: A Linguistic Description of Processing Varieties and the Effect of Discourse." *DAI* 49 (December 1988): 1445A.

Concludes that oral and written texts differed across genres.

798. Mansbridge, Ronald. "Purist." *EngT* 4 (April 1988): 21–23.

Chronicles how the author came to relax his hardline stance in favor of maintaining language purity.

799. Matthews, Alison, and Martin S. Chodorow. "Pronoun Resolution in Two-Clause Sentences: Effects of Ambiguity, Antecedent Location, and Depth of Imbedding." *JML* 27 (June 1988): 245–260.

Studies connections between gender cues and pronoun resolution, examining how antecedents are determined in ambiguous sentences.

800. McArthur, Tom. "The Cult of Abbreviation." *EngT* 4 (July 1988): 36–42.

Favors a continuum model for classifying abbreviations, which includes as "focal points" four traditional categories: initialism, acronyms, clipping, and blends.

801. McCann, Robert S., Derek Besner, and Eileen Davelaar. "Word Recognition and Identification: Do Word-Frequency Effects Reflect Lexical Access?" *JEPH* 14 (November 1988): 693–706.

Reports on experiments showing that lexical access is not frequency sensitive.

802. McKenna, Marian J. "The Development and Validation of a Model for Coherence." *DAI* 48 (February 1988): 2032A.

Examines the differences between cohesion and coherence and seeks to determine the validity of certain variables to predict coherence in written texts.

803. Meyer, Charles F. *A Linguistic Study of American Punctuation*. American University Studies, Linguistics, vol. 5. New York: Peter Lang, 1987. 159 pages

A descriptive account of American punctuation that analyzes data from style manuals and Brown University's *Standard Corpus of Present-Day Edited American English*. Postulates a system of punctuation governed by syntactic, semantic, and prosodic considerations.

804. Miller, Joanne L., and Emily R. Dexter. "Effects of Speaking Rate and Lexical Status on Phonetic Perception." *JEPH* 14 (August 1988): 369–378.

Investigates how listeners use later occurring sounds to clarify initial sounds.

805. Morriss, James E., and Joan M. Boyle. "The Mirror of Time: Images of Aging." *ETC* 45 (Spring 1988): 57–62.

Explores relationships between characterizing groups in language and resultant attitudes toward aging and the elderly in American society.

806. Mulac, Anthony, John M. Wiemann, Sally J. Widenmann, and Toni W. Gibson. "Male-Female Language Differences and Effects in Same Sex and Mixed Sex Dyads: The Gender-Linked Language Effect." *ComM* 55 (December 1988): 315–335.

Findings indicate that male-female language in cooperative problem solving differs but diminishes in opposite-sex dyadic interactions.

807. Myhill, John. "Categoriality and Clustering." *SLang* 12 (1988): 261–297.

Formulates a theory about the structure of clauses to explain diverse morphological and syntactic phenomena.

808. Nairne, James S., and Robert L. Widner, Jr. "Familiarity and Lexicality as Determinants of the Generation Effect." *JEPL* 14 (October 1988): 694–699.

Lexical representation is neither a necessary nor a sufficient condition to produce the generation effect.

809. Newsom, David. "Misuse and Abuse of Democracy." *QRD* 14 (January 1988): 11–12.

Analyzes the meaning of *democracy* as used to promote the "Reagan Doctrine."

810. Nippold, Marilyn A., ed. *Later Language Development: Ages 9 through 19*. Boston: Little, Brown, 1988. 271 pages

Attempts to describe what is and is not known about normal language development in adolescence. Chapters treat the nature of literacy, the lexicon, syntax, reading and writing, cognition, verbal reasoning, figurative language, linguistic ambiguity, language and socialization, and pragmatics.

811. Noble, W. Vernon. "A Sheepish Tongue." *EngT* 4 (April 1988): 24–25.

Discusses English aphorisms, colloquialisms, and metaphors borrowed from the occupation of sheep-rearing.

812. Oppenheim, Ross. "The Mathematical Analysis of Style: A Correlation-Based Approach." *CHum* 22 (1988): 241–252.

Describes the potential value of studying lengths of successive sentences in order to examine style shifts.

813. Ostler, Shirley E. "A Study of the Contrastive Rhetoric of Arabic, English, Japanese, and Spanish." *DAI* 49 (August 1988): 245A.

Uses syntactic and discourse-bloc analysis to test the notion of contrastive rhetoric.

814. Paivio, Allan, James W. Clark, and Wallace E. Lambert. "Bilingual Dual-Coding Theory and Semantic Repetition Effects on Recall." *JEPL* 14 (January 1988): 163–172.

Concludes that dual-coding theory and the independence of the storage hypothesis of bilingual memory predicts the recall of concrete and abstract words among bilingual speakers.

815. Parker, Frank, Kathryn Riley, and Charles Meyer. "Case Assignment and the Ordering of Constituents in Coordinate Constructions." *AS* 63 (Fall 1988): 214–233.

Provides explanations for the suspension of case assignment rules in English grammar. Demonstrates that the order of noun phrases is systematic and pragmatic.

816. Payne, Thomas E. "Referential Distance and Discourse Structure in Yagua." *SLang* 12 (1988): 345–392.

Finds that the quantitative methodological procedure known as "topic continuity" is a useful base for building observations about coding devices in discourse.

817. Pointon, Graham. "The BBC and English Pronunciation." *EngT* 4 (July 1988): 8–12.

The Director of the Pronunciation Unit describes how the British Broadcasting Corporation has responded to changes in public usage.

818. Prince, Moneta Speaker. "The Development of Perception of English Vowels by Indonesian Students." *DAI* 49 (December 1988): 1395A.

Discusses implications for ESL teaching.

819. Radwan, Mohammad Ali. "A Linguistic Analysis of the Grammatical and Lexical Errors in the Nominal Group Found in the Written English of Syrian University Students." *DAI* 49 (December 1988): 1392A.

Describes, analyzes, and classifies the types of errors Syrian students of English make.

820. Rager, John E. "Multi-Level Structures for Natural Language Processing." *DAI* 48 (April 1988): 3029B.

Discusses the advantages of using two-level grammars in processing the syntax of natural language.

821. Rapoport, Nantol. "War without Hatred." *ETC* 45 (Fall 1988): 211–217.

Explores linguistic and historical distinctions between aggression and predation, using evolutionary theory to clarify our views of war. Warns of increasing intellectualization about war.

822. Ren, Hongmo. "On the Acoustic Structure of Diphthongal Syllables." *DAI* 48 (April 1988): 2618A.

Develops an approach to the problems of interface between linguistic transcriptions and physical properties of speech.

823. Ricento, Thomas K. "Aspects of Coherence in English and Japanese Expository Prose." *DAI* 48 (January 1988): 1754A.

Analyzes cross-linguistic rhetorical patterns and access to translated texts by measuring thematic continuity, reader-writer responsibility, paragraph linking, and cultural values.

824. Richards, Julie Becker. "Language, Education, and Cultural Identity in a Mayan Community of Guatemala." *DAI* 49 (October 1988): 864A.

Examines the role of language in elaborating and symbolizing cultural identity.

825. Riley, Kathryn, and Frank Parker. "Tone as a Function of Presupposition in Technical and Business Writing." *JTWC* 18 (1988): 325–343.

Argues that the linguistic concept of presupposition helps to explain how and why problems in tone arise.

826. Roesler, Janet Ruth. "Control of Information and Ways of Speaking in an Indigenous Settlement in Michoacan, Mexico." *DAI* 48 (June 1988): 3145A.

Focuses on the Nahuatl Indians' ways of speaking, which are rooted in social relationships.

827. Rooks, Mark Curtis. "A Subversive Account of Linguistic Metatheory." *DAI* 48 (March 1988): 2358A.

Criticizes Chomsky's explanation of linguistic structure in terms of innate mental structure. Supports Harris's theory, which explains language in terms of mental demands.

828. Schwanenflugel, Paula J., and Kathy L. LaCount. "Semantic Relatedness and the

Scope of Facilitation for Upcoming Words in Sentences." *JEPL* 14 (April 1988): 344–354.

Examines how sentence-level information is interrelated and combined with semantic representations during word processing. Sentence structure and semantics influence word recognition.

829. Schwartz, Bonnie Dale. "The Modular Basis of Second Language Acquisition." *DAI* 49 (August 1988): 246A.

Using Fodor's theory of epistemology and Chomsky's theory of linguistics, develops a model to explain the study's native-like and less-than-native-like results.

830. Sequeira, Debra-Lynn Marie. "Personal Address in American Culture: A Case Study." *DAI* 48 (April 1988): 2666A.

Identifies 20 forms of personal address, two patterns of interaction, and five semantic dimensions of social meaning in use. Revises earlier models of personal address.

831. Shen, Dan. "On the Aesthetic Function of Intentional Illogicality in English-Chinese Translation of Fiction." *Style* 22 (Winter 1988): 628–645.

Considers the nature of illogicality as a stylistic feature that violates readers' stereotypic conceptual frames and may separate literary discourse from ordinary discourse.

832. Shina, Chris. *Language and Representation: A Socio-Naturalistic Approach to Human Development.* New York: New York University Press, 1988. 240 pages

Presents a synthetic approach to linguistic and cognitive development, drawing from linguistics, philosophy, semiotics, biology, and cognitive and developmental psychology.

833. Shults, David. "Soothespeak." *QRD* 15 (October 1988): 11–12.

Defends the use of some euphemisms such as *honorable,* not *roguish.*

834. Sinclair, John. "Models and Monuments." *EngT* 4 (July 1988): 3–6.

Argues that British English should serve as a model for international use.

835. Sledd, James. "Product in Process: From Ambiguities of Standard English to Issues That Divide Us." *CE* 50 (February 1988): 168–176.

Argues that Standard English was created by the dominant culture to dominate. Explores ways in which teachers evade this issue. Questions how much variation to accept or encourage.

836. Sloan, Gary. "Relational Ambiguity between Sentences." *CCC* 39 (May 1988): 154–165.

Analyzes one paragraph to illustrate that schemes designed to classify semantic relationships between sentences do not account for frequent relational ambiguity.

837. Starling, Betty R. "An Analysis of Cohesion in Selected Texts of Referential Discourse." *DAI* 48 (April 1988): 2618A.

Finds differences in the sources of intersentential cohesion in exploratory, informative, and scientific discourse.

838. Stein, Samuel H. "The Language of Inequality." *ETC* 45 (Spring 1988): 52–56.

Explores the effects of language that promotes inequality among sexes, races, the elderly, and health professionals. Argues for individual treatment of individuals.

839. Summers, Della. "English Language Teaching Dictionaries: Past, Present, and Future." *EngT* 4 (April 1988): 10–14.

Briefly reviews the development of English dictionaries for foreign students, then compares the coverage of three monolingual English language teaching dictionaries.

840. Treiman, Rebecca, and Catalina Danis. "Short-Term Memory Errors for Spoken Syllables Are Affected by the Linguistic Structure of the Syllables." *JEPL* 14 (January 1988): 145–152.

Argues that short-term memory of speech needs to be studied with reference to specific linguistic structures because certain groups of phonemes behave more strongly as groups.

841. "Tried Any Initiatives Lately?" *QRD* 14 (April 1988): 11.

Analyzes the use of the word *initiative*. Reprinted from *New York Times,* 29 July 1987, p. D23.

842. Tucker, Dan. "Syntax as Pregnant as a Puff of Smoke." *QRD* 14 (January 1988): 10.

Examines the language of cigarette advertising as "verbal vacuums."

843. Tumas-Serna, Jane Anne. "An Investigation of the Primitive in Rock and Roll Performance: Steps toward a Cultural Approach to the Analysis of Mass Media Texts." *DAI* 49 (August 1988): 163A.

Analyzes texts of rock and roll performances, studying not only the lyrics but also the semiotics of open and closed texts.

844. "The Unknown Holiday." *QRD* 14 (April 1988): 9.

Designates 1 June as National Simple Speak Day and speculates on its meaning.

845. Valian, Virginia, and Seana Coulson. "Anchor Points in Language Learning: The Role of Marker Frequency." *JML* 27 (February 1987): 71–85.

Reports on two experiments involving dialects of a miniature artificial language with and without reference fields.

846. Villaume, William A., and Donald J. Cegala. "Interaction Involvement and Discourse Strategies: The Patterned Use of Cohesive Devices in Conversation." *ComM* 55 (March 1988): 22–40.

Examines the relationship between communicative competence and some explicitly clued verbal parameters of conversational coherence.

847. Webster, Eric. "The Power of Negative Thinking: 22 Convenient Ways to Bury an Idea." *ETC* 45 (Fall 1988): 246–249.

An analysis of verbal and nonverbal responses that reveal how listeners can bias their own evaluations or sabotage the evaluations of others.

848. Willett, Thomas. "A Cross-Linguistic Survey of the Grammaticization of Evidentiality." *SLang* 12 (1988): 51–97.

Synthesizes hypotheses about the nature of evidentials and their relation to each other and to other grammatical areas. Also proposes his own hypothesis.

849. Williamson, John. "Proper Words in Improper Places: Some Problems of Word Frequency Counts." *EQ* 21 (1988): 91–92.

Cautions against using word frequency counts that ignore context.

850. Wilson, Kenneth G. *Van Winkle's Return: Change in American English, 1966–1986.* Hanover, N.H.: University Press of New England, 1987. 208 pages

"Informal observations on some aspects of the present state of American English and our opinions of it," compared with views of 20 years ago.

851. Witt, Linda. "A Verbal Fig Leaf to Hide a Naked Truth." *QRD* 14 (January 1988): 11.

Analyzes the origins, use, and meanings of *micromanage.*

852. Wittenburg, Kent Barrows. "Natural Language Parsing with Combinatory Categorical Grammar in a Graph-Unification-Based Formalism." *DAI* 48 (April 1988): 2619A.

Reviews computational formalism, provides an overview of grammar theory, and considers issues connected with published analyses of English extraction and conjunction.

853. Yantis, Steven, and David E. Meyer. "Dynamics of Activation in Semantic and Episodic Memory." *JEPG* 117 (June 1988): 130–147.

Studies experimental methods for describing interactions between subcomponents of the human information-processing system.

Concludes that both discrete and continuous processes are involved.

854. Yellin, Daniel M. "Attribute Grammar Inversion and Source-to-Source Translation." *DAI* 48 (February 1988): 2386B.

Investigates attribute grammar inversion and shows how the technique can build translators between computer languages.

855. Yule, Valerie. "English Spelling and Pidgin." *EngT* 4 (July 1988): 29–35.

Discusses how orthographic systems are developed for English pidgins. Outlines factors influencing how closely pidgin spelling matches English spelling.

856. Zeidner, M. A. "Experts: A Definition." *QRD* 15 (October 1988): 10–11.

Examines the current usage of the term *expert*.

See also 55, 110, 190, 347, 557, 576, 613, 644, 664, 671, 681, 863, 889, 891, 898, 900, 908, 909, 911, 912, 917, 920, 927, 1010, 1211, 1263, 1491

2.9 PSYCHOLOGY

857. Adams, Michael. "The Interpretation of Unconscious Speech Acts: Conventions, Intentions, and the Profounder Self." *CEAC* 51 (Fall 1988): 114–128.

Analyzes the roles of intention, convention, and subjective context in the interpretation of meaning.

858. Archer, Sally L., and Alan S. Waterman. "Psychological Individualism: Gender Differences or Gender Neutrality." *HD* 31 (March–April 1988): 65–81.

Surveys studies on psychological individualism and concludes that this concept is gender neutral. Gilligan's "principled female voice" should represent males and females.

859. Baddeley, Alan, Robert Logie, and Nick Ellis. "Characteristics of Developmental Dyslexia." *Cognition* 29 (1988): 197–228.

Evaluates whether the patterns of reading performance among developmental dyslexic boys resemble patterns observed in patients with acquired dyslexia.

860. Bidell, Thomas. "Vygotsky, Piaget, and the Dialectic of Development." *HD* 31 (November 1988): 329–348.

Proposes that the dialectical approach shared by Vygotskian and Piagetian theories can work together in "framing developmental research."

861. Brand, Alice G. "Hot Cognition: Emotion and Writing Behavior." *CEAF* 18 (1988): 21–25.

Argues that composition studies should not neglect the influences of writers' emotions on their writing.

862. Brand, Alice G., and Phoebe A. Leckie. "The Emotions of Professional Writers." *JPsy* 122 (September 1988): 421–439.

An analysis of 24 professional writers' emotions before, during, and after writing activities.

863. Burgess, Curt, and Greg B. Simpson. "Cerebral Hemispheric Mechanisms in the Retrieval of Ambiguous Word Meanings." *BL* 33 (January 1988): 86–103.

Compares the retrieval of ambiguous word meanings from the right hemisphere, which retrieves subordinate meanings, to the left hemisphere, which retrieves more frequent meanings.

864. Campbell, Robert L., and Mark H. Bickhard. "A Deconstruction of Fodor's Anticonstructivism." *HD* 30 (January–February 1987): 48–59.

Counters Fodor's arguments by not "equating knowledge with encodings" but by building "consistently interactive models of knowledge and development."

865. Carlson, Richard, and Don E. Dulany. "Diagnostic Reasoning with Circumstantial Evidence." *CPsy* 20 (October 1988): 463–492.

Subjects used "forward and backward implications relating facts and possible causes" as a means of reasoning with circumstantial evidence.

866. Carlton, Carol Ann. "Thought Processes in Writing: A Case Study." *DAI* 49 (July 1988): 51A.

Using observations, interviews, journals, and manuscripts, this study describes thought processes of a professional writer over a two-year period.

867. Chapman, Michael. "Contextuality and Directionality of Cognitive Development." *HD* 31 (March 1988): 92–106.

Argues that cognitive development is contextual, multidirectional, and defined retrospectively as individuals move away from an initial state. Cognitive development is not universal, unidirectional, or defined teleologically.

868. Chebat, Jean-Charles, Pierre Filiatraoul, Michel LaRoche, and Catherine Watson. "Compensatory Effects of Cognitive Characteristics of the Source, the Message, and the Receiver upon Attitude Change." *JPsy* 122 (November 1988): 609–621.

A study of 236 Canadian students showed a positive and significant main effect of initial attitude on attitude change.

869. Cravens, Hamilton. "Recent Controversy in Human Development: A Historical View." *HD* 30 (November–December 1987): 325–335.

Places the current state of the field in the context of past states, discussing how they each reflect their then-current world views.

870. Cummins, Denise Dellarosa, Walter Kintsch, Kurt Reusser, and Rhonda Weimer. "The Role of Understanding in Solving Word Problems." *CPsy* 20 (October 1988): 405–438.

Suggests that text comprehension influences one's choice of heuristics and is crucial for solving word problems of any nature.

871. Custer, Harriet Howell. "The Cognitive Development of Women: A Grounded Theory Derived from Fiction." *DAI* 49 (August 1988): 206A.

Uses six novels written by women to analyze sources of knowledge. Investigates cognition, personal development, and self-esteem.

872. Dixon, Peter, Jo-Anne LaFeure, and Leslie Twilley. "Word Knowledge and Working Memory as Predictors of Reading Skill." *JEdP* 80 (1988): 465–472.

Working memory capacity and word knowledge were used as predictors of reading skill. Results suggest that concepts are multidimensional constructs.

873. Eysenck, Hans J. "The Concept of 'Intelligence': Useful or Useless?" *Intell* 12 (January–March 1988): 1–16.

An editorial that discusses three concepts of intelligence: biological, psychometric, and social. Argues that, in the interests of scientific advancement, the use of "social intelligence" must be resisted.

874. Gellatly, Angus R. H. "Acquisition of a Concept of Logical Necessity." *HD* 30 (January–February 1987): 32–47.

Analyzes Piaget's concept of logical necessity as a cultural construction. Ties the argument to the development of literacy.

875. Goldsmith, Ronald E., and Timothy A. Matherly. "Creativity and Self-Esteem: A Multiple Operationalization Validity Study." *JPsy* 122 (January 1988): 47–56.

Supports the hypothesis that creativity and self-esteem are related, particularly for females.

876. Graham, Janet Gorman. "A Comparison of the Writing of College Freshmen and College Seniors with a Focus on Indications of

Cognitive Development." *DAI* 48 (February 1988): 2007A.

Examines differences in writing and cognitive development across age groups.

877. Harding, Carol Gibb. "A Developmental Model for the Invention of Dilemmas." *HD* 30 (September–October 1987): 282–290.

Developing the concept of dilemma "requires the ability to act with intention," to see others' behavior as intentional, and to deal with contradictions.

878. Harris, Richard Jackson, D. John Lee, Deana L. Hensley, and Lawrence M. Schoen. "The Effect of Cultural Script Knowledge on Memory for Stories over Time." *DPr* 11 (October–December 1988): 413–431.

The effects of script-based knowledge on memory depended partly on the cultural context of discourse. Memory distortions were more likely with culturally unfamiliar scripts.

879. Hays, Janice N. "Socio-Cognitive Development and Argumentative Writing: Issues and Implications from One Research Project." *JBW* 7 (Fall 1988): 42–67.

Continues the journal's colloquy on developmental research by explaining research using Perry's scheme. Emphasizes that "socio-cognitive structures cannot be ignored as contributors to students' writing performance."

880. Hirshman, Elliot. "The Expectation-Violation Effect: The Paradoxical Effects of Semantic Relatedness." *JML* 27 (February 1988): 40–58.

Finds that weakly related items in a word pair can be more easily remembered than strongly related items.

881. Honey, Margaret A. "The Interview as Text: Hermeneutics Considered as a Model for Analyzing the Clinically Informed Research Interview." *HD* 30 (March–April 1987): 69–82.

Utilizes Ricoeur's discussion of the dichotomy between explanation and understand-ing to determine if the clinical interview satisfies his criteria of textuality.

882. Humphreys, Glyn W., Derek Besner, and Philip T. Quinlan. "Event Perception and the Word Repetition Effect." *JEPG* 117 (March 1988): 51–67.

Evaluates the relationship between word repetition effect and event perception.

883. Jacoby, Larry L., Lorraine G. Allan, Jane C. Collins, and Linda K. Larwill. "Memory Influences Subjective Experience: Noise Judgments." *JEPL* 14 (April 1988): 240–247.

People perceived noise as being louder when they were trying to identify unfamiliar words and sentences than when they were listening for familiar ones.

884. Kagan, Dona M., and Kris E. Berg. "The Relationship between Aerobic Activity and Cognitive Performance under Stress." *JPsy* 122 (September 1988): 451–462.

Finds that inherent cognitive aptitude and personality traits are stronger factors in cognitive performance than aerobic exercise conditioning.

885. Keen, Sam. "Stories We Live By." *PsyT* 22 (December 1988): 42–47.

Shows ways of reinventing the self through retelling personal myths.

886. Klouda, Gayle V., Donald A. Robin, Neill R. Graff-Radford, and William E. Cooper. "The Role of Collosal Connections in Speech Prosody." *BL* 35 (September 1988): 154–171.

Studies collosal involvement in speech prosody. Shows evidence that the left hemisphere can perform the right hemisphere's task of frequency programming following collasal damage.

887. Kosslyn, Stephen M., Carolyn Backer Cave, David A. Provost, and Susanne M. Von Gierke. "Sequential Processes in Image Generation." *CPsy* 20 (July 1988): 319–343.

Suggests that images are not typically perceived holistically but rather are constructed when separate "perceptual units" are activated.

888. Kozulin, Alex. "Social Constructs Misconstrued: The Case of Soviet Developmental Psychology." *HD* 30 (November–December 1987): 336–340.

Disputes Wertsch and Youniss's article [*HD* 30 (January–February 1987)]. Vygotsky's theory was not the result of nation-building but of the European tradition emphasizing conceptual reasoning.

889. Leadbeater, Bonnie J. "Relational Processes in Adolescent and Adult Dialogues: Assessing the Intersubjective Context of Conversation." *HD* 31 (September 1988): 313–326.

Investigates relational processes through transactive statements of same-sex peer dialogues. Finds "noncompetitive" transacts for female subjects, but "competitive and ego-focused" transacts for male subjects.

890. Lewicki, Pawel, Thomas Hill, and Elizabeth Bizot. "Acquisition of Procedural Knowledge about a Pattern of Stimuli That Cannot Be Articulated." *CPsy* 20 (January 1988): 24–37.

Argues that "nonconsciously acquired knowledge can automatically be utilized to facilitate performance" without conscious awareness or control over this knowledge.

891. Lieberman, Philip. *On the Origins of Language: An Introduction to the Evolution of Human Speech*. Lanham, Md.: University Press of America, 1988. 202 pages

Examines studies of cognitive behavior in primates, of the neural bases of auditory perception, and of play activity in rhesus monkeys. Attempts to synthesize a large body of data into a coherent theory of language development. Originally published in 1975.

892. MacNeal, Edward. "MacNeal's Master Atlas of Decision Making: Logics for Interconnected Decisions." *ETC* 45 (Fall 1988): 218–230.

Examines and illustrates transformative, recursive, and allocative procedures whereby individuals link decisions in problem solving. Discusses the costs and benefits of each.

893. MacNeal, Edward. "MacNeal's Master Atlas of Decision Making: Logics for Interconnected Decisions." *ETC* 45 (Winter 1988): 311–324.

Analyzes and illustrates processes of group decision making. Discusses strengths and weaknesses in these processes.

894. MacNeal, Edward. "MacNeal's Master Atlas of Decision Making: Logics for the Single Decision." *ETC* 45 (Spring 1988): 3–14.

Classifies patterns of simple decision making, separating them from the rationalization given for choices made. Points to essential differences between decision making and problem solving.

895. MacNeal, Edward. "MacNeal's Master Atlas of Decision Making: Logics for the Single Decision." *ETC* 45 (Summer 1988): 118–127.

Analyzes the roles and dangers of originative maps and scorecards in decision making. Both may be inefficient and confusing but serve important creative functions.

896. McKoon, Gail, and Roger Ratcliff. "Contextually Relevant Aspects of Meaning." *JEPL* 14 (April 1988): 331–343.

Studies the conditions for incorporating general knowledge into the memory representation of a text.

897. Medin, Douglas L., and Edward J. Shoben. "Context and Structure in Conceptual Combination." *CPsy* 20 (April 1988): 158–190.

Argues that centrality of meaning and theoretical knowledge are important constructs for understanding how individuals combine concepts.

898. Mehler, Jacques, Peter Jusczyk, Ghislaine Lambertz, Nilofar Halsted, and Josiane Ber-

toncini. "Amiel-Tiscon Claudine A Precursor of Language Acquisition in Young Infants." *Cognition* 29 (1988): 143–178.

A study of French and American infants' ability to distinguish utterances. Findings suggest that the basis for classifying utterances may be provided by prosodic cues.

899. Miller, Lawrence. "The Emotional Brain." *PsyT* 22 (February 1988): 34–42.

Describes research on how the brain hemispheres control different types of emotions, indicating that emotional control depends on the tight balance of spheres.

900. Mirel, Barbara. "Cognitive Processing, Text Linguistics, and Documentation Writing." *JTWC* 18 (1988): 111–133.

Based on a survey and discussion of research, this article proposes and illustrates a set of principles for writing effective computer manuals.

901. Nairne, James S. "The Mnemonic Value of Perceptual Identification." *JEPL* 14 (April 1988): 248–255.

Attempts to discover whether words presented for identification might be remembered better than ones that are read. Results varied by the measure of recall.

902. Nilsson, Lars-Goran, Janine Law, and Endel Tulving. "Recognition Failure of Recallable Unique Names: Evidence for an Empirical Law of Memory and Language." *JEPL* 14 (April 1988): 266–277.

Discusses an empirical law concerning recognition and recall. People recognized famous names previously studied when they were presented in the context studied but not in isolation.

903. Onuf, N. G. "Rules in Moral Development." *HD* 30 (September–October 1987): 257–267.

Discusses how various cultures mix types of rules that themselves depend on basic types of speech acts. Concludes that "no developmental logic is implied."

904. Oser, Fritz K., and K. Helmut Reich. "The Challenge of Competing Explanations: The Development of Thinking in Terms of Complementarity of Theories." *HD* 30 (May–June 1987): 178–186.

Hypothesizes a developmental sequence for the postformal ability to synthesize two complementary theories into one. Refers particularly to the growth of epistemic cognition.

905. Pohl, Gayle Marechia. "Anxiety and Message-Induced Persuasion: A Meta-Analytical Approach." *DAI* 49 (August 1988): 167A.

A quantitative study concluding that anxiety increased the effect of persuasive messages and altered the hearer's level of anxiety.

906. Reeke, George N., Jr., and Gerald M. Edelman. "Real Brains and Artificial Intelligence." *Daedalus* 117 (Winter 1988): 143–174.

"Nervous systems" (perception, cognition, expression) "do not work like the standard AI paradigm." "A real organism capable of intelligent behavior reveals a staggering number of non-linear interactions."

907. Richards, D. Dean. "Dynamic Concepts and Functionality: The Influences of Multiple Representations and Environmental Constraints on Categorization." *HD* 31 (January 1988): 11–19.

Suggests that concepts should be considered dynamic and context-sensitive rather than static.

908. Rivera, Hector Anibal. "The Relationship between Bilingualism and Primary Process Thinking." *DAI* 48 (January 1988): 1713A.

Studies 32 adult male Spanish-English bilinguals to test whether memories and experiences are stored in common and can be tapped equally by either language.

909. Ross, Elliot D., Jerold A. Edmondson, G. Burton Seibert, and Richard W. Homan. "Acoustic Analysis of Affective Prosody during Right-Sided Wada Test: A Within-Sub-

jects Verification of the Right Hemisphere's Role in Language." *BL* 33 (January 1988): 128–145.

Results support the view that the right hemisphere "modulates dominantly the affective components of language."

910. Schmid-Kitsikis, Elsa. "Development of Mental Functioning: Integrative Approach to Psychoanalytic and Psychogenetic Theory." *HD* 30 (July–August 1987): 189–209.

Presents an argument for "new syntheses of Piaget's psychological and epistemological theory and Freud's psycholanalytic metapsychology," one sensitive to sexual, cultural, and social factors.

911. Schneiderman, Eta I., and J. Douglas Saddy. "A Linguistic Deficit Resulting from Right-Hemisphere Damage." *BL* 34 (May 1988): 38–53.

Researches the involvement of the right hemisphere in aspects of grammar that had previously been considered inaccessible to the right hemisphere.

912. Shipley-Brown, Frances, William O. Dingwall, Charles I. Berlin, Grace Yeni-Komshian, and Sandra Gordon-Salant. "Hemispheric Processing of Affective and Linguistic Intonation Contours in Normal Subjects." *BL* 33 (January 1988): 16–26.

Empirical evidence suggests that the right hemisphere is involved in processing both affective and linguistic prosody.

913. Simpson, Evan. "The Development of Political Reasoning." *HD* 30 (September–October 1987): 268–281.

Discusses political argument from the perspective primarily of Habermas, but also includes Kohlberg, Piaget, and Marxist ideology.

914. Sloman, Steven A., C. A. Gordon Hayman, Nobuo Ohta, Janine Law, and Endel Tulving. "Forgetting in Primed Fragment Completion." *JEPL* 14 (April 1988): 223–239.

Finds that brief study improves word-fragment completion. The effect decreases rapidly during the first five minutes, then decreases much more slowly. Benefits still persist after 16 months.

915. Smith, Leslie. "A Constructive Interpretation of Formal Operations." *HD* 30 (November–December 1987): 341–354.

Returns to Piaget's 16 patterns to reinterpret his theory, stressing the two key features of constructivism: differentiation and integration of understanding.

916. Sokolowski, Robert. "Natural and Artificial Intelligence." *Daedalus* 117 (Winter 1988): 45–64.

Analogizes writing with artificial intelligence and speech with "natural" intelligence. Finds writing "a bridge" to artificial intelligence, which is "straight-line inferential thinking," not "quotation, making distinctions, and desire."

917. Sommers, Ronald K. "Prediction of Fine Motor Skills of Children Having Language and Speech Disorders." *PMS* 67 (1988): 63–72.

Studies the relationships between motor skills and linguistic abilities among 39 developmentally delayed children. Results indicate a strong relationship between motor skills and expressive-receptive language.

918. Sternberg, Robert J. "Mental Self-Government: A Theory of Intellectual Styles and Their Development." *HD* 31 (July 1988): 197–221.

Theorizes a set of intellectual styles that serve as a bridge between intelligence and personality.

919. Sweller, John. "Cognitive Load during Problem Solving: Effects on Learning." *CSc* 12 (1988): 257–285.

Argues that domain-specific knowledge in the form of schemas is a primary factor distinguishing experts from novices in problem-solving skill. Discusses theoretical and practical implications.

920. Todorovic, Dejan. "Hemispheric Differences in Case Processing." *BL* 33 (March 1988): 365–389.

Researches the linguistic capacity of the right hemisphere.

921. van Goert, Paul. "The Structure of Developmental Theories: A Generative Approach." *HD* 30 (May–June 1987): 160–177.

Uses the theories of Piaget, Erikson, Jakobson, and Gal'perin to construct a possible "generative grammar" for any developmental theory.

922. Vernon, Philip A., and Steven Strudensky. "Relationship between Problem Solving and Intelligence." *Intell* 12 (October–December 1988): 435–453.

Concludes that "general intelligence" insufficiently explains the relationships between problem solving and intelligence. Subjects cope with novelty via verbal strategies until pressing demands "become increasingly automatized."

923. Wertsch, James V. "L. S. Vygotsky's 'New' Theory of Mind." *ASch* 57 (Winter 1988): 81–89.

Investigates Vygotsky's lasting influence on theories of mind, using as a context the sociocultural settings in which he worked.

924. Wertsch, James V. *Vygotsky and the Social Formation of Mind.* Cambridge, Mass.: Harvard University Press, 1988. 280 pages

Outlines Vygotsky's principal tenets. Draws on current research in cognitive studies, cross-cultural psychology, and linguistics in an attempt to synthesize his work with contemporary research in related fields.

925. Wertsch, James V., and James Youniss. "Contextualizing the Investigator: The Case of Developmental Psychology." *HD* 30 (January–February 1987): 18–31.

Studies the influence of social, political, and historical forces on how issues are formulated in developmental psychology. Also discusses relationships between nation-building and developmental psychology.

926. Williams, Wendy M., and Robert J. Sternberg. "Group Intelligence: Why Some Groups Are Better Than Others." *Intell* 12 (October–December 1988): 351–377.

Defines "group intelligence." Studies its relationship to characteristics of group performance and to the relative quality of the product produced by the group.

927. Winner, Ellen. *The Point of Words: Children's Understanding of Metaphor and Irony.* Cambridge, Mass.: Harvard University Press, 1988. 256 pages

Examines the development of the child's ability to use and understand metaphor and irony. Argues that metaphor serves a cognitive function while irony serves a social function.

928. "Words Count." *QRD* 15 (October 1988): 9–10.

Cites an article by Harold A. Herzog in *American Psychologist* (June 1988) for its analysis of labels and their effects.

929. Zolten, J. Jerome. "Joking in the Face of Tragedy." *ETC* 45 (Winter 1988): 345–350.

Explains why we joke when facing adversity. Joking establishes community, releases aggression and anger, enhances the teller's appeal, and imposes order on perceived chaos.

See also 71, 159, 535, 613, 652, 663, 684, 691, 693, 704, 758, 768, 776, 832, 1769

2.10   EDUCATION

930. Ackerman, Phillip L. "Determinants of Individual Differences during Skill Acquisition: Cognitive Abilities and Information Processing." *JEPG* 117 (September 1988): 288–312.

Broad phases of skill acquisition correspond to the cognitive abilities of general intelligence, perceptual speed, and psychomotor ability.

931. Brenders, David A. "Some Perplexities of Power in the Classroom: A Pragmatic Perspective on Instructional Relationships." *JT* 22 (Winter 1988): 51–56.

Argues for a shared role in defining classroom control. The interested, courteous instructor who acts without an obvious need for approval seems most effective.

932. Buriel, Raymond, and Desdemona Cardoza. "Sociocultural Correlates of Achievement among Three Generations of Mexican American High School Seniors." *AERJ* 25 (Summer 1988): 177–192.

Counters the position that Spanish language impedes Hispanic achievement by examining the backgrounds of first-, second-, and third-generation Americans.

933. Campbell, Wanda J., and Gary L. Allen. "Experimentally Assessed Learning Rate as a Determinant of Performance under Self-Paced and Instructor-Paced Instruction." *JPsy* 122 (January 1988): 69–78.

Compares the performances of slow, average, and fast learners under self-paced and instructor-paced instruction.

934. Carnegie Foundation for the Advancement of Teaching. *Report Card on School Reform: The Teachers Speak*. Princeton, N.J.: Carnegie Foundation for the Advancement of Teaching, 1988. 85 pages

Reports on a survey of 13,500 teachers. Although reform efforts have clarified schools' goals and led to higher expectations of students' performance, teachers believe that political interference has increased, that working conditions have not improved, and that morale has declined.

935. Chang, Kuang-Fu. "The Educational Philosophy of Robert Maynard Hutchins." *DAI* 49 (December 1988): 1400A.

Explicates and evaluates Hutchins's concept of a liberal, great books education as necessary to his doctrine of equality of opportunity.

936. Chase, Geoffrey. "Accommodation, Resistance, and the Politics of Student Writing." *CCC* 39 (February 1988): 13–22.

Provides examples of accommodation, opposition, and resistance, categories Giroux uses to describe how students respond in their learning to the dominant culture, by describing how three students approached their senior projects.

937. Commission on the Future of Community Colleges. *Building Communities: A Vision for a New Century*. Washington, D.C.: American Association of Community and Junior Colleges, 1988.

Seeks to identify the direction of the community, technical, and junior colleges for the twenty-first century.

938. Farrell, Edwin, George Peguero, Rasheed Lindsey, and Ronald White. "Giving Voice to High School Students: Pressure and Boredom, Ya Know What I'm Sayin'?" *AERJ* 25 (Winter 1988): 489–502.

Students collaborated in producing this ethnography, finding that outside social pressures and boredom were negative forces on at-risk students.

939. Friedrich, Gustav W. "Instructional Communication Research." *JT* 22 (Winter 1988): 4–10.

Summarizes research in instructional communication. Concludes that it relies too much on one empirical methodology and should be broadened into interpretive and critical frameworks.

940. Giroux, Henry A. *Schooling and the Struggles for Public Life: Critical Pedagogy in the Modern Age*. American Culture Series. Minneapolis: University of Minnesota Press, 1988. 258 pages

Proposes a theory and practice of education linking schooling to the quest for a radical concrete form of democracy. Rejects the discourse of reformers who focus on the labor market, testing, and cultural artifacts, calling instead for a language of hope and possibility that moves beyond critique to ethical vision.

941. Gluck, Mark, and Gordon H. Bower. "From Conditioning to Category Learning: An Adaptive Network Model." *JEPG* 117 (September 1988): 227–247.

Considers whether the "least mean squares" rule provides an empirically accurate account of how people learn.

942. Hanson, Sandra L., and Alan L. Ginsburg. "Gaining Ground: Values and High School Success." *AERJ* 25 (Fall 1988): 334–365.

Findings support the position that the values of students, family, and peers affect behavior and achievement in school. The story involves more than ability and socioeconomic status.

943. Kearney, Patricia. "Power in the Classroom." *JT* 22 (Winter 1988): 45–50.

Reports on studies of the verbal and nonverbal means of influencing students' behavior. Immediate teachers who used "prosocial" techniques were most effective.

944. Kleinert, Harold Lawrence. "Single and Multiple Print Exemplar Strategies in Enhancing Generalized Sight Word Reading with Students with Moderate Retardation." *DAI* 49 (August 1988): 234A.

Reports on two studies in which four students with slight retardation were taught expressively to label 12 functional sight words.

945. Lomawaima, Kimberly T. " 'They Called It Prairie Light': Oral Histories from Chilocco Indian Agricultural Boarding School, 1920–1940." *DAI* 48 (May 1988): 2917A.

Uses an ethnohistoric method to reconstruct the "school culture" at Chilocco from 1920 to 1940.

946. Lundquist, Arlene J. "Remediating Language Deficient/Dyslexic College Students: An Interview with Robert Nash." *JDEd* 12 (September 1988): 16–19.

An authority on language handicapped college students asserts that we cannot continue to ignore their social and psychological problems.

947. Markee, Numa P. "An Appropriate Technology Model of Communicative Course Design." *DAI* 49 (October 1988): 806A.

Concludes that an appropriate technology approach must balance what is desirable with what is feasible.

948. Miller, Sandra E., Gaea Leinhardt, and Naomi Zigmond. "Influencing Engagement through Accommodation: An Ethnographic Study of At-Risk Students." *AERJ* 25 (Winter 1988): 465–487.

Presents ethnographic findings suggesting that the accommodating approach of a school may keep at-risk students from dropping out.

949. Minnich, Elizabeth, Jean O'Barr, and Rachel A. Rosenfeld. *Reconstructing the Academy: Women's Education and Women's Studies*. Chicago: University of Chicago Press, 1988. 320 pages

Thirteen essays discuss the social forces that shape women's educational experiences. Treats women's access to education, the development of women's studies, the impact of women's colleges, and the future of curricular transformations. Authors are not indexed separately in this volume.

950. Priestley, Jack Greaves. "Moral Education and Religious Story: An Essay in Support of Whitehead's Contention That the Essence of Education Is That It Be Religious." *DAI* 49 (December 1988): 1400A.

Suggests that the narrative form holds together facts and values, making the current movement toward a concern for controlled narrative logical.

951. Soffree-Cady, Flora F. "A Pedagogical and Practice for College Writing Courses and Writing across the Curriculum Courses: A Social Constructionist Perspective on Learning through Argument." *DAI* 49 (August 1988): 247A.

Provides a writing pedagogy grounded in theory drawn from various sources.

952. Stahl, Fred. *Minorities in Urban Community Colleges: Tomorrow's Students Today.* Washington, D.C.: American Association of Community and Junior Colleges, 1988.

Synthesizes several research studies, providing data on minority retention, recruitment, and the successful transfer of students to baccalaureate degree-granting institutions.

953. Yoon, Byung Hee. "An Epistemological Analysis of Contemporary Curriculum Theories." *DAI* 48 (March 1988): 2238A.

Investigates the knowledge claims of 15 curriculum theories, analyzing them according to four criteria: the nature, the origin, the values, and the scope of knowledge.

See also 198, 810, 987, 1023, 1044, 1197, 1721

2.11   JOURNALISM, PUBLISHING, TELEVISION, AND RADIO

954. Babrow, Austin S., and David L. Swanson. "Disentangling Antecedents of Audience Exposure Levels: Extending Expectancy-Value Analyses of Gratifications Sought from Television News." *ComM* 55 (March 1988): 1–21.

Refines and extends a conceptual innovation to unify the applications of expectancy-value theory.

955. Belford, Barbara. *Brilliant Bylines: A Biographical Anthology of Notable Newspaperwomen in America.* Irvington-on-Hudson, N.Y.: Columbia University Press, 1988. 385 pages

Traces the historical development of leading women journalists. Includes biographical profiles and samples of their writing.

956. Bineham, Jeffery L. "A Historical Account of the Hypodermic Model in Mass Communication." *ComM* 55 (September 1988): 230–246.

Relates different historical conceptions to different ideological, theoretical, and methodological commitments.

957. Carbaugh, Donal. "Cultural Terms and Tensions in the Speech at a Television Station." *WJSC* 52 (Summer 1988): 216–237.

Uses an ethnographic approach to discover the meaning of organizational speech through local symbols, forms, and meanings.

958. Carrard, Phillipe. "Telling the Game: Baseball as an AP Report." *JNT* 18 (Winter 1988): 47–60.

Using narrative theory, examines the structure, audience, and rhetorical context of 402 Associated Press capsules in an attempt to understand the relationship between reader and text.

959. Chan, Joseph Man, and Chin-Chuan Lee. "Press Ideology and Organizational Control in Hong Kong." *ComR* 15 (April 1988): 185–197.

A survey of Hong Kong journalists shows how news organizations exercised institutional control in recruiting journalists and conducting newswork in a politicized environment.

960. Dionisopoulos, George N. "A Case Study in Print Media and Heroic Myth: Lee Iacocca, 1978–1985." *SSCJ* 53 (Spring 1988): 227–243.

Examines rhetorical strategies that present mediated actions and actors as "heroic" within the mythopoetic role of the media.

961. Ettema, James S., and Theodore L. Glasser. "Narrative Form and Moral Force: The Realization of Innocence and Guilt through

Investigative Journalism." *JC* 38 (Summer 1988): 8–26.

An analysis of one broadcast news and two print journalism reports indicates how facts in story form can shape history and create reality.

962. Glasser, Ira. "Television and the Construction of Reality." *ETC* 45 (Summer 1988): 156–162.

Analyzes the power of television to impose a false reality on everyday experience by altering our perceptions.

963. "How to Analyze the News." *QRD* 15 (October 1988): 9.

Summarizes Frank Brodhead's suggestions for analyzing news reports on Nicaragua and Central America.

964. Kennamer, J. David. "News Values and the Vividness of Information." *WC* 5 (January 1988): 108–123.

Argues that information selected on the basis of "vividness" may be inadequate for decision making and drawing inferences.

965. Kennedy, George. "How Journalists Select News." *ETC* 45 (Summer 1988): 164–173.

Finds that journalists decided what news was in relation to their audience. Impact on, proximity to, timeliness for, prominence in relation to, novelty for, and conflict for readers determined what was newsworthy.

966. Kupfersmid, Joel. "Improving What Is Published: A Model in Search of an Editor." *AmP* 43 (August 1988): 635–642.

Describes problems affecting a manuscript's acceptance: irrelevant topics, meaningless or unusable findings in "statistical significance testing," and editorial bias. Focuses on scientific journals.

967. Ludlow, Lynn. "Headlines: The Unappreciated Art." *ETC* 45 (Fall 1988): 236–245.

Offers a history of headline writing, presenting and analyzing generally accepted professional practices.

968. Marsh, Harry Lynn. "Crime and the Press: Does Newspaper Crime Coverage Support Myths about Crime and Law Enforcement?" *DAI* 49 (October 1988): 959A.

Analyzes the content of six Texas newspapers to determine if their news coverage supports myths about crime and law enforcement.

969. McLeod, Jane A. "A Social Study of Printers and Booksellers in Bordeaux from 1745 to 1810." *DAI* 48 (June 1988): 3181A.

Assesses the effects of Bordeaux's prosperity on the printing and bookselling community.

970. Morello, John T. "Argument and Visual Structuring in the 1984 Mondale-Reagan Debates: The Medium's Influence on the Perception of Clash." *WJSC* 52 (Fall 1988): 277–290.

Concludes that media commentary and camera shots shaped viewers' perceptions and altered the content of arguments.

971. Nelkin, Dorothy. "The High Cost of Hype." *ETC* 45 (Fall 1988): 262–272.

Analyzes fundamental differences between scientists and journalists regarding scientific journalism. Concludes that the groups must accept an uneasy, often adversarial relationship.

972. Parsons, Paul Fowler. "Getting Published: The Acquisitions Process at University Presses." *DAI* 48 (January 1988): 1571A.

Investigates how presses select the manuscripts they publish, thus playing a gatekeeping role in advancing knowledge.

973. Portnoy, Jeffrey A. "Transition to Print: Editorial Presence and Literary Community." *DAI* 49 (December 1988): 1464A.

Concludes that, since the printing press changed the sense of community among scribes and readers, some writers used editorial presence to educate their new audiences.

974. "Project Censored." *QRD* 14 (July 1988): 12.

Describes a research project for identifying and publicizing news stories deserving public attention.

975. Reep, Diana C., and Faye H. Dambrot. "In the Eye of the Beholder: Viewer Perceptions of Television's Male-Female Working Partners." *ComR* 15 (February 1988): 51–69.

Finds that viewers are able to distinguish differences in sex role stereotypes even among characters that would be coded identically in content analysis.

976. Rozell, Mark J. "Journalistic Perceptions of the Carter Presidency: Evaluating Presidential Leadership and Performance." *DAI* 49 (September 1988): 609A.

A study of presidential journalism during the Carter years.

977. Rubin, Alan M., Elizabeth M. Perse, and Donald S. Taylor. "A Methodological Examination of Cultivation." *ComR* 15 (April 1988): 107–134.

Finds that television affects personal perceptions, not through inordinate exposure, but by individual differences in selecting content and by an audience's attitudes and activities.

978. Salazar, Leonardo Alberto. "Discourses on Terrorism and Nicaragua: A Case Study of Television News, Ideology, and Cultural Impoverishment." *DAI* 49 (December 1988): 1303A.

Uses Habermas's social theory to analyze the relationship between commercial television discourse and the language of the U.S. administration.

979. Scripps, Charles E. "Labeling Journalists as Professionals." *ETC* 45 (Winter 1988): 329–330.

Explores the semantic and rhetorical implications of labeling journalism a profession. Concludes that journalism is a "calling."

980. Thomas, Margaret Bigham. "Writing for Publication: Personal Attributes and Work-Environment Factors Associated with Authors Who Publish in an Adult Education Journal for Practitioners." *DAI* 49 (December 1988): 1348A.

Describes 43 authors' reasons for writing for publication. Discusses personal attributes, obstacles in writing, the work environment, and schedules for writing. Includes their advice to aspiring authors.

981. Thompson, Patricia J. "Writing a Textbook: From Theoretical Knowledge to Tacit Knowledge—And Back Again." Paper presented at the AERA, Washington, D.C., April 1987. ERIC ED 289 170. 27 pages

Offers a systems model to clarify the writing of a textbook.

982. van Driel, Barend, and James T. Richardson. "Print Media Coverage of New Religious Movements: A Longitudinal Study." *JC* 38 (Summer 1988): 37–61.

Traces how four newspapers and three newsweeklies covered "movements in conflict with mainstream society" from May 1972 to April 1984.

983. Waller, Mary E. "Popular Women's Magazines, 1890–1917." *DAI* 49 (September 1988): 601A.

Traces the development of major women's magazines at the turn of the century.

984. Warner, Judith Ann. "Marginality and Selective Reporting: Ethnic and Gender Issues in the Press." *DAI* 48 (March 1988): 2461A.

Analyzes imbalanced coverage of illegal Mexican immigration and the 1984 Ferraro-Bush campaign, finding diminished access to the press for minorities.

985. Zizi, Khadija. "Contrastive Discourse Analysis of Argumentative and Informative Newspaper Prose in Arabic, French, and English: Suggestions for Teaching/Learning English as a Foreign Language for Journalistic Purposes (EJP) in Morocco." *DAI* 49 (July 1988): 86A.

Compares journalistic writing in three languages, discussing coherence, organization of the discourse, repetition, and speech acts.

See also 367, 368, 369, 420, 441, 442, 466, 480, 501, 502, 817

2.12 PHILOSOPHY

986. Hallett, Garth L. *Language and Truth.* New Haven: Yale University Press, 1988. 224 pages

Argues that truth corresponds with reality, but not in the way traditional views have envisaged. Following Wittgenstein, the author examines the use of the concept "true" and locates it on the map of language.

987. Harden, George Daniel. "The Perennial Vision: From Cardinal Newman to Mortimer Adler." *DAI* 48 (February 1988): 2014A.

Surveys classical and educational philosophers who have had an impact on liberal arts curricula.

988. Heddendorf, David. "William James and the Rhetoric of Popular Philosophy." *DAI* 49 (December 1988): 1456A.

Analyzes James's writings with attention to the rhetorical considerations that influenced his work.

989. Kenat, Ralph Carl, Jr. "Physical Interpretation: Eddington, Idealization, and the Origin of Stellar Structure Theory." *DAI* 48 (February 1988): 2078A.

Examines the use of idealizations in scientific theorizing, the use of theories as conceptual devices, and the problem of scientific realism.

990. Marassi, Massimo. "Rhetoric and Historicity (An Introduction)." *P&R* 21 (Fall 1988): 245–259.

Discusses the historiographical and theoretical relationship between philosophy and rhetoric.

991. Phillips, John. "A Study of Plato's *Hippias Minor.*" *DAI* 49 (December 1988): 1448A.

Analyzes the work and responds to previous criticism.

992. Smith, Nicholas D. "Collaborating Philosophically." *RSQ* 17 (Summer 1987): 247–262.

A philosopher discusses why many philosophers work in isolation and what advantages and disadvantages collaborative intellectual work has.

993. Southwell, Samuel. *Kenneth Burke and Martin Heidegger: With a Note against Deconstruction.* University of Florida Humanities Monograph, no. 60. Gainesville, Fla.: University of Florida Press, 1988.

Compares Burke and Heidegger and finds their ideas antithetical to deconstruction. Compares Burke's pentad with Heidegger's "four-fold."

994. Toulmin, Stephen. "The Recovery of Practical Philosophy." *ASch* 57 (Summer 1988): 337–352.

Discusses the nature of philosophy, setting aside many of those topics addressed as philosophical inquiry. Reexamines issues spanning antiquity through the middle ages.

995. Tuttleton, James. "The Vexations of Modernism: Edmund Wilson's *Axel's Castle.*" *ASch* 57 (Spring 1988): 262–272.

Explores one aspect of the problem of modernism, the complex relationship between the radical aesthetic and the conservative ideology that often accompanies it.

See also 245, 594, 719

2.13 SCIENCE AND MEDICINE

996. "Aidspeak." *QRD* 15 (October 1988): 11.

Cites Randy Shilts for examples of double-speak used in reference to AIDS.

997. Barker, Thomas T. "Feedback in High-Tech Writing." *JTWC* 18 (1988): 35–54.

Examines the literature to determine problems, types, theories, and elements of feedback specific to high-tech writing.

998. Bazerman, Charles. *Shaping Written Knowledge: The Genre and Activity of the Experimental Article in Science*. Madison, Wis.: University of Wisconsin Press, 1988. 356 pages

Traces the emergence of the experimental article in science. Sees the appearance of argumentative forms of scientific writing as coincident with the rise of the scientific community and the development of experimental procedures.

999. Brown, Mary Helen. "Relational Referents in the Nursing Home: The Staff to Referent Link." *SSCJ* 53 (Summer 1988): 406–419.

Reviews the literature on relational language and applies discourse analysis to conversational interviews.

1000. Casari, Laura E., and Joyce T. Povlacs. "Practices in Technical Writing in Agriculture and Engineering Industries, Firms, and Agencies." *JTWC* 18 (1988): 143–159.

Data from questionnaires and on-site interviews confirm the importance and frequency of writing, demonstrate the importance of context, and reveal variations in types of documents, genres, and strategies.

1001. Cialdini, Robert B. "Communicating Responsibly with the Public: Researcher as Edifier." *ComR* 15 (December 1988): 781–792.

A review essay discussing ways to inform the public of scientific research in ways that satisfy both the public's and the researcher's communication goals.

1002. Downs, Valerie C., Manoochehr Javidi, and Jon F. Nussbaum. "A Comparative Analysis of the Relationship between Communication Apprehension and Loneliness for Elderly

Nursing Home and Non-Nursing Home Residents." *WJSC* 52 (Fall 1988): 308–320.

Provides evidence that communicative traits can significantly affect the elderly. The impact is moderated by the living environment.

1003. Drass, Kriss. "Discourse and Occupational Perspectives: A Comparison of Nurse Practitioners and Physician Assistants." *DPr* 11 (April–June 1988): 163–181.

As compared with two physician assistants, the nurse practitioner produced speech showing greater sensitivity to the subjective understandings and experiences of patients.

1004. Dubois, Betty Lou. "Citation in Biomedical Journal Articles." *ESP* 7 (1988): 181–193.

Studies how biomedical scientists cite others in published journal articles by using chiefly summary and generalization.

1005. Edgar, Timothy, and Mary Anne Fitzpatrick. "Compliance-Gaining in Relational Interaction: When Your Life Depends on It." *SSCJ* 53 (Summer 1988): 385–405.

The Verbal Interaction Scheme provides assistance in understanding unique health-related problems.

1006. Freeman, Sarah Hosford. "Doctor-Patient Encounters as Communicative Tasks: Culture, Meaning, and Organizational Constraints." *DAI* 48 (March 1988): 2373A.

Analyzes the importance of shared organizational and technical schematics in successful communication between doctors and patients.

1007. Gambrell, Patricia G. "Rhetorical Persona in the Writing of Chemical Engineers." *DAI* 48 (April 1988): 2613A.

Argues that scientific and technical writing is not objective, that writers are present in various features of scientific and technical texts.

1008. Harrison, Teresa M., and Mary Beth Debs. "Conceptualizing the Organizational Role of Technical Communicators: A Systems Approach." *JBTC* 2 (September 1988): 5–21.

Presents a conceptual model, arguing from systems theory that technical communicators gather, review, mediate, translate, edit, and synthesize material, thus functioning as "boundary spanners" both within and across organizations. Sketches management and pedagogical strategies.

1009. Heim, Michael. "The Technological Crisis of Rhetoric." *P&R* 21 (First Quarter 1988): 48–59.

Examines today's technology-based rhetoric, calling for a theory that takes into account the erosion of direct verbal persuasion between human beings.

1010. Hoffmann, Gregg. "How We Coped with Cancer." *ETC* 45 (Winter 1988): 325–328.

An example of using general semantics thinking strategies to cope more effectively with serious problems like cancer.

1011. Huckin, Thomas. "Surprise Value in Scientific Discourse." Paper presented at the CCCC Convention, Atlanta, March 1987. ERIC ED 284 291. 17 pages

Finds that current scientific articles in physics and molecular biology foreground the most newsworthy information, using conventions analogous to news reports.

1012. Kreps, Gary L. "Relational Communication in Health Care." *SSCJ* 53 (Summer 1988): 344–359.

Offers a perspective for enhancing the quality of health communication. Identifies areas for additional research.

1013. Lehman, Darrin R., Richard O. Lempert, and Richard E. Nisbett. "The Effects of Graduate Training on Reasoning: Formal Discipline and Thinking about Everyday Life Events." *AmP* 43 (June 1988): 431–442.

Looks at graduate training in law, medicine, psychology, and chemistry, examining the implications of instruction in abstract rule systems.

1014. Lipson, Carol. "A Social View of Technical Writing." *JBTC* 2 (January 1988): 7–20.

Discusses some effects of different social structures and conditions in science and engineering on the uses of language. A key differentiating factor is the degree of professionalization.

1015. Moss, Jean Russell. "Walking the Tightrope: The Story of Nursing as Told by Nineteenth-Century Nursing Journals." *DAI* 49 (October 1988): 856A.

A thick description of how nursing journals formed the characteristics, behaviors, and assumptions of the nursing profession.

1016. Pace, Roger C. "Technical Communication, Group Differentiation, and the Decision to Launch the Space Shuttle Challenger." *JTWC* 18 (1988): 207–220.

An analysis of testimony reveals that the loss of the space shuttle and crew can be blamed, in part, on flaws in the process of group communication.

1017. Rainey, Kenneth T. "Technical Editing at the Oak Ridge National Laboratory." *JTWC* 18 (1988): 175–181.

Examines the types of documents prepared, audiences for whom the documents are intended, and the editing process employed by the Technical Publications Department.

1018. Wheeler, Daniel R. "Foreword to Psychotherapy." *ETC* 45 (Spring 1988): 68–71.

Describes and analyzes relationships between language, self-concept, and psychotherapy, explaining why *disease* is a term preferable to *mental illness*.

1019. Worms, Tom. "A Study of a Scientific Sub-Language of English." *DAI* 49 (December 1988): 1446A.

Uses Harris's transformational analysis to analyze tests in cardiac pharmacology.

Finds that the use of certain quantificational terms was dependent upon context.

See also 307, 460, 478, 650, 966, 971, 989

2.14 CROSS-DISCIPLINARY STUDIES

1020. Allured, Janet L. "Families, Food, and Folklore: Women's Culture in the Postbellum Ozarks." *DAI* 49 (January 1989): 1937A.

Examines the culture of rural women in the Ozarks during the late nineteenth and early twentieth centuries.

1021. Anderson, Richard Walter. "Taiken: Personal Narratives and Japanese New Religion." *DAI* 49 (October 1988): 915A.

Analyzes the structure and content of personal experience narratives in three Japanese new religions.

1022. Beniger, James R. "Information and Communication: The New Convergence." *ComR* 15 (April 1988): 198–218.

A review of publications across academic disciplines that converge on the concept of information. Finds that communication scholars remain largely oblivious to this convergence.

1023. Brehm, Mary Ann. "Margaret H'Doubler's Approach to Dance Education and Her Influence on Two Dance Educators." *DAI* 49 (December 1988): 1296A.

Finds support for H'Doubler's approach to dance education. She argued that education should further an individual's development and be based upon pertinent facts of human life.

1024. Cruikshank, Julia Margaret. "Life Lived like a Story: Cultural Constructions of Life History by Tagish and Tutchone Women." *DAI* 49 (November 1988): 1184A.

Shows how individuals may use traditional dimensions of culture as a resource in creating and telling life history.

1025. Cummings, L. A. "A Semiotic Account of Gothic Serialization." *Style* 22 (Summer 1988): 324–340.

Adopts semiotic techniques to study forms of medieval expression: poetry, painting, sculpture, architecture, city plans, and military science. Discovers an unconscious Gothic "signature."

1026. Gelfenbien, Gary Paul. "Spheres of Light: Light as the Common Element of the Byzantine East and the Gothic West." *DAI* 48 (May 1988): 2762A.

An interdisciplinary study of the rhetorical content inherent in the art and architectural forms influenced by Platonic and Aristotelian philosophies.

1027. Gumport, Patricia J. "The Social Construction of Knowledge: Individual and Institutional Commitments to Feminist Scholarship." *DAI* 48 (May 1988): 2817A.

Concludes that feminist scholarly achievements reflect changing individual and institutional definitions of what counts as knowledge.

1028. Lotto, Edward. "The Texts and Contexts of Writing." *WCJ* 9 (Fall-Winter 1988): 13–20.

Examines differences and similarities in the relationship between texts and contexts and between language and knowledge in three disciplines: computer science, government, and history.

1029. Martin, Andrew Victor. "Critical Approaches to American Cultural Studies: The Vietnam War in History, Literature, and Film." *DAI* 49 (October 1988): 856A.

Analyzes a range of textual practices to examine how popular culture treats an unresolved cultural crisis.

1030. Mulcahy, Joanne Burke. " 'Knowing Women': Narratives of Healing and Traditional Life from Kodiak Island, Alaska." *DAI* 49 (December 1988): 1545A.

Uses oral history interviews to explore the differences between women's perceptions, values, and beliefs and those reflected in visible, dominant cultural forms.

1031. O'Hair, Dan, Michael J. Cody, Blaine Goss, and Karl J. Krayer. "The Effect of Gender, Deceit Orientation, and Communicator Style on Macro-Assessments of Honesty." *ComQ* 36 (Spring 1988): 77–93.

A study of 385 students finds that certain attributes of communication style predict evaluations of honesty and dishonesty.

1032. Pages, Myrtha E. Ruiz de. "Narratives as Structural Models of Thought: A Comparison of Folktales from the Humahuaca Canyon of Argentina and the Pueblo Southwest." *DAI* 48 (May 1988): 2807A.

Concludes that the stories studied functioned as "cultural grammars" for transmitting traditions and values.

1033. Paul, Angus. "Writing about Writing: Leading Anthropologist Casts a Literary Eye on Classic Works in His Field." *CHE* 34 (10 February 1988): A4-A6.

Clifford Geertz's *Works and Lives* argues for literary and rhetorical analyses of anthropologists' writings, enabling scholars to comprehend their strengths and limitations.

1034. Richardson, Herbert N. "Black Workers and Their Responses to Work through the Songs They Sang." *DAI* 48 (March 1988): 2427A.

Focuses on songs from agriculture, mining, and farming to illustrate how black workers responded to the experience of work.

1035. Rushing, James A., Jr. "Adventures beyond the Text: Ywain in the Visual Arts." *DAI* 49 (October 1988): 815A.

Pictorial manifestations of a medieval narrative reveal that the story and character existed independent from the text in a variety of nonverbal forms.

1036. Rutherford, Susan Dell. "A Study of

American Deaf Folklore." *DAI* 48 (March 1988): 2420A.

Examines ways of studying and understanding the deaf community and its folklore.

1037. Savedoff, Barbara Elissa. "Art Interpretation." *DAI* 49 (December 1988): 1479A.

Compares the interpretation of art with speech, concluding that interpretation depends on the conventions, history, and traditions of the medium in question.

1038. Thompson, Leslie. "As a Matter of Fact." *JT* 23 (Spring-Summer 1988): 61–76.

Discusses the difference between facts and meaning, knowledge and wisdom. Argues that we must "rise above facts" to respond to real human needs.

1039. Timpunza Mrula, Enoch Selestine. "Women's Oral Poetry as a Social Strategy in Malawi." *DAI* 48 (March 1988): 2420A.

Examines the use of sung poetry as a social and communicative strategy that defines, evaluates, and interprets women's positions.

1040. Varga, A. Kibedi. "Stories Told by Pictures." *Style* 22 (Summer 1988): 194–208.

Examines types of paintings. Concludes that fixed images tell a story but that autonomous visual stories developed alongside existing stories cannot.

1041. Wa-Gachanja, Muigai. "The Gikuyu Folk Story: Its Structure and Aesthetics." *DAI* 48 (June 1988): 3174A.

Analyzes the social, ethical, and psychological implications of 12 Gikuyu folktales.

1042. Winkler, Gail Caskey. "Influence of Godey's *Lady's Book* on the American Woman and Her Home: Contributions to a National Culture 1830–1877." *DAI* 49 (December 1988): 2154B.

Analyzes the contributions of *Lady's Book* to the cult of domesticity and to the homogenization of the American domestic interior.

See also 95, 103, 843, 1013, 1692

3
Teacher Education, Administration, and Social Roles

3.1   TEACHER EDUCATION

1043. Aber, John. "Composition Teachers Need to Become Teacher-Researchers: Reflections Based on an Ethnography of Teacher Training Sessions." Paper presented at the CCCC Convention, St. Louis, March 1988. ERIC ED 293 134. 13 pages

In-service programs to train writing teachers, driven by university research, received negative responses from teachers. Recommends that teachers become active participants in their own research projects.

1044. Angelotti, Michael, Rita Brause, John Mayher, Gordon Pradl, and Bruce Appleby. "On the Nature and Future of English Education: What the Grayhair's Gathering Was Really About." *EEd* 20 (December 1988): 230–244.

A report on the issues discussed at an English educator's conference in each of three working groups: graduate programs and research, teacher education, and English studies.

1045. Bain, Bob. "Attacking Ignorance and Apathy in High Places." *TETYC* 15 (October 1988): 202–209.

Discusses issues facing the profession, emphasizing the relationships between two-year college and university faculties.

1046. Betz, Renee, and William E. Rivers. "Dialogue: Readers and Authors." *JBTC* 2 (September 1988): 91–100.

Betz criticizes conclusions drawn in Rivers's article [*JBTC* 1 (January 1987)] on doctoral programs and job placement in business and technical writing. Rivers responds.

1047. Bogel, Fredric B., and Katherine K. Gottschalk, eds. *Teaching Prose: A Guide for Writing Instructors*. New York: Norton, 1988. 423 pages

A guide for teachers of composition, developed by instructors in Cornell's Freshman Seminar Program. Gives advice about composition theory, designing a course, classroom activities, developing assignments, responding to students' essays, understanding prose, improving sentences, and computers. Includes a bibliographical guide to the profession.

1048. Danish, Barbara. "A Descriptive Study of the Complexity of Factors Involved in Three Teachers' Classroom Uses of Writing." *DAI* 49 (July 1988): 74A.

Focuses upon the personal, teaching, and environmental issues that influence a writing-to-learn model, suggesting that these issues often impede classroom writing.

1049. Diamond, C. T. Patrick. "Construing a Career: A Developmental View of Teacher Education and the Teacher Educator." *JCS* 20 (March–April 1988): 133–140.

A reflective case study of stage-related teacher training in English, concentrating on the teacher as researcher and learner.

1050. Diaz, Diana M. "The Writing Process: What's Gone Wrong?" *ArEB* 31 (Fall 1988): 31–33.

Warns that writing process instruction may go the way of New Math if teachers fail to learn underlying theory or avoid becoming writers themselves.

1051. Downs, Valerie C., Manoochehr Javidi, and Jon F. Nussbaum. "An Analysis of Teachers' Verbal Communication within the College Classroom: Use of Humor, Self-Disclosure, and Narratives." *ComEd* 37 (April 1988): 127–141.

Presents the results of two studies in which teachers' verbal behaviors were identified, coded, and tested.

1052. Farris, Christine R. "Constructing a Theory of Composition in the First Year: An Ethnographic Study of Four New Teaching Assistants of English." *DAI* 49 (October 1988): 752A.

Confirms that new teaching assistants construct composition theory through a kinetic recursive process informed by experience prior to and resulting from teaching.

1053. Fortune, Ron, and Janice Neulieb. "The Creative Process in Prose Fiction: Connecting Writing and Literary Studies (An Overview of the Project)." *IlEB* 76 (Fall 1988): 5–8.

Discusses a summer institute at Illinois State University that integrates literature and composition studies for secondary and college English teachers.

1054. Giroux, Henry A. *Teachers as Intellectuals: Toward a Pedagogy of Practical Learning*. Critical Studies in Education Series. South Hadley, Mass.: Bergin Garvey, 1988. 288 pages

Argues that teachers must be seen as intellectuals capable of linking conception to practice, connecting schooling with a democratic vision, and maintaining some control over the nature of their jobs. Students must also be treated as intellectuals engaged in critical pedagogy so that they can better understand their own voices.

1055. Goggin, Maureen Daly. "Training Tutors to Work with Student Writers." *WLN* 12 (March 1988): 8–11.

Describes five techniques to help train tutors: evaluating writing samples, roleplaying, group discussions, reading about current theories and practices, and evaluating dramatizations. Also describes professional development and components of training workshops.

1056. Herrmann, Andrea W. "Teaching Teachers to Use Computers as Writing Tools." *EEd* 20 (December 1988): 215–229.

Describes a three-week in-service course in computers and writing. Explains how the course influenced the behavior of teachers as they taught writing with the assistance of a microcomputer.

1057. Hilbert, Betsy. "A Community of Teachers: From East to West, and through the English Coalition Conference." *TETYC* 15 (October 1988): 165–169.

A teacher exchange with a nontraditional college gives a community college teacher a perspective on the English Coalition Conference and on her own work.

1058. Javidi, Manoochehr, Valerie C. Downs, and Jon F. Nussbaum. "A Comparative Analysis of Teachers' Use of Dramatic Style Behaviours at Higher and Secondary Educational Levels." *ComEd* 37 (October 1988): 278–288.

Studies the use of humor, self-disclosure, and narrative by 15 college, 15 high school, and 15 mid-high instructors.

1059. Knodt, Ellen Andrews. "Taming Hydra: The Problem of Balancing Teaching and Scholarship at a Two-Year College." *TETYC* 15 (October 1988): 170–174.

Offers suggestions for maintaining faculty research in the face of heavy course loads.

1060. Laird, Susan. "Reforming 'Woman's True Profession': A Case for Feminist Pedagogy in Teacher Education?" *HER* 58 (November 1988): 449–463.

Critiques ahistorical, gender-neutral proposals such as the report of the Carnegie Forum's Task Force on Teaching as a Profession. Considers the difficulties and promise of feminist pedagogy for educating teachers.

1061. Loeher, Larry, ed. *The TA at UCLA Newsletter* (1979–1985). ERIC ED 289 441 and 443. 85 pages

Offers ten issues of a newsletter for English teaching assistants. ERIC ED 289 441 includes issues one, three, and five through eight (1979–1981); ERIC ED 289 443 includes issues 12–15 (1984–1985).

1062. McCleary, Bill. "UNH's Apostle of Conferencing and the Process Approach Retires from Teaching." *CompC* 1 (February 1988): 1–2.

Summarizes Donald Murray's career as a writer and teacher.

1063. McEwan, Hunter. "Interpreting the Subject Domains for Students: Towards a Rhetorical Theory of Teaching." *DAI* 48 (June 1988): 3069A.

Examines the relationships among teacher, student, and subject, finding that the teacher remains the pedagogical interpreter.

1064. McKay, Sandra Lee, and Sau-Ling Cynthia Wong. "Language and Teaching in Nativist Times: A Need for Sociopolitical Awareness." *MLJ* 72 (Winter 1988): 379–388.

Analyzes the contents of four professional journals and regrets finding little sensitivity on the part of language teachers to social and political forces.

1065. Niemloy, Araya. "Teaching Students to Do: Teacher Talk in Technical Classrooms." *DAI* 49 (September 1988): 486A.

Studies the language of teachers in two technical classes at the graduate level, an engineering and a computer science course.

1066. Nist, Elizabeth A. "Colloquium: A Conversation about Excellence." Paper presented at the Conference of Writing Program Administrators, Logan, Utah, August 1987. ERIC ED 288 200. 9 pages

Describes staff development colloquia at Utah Valley Community College.

1067. Nussbaum, Jon F., Sherry J. Holladay, and Mark E. Comadena. "Classroom Verbal Behavior of Highly Effective Teachers." *JT* 22 (Winter 1987): 73–80.

Three highly effective teachers exhibited more humor, disclosed more ideas about themselves, and used more narratives in class. They were more "dramatic" in style.

1068. Office of Instructional Development. *Teaching Tips for TAs: A Sourcebook of Suggestions and Guidelines for Teaching Assistants*. Los Angeles: UCLA, 1987. ERIC ED 289 439. 113 pages

Offers teaching suggestions for beginning teaching assistants.

1069. Parker, Robert P. "Theories of Writing Instruction: Having Them, Using Them, Changing Them." *EEd* 20 (February 1988): 18–40.

Advocates a balanced concern for theories in relation to methods. Presents procedures for identifying teachers' theories and using journals to construct and analyze theories.

1070. Pestel, Beverly C. "Some Practical Distinctions between Preaching, Teaching, and Training." *JCST* 18 (September–October 1988): 26–31.

To be more effective, teachers must examine their preconceptions and analyze critically their classroom performances. Offers suggestions and examples for doing so.

1071. Pickering, Miles. "Can Ability as a Teaching Assistant Be Predicted?" *JCST* 18 (September–October 1988): 55–56.

Significant predictors of a teaching assistant's ability are knowing the subject (as indicated by GRE scores) and having received an undergraduate education at a school with fewer than 7,000 students.

1072. Pickering, Miles. "Improving the Flow of Information in Large Courses." *JCST* 17 (March–April 1988): 385–386.

Describes training techniques and writing strategies that enhance the teaching effectiveness of teaching assistants.

1073. Piper, David. "Perspectives on Language in Content Area Teacher Education." *EQ* 21 (1988): 174–182.

Recommends that the relationship between language and ideology and between language and social identity be included in teacher preparation curricula to increase teacher's awareness of language.

1074. Pitts, Beverley. "Improving Writing for Student Publication." *JTW* 7 (Fall-Winter 1988): 205–214.

Offers eight suggestions for high school publications advisors.

1075. Reagan, Sally Barr. "Teaching TAs to Teach: Show, Don't Tell." *WPA* 11 (Spring 1988): 41–51.

Describes a seven-step process to train teaching assistants and to introduce them to empirical research.

1076. Rottenberg, Annette T. "Learning to Teach by Tutoring." *WLN* 12 (June 1988): 11–12.

When graduate students work as tutors, they develop interpersonal skills for working with students and learn about the writing process, effective assignments, and evaluation standards.

1077. Schultz, Lucille M., Chester H. Laine, and Mary C. Savage. "Interaction among School and College Writing Teachers: Toward Recognizing and Remaking Old Patterns." *CCC* 39 (May 1988): 139–153.

Describes interactions among school and college teachers as historically unsuccessful, arguing that the teachers' "cultures" deter collaboration. Poses initiatives for improving collaborative efforts.

1078. Sledd, James. "Pie in the Sky; or, Teaching New Paradigms Old Tricks." Paper presented at the CCCC Convention, St. Louis, March 1988. ERIC ED 294 179. 11 pages

Argues that writing teachers should investigate their roles to avoid producing a brainwashed and uncritical workforce.

1079. Sparks, Georgea. "Teachers' Attitudes toward Change and Subsequent Improvements in Classroom Teaching." *JEdP* 80 (1988): 111–117.

Investigates the relationship between teachers' attitudes toward teaching practices presented in in-service training and teachers' subsequent use of these practices.

1080. Stevens, Ellen Anne. "The Process of Change in College Teaching." *DAI* 49 (September 1988): 467A.

Analyzes tape recorded interviews with 12 professors, focusing on their attitudes, self-initiated change, and perceptions of the university's emphasis on teaching.

1081. Tarvers, Josephine Koster. *Teaching Writing: Theories and Practices*. Glenview, Ill.: Scott, Foresman, 1988. 216 pages

A guide for teachers of composition, arranged in three parts. Five chapters review theoretical bases for teaching writing. Seven chapters cover practical aspects of writing instruction, from organizing courses to evaluating students' work. The final section reprints 13 position statements and articles on the teaching of writing. Includes a bibliography.

1082. Tate, Gary, and Edward P. J. Corbett, eds. *The Writing Teacher's Sourcebook*. New York: Oxford University Press, 1988. 384 pages

A new edition of 34 essays on the teaching of college composition. Ten sections cover history, overviews, writing and learning, the composing process, audience, style, teaching, responding to writing, basic writing, and questioning traditions. Bibliographies conclude each section. Authors of these essays are not indexed separately in this volume.

1083. Tchudi, Stephen. "A Personal Bibliography on Teaching Composition." *JR* 31 (February 1988): 462–465.

Reviews for teachers current thinking in composition instruction.

1084. Tesi, Roger Frank. "The Evolution of Teachers' Personal Theories about Writing as Process: Five Case Studies." *DAI* 49 (October 1988): 794A.

Interviews teachers following a writing process workshop. Finds that the process training program had a significant influence on teachers' theories about writing.

1085. Tifft, Susan. "Who's Teaching Our Children?" *Time* (14 November 1988): 58–64.

Discusses the frustration and satisfactions of teaching, focusing on several public school teachers.

1086. Uchida, Rita Jean. "Toward a Theory of a Theoretical Oriented Reading Teacher." *DAI* 48 (February 1988): 2033A.

Examines conceptual frameworks that influence teachers and proposes a system to characterize, classify, and integrate these orientations to teaching.

1087. Vitanza, Victor J. "Rhetoric's Past and Future: A Conversation with Edward P. J. Corbett." *Pre/Text* 8 (Fall-Winter 1987): 247–264.

Corbett describes his early training and teaching experiences, his history as a member of CCCC, and his editorship of *CCC*. He also discusses current developments in the field.

1088. Williams, Margaret. "Composition's Philosopher and Advocate for the Power of the Imagination Retires from UMass." *CompC* 1 (April 1988): 1–3.

Summarizes the scholarship and career of Anne Evans Berthoff.

1089. Wilson, David E. "Writing Projects and Writing Instruction: A Study of Teacher Change." Paper presented at the CCCC Convention, St. Louis, March 1988. ERIC ED 295 148. 16 pages

Examines how participation in the Iowa Writing Project changed a teacher.

See also 189, 417, 931, 934, 943, 1163, 1280, 1521, 1622, 1736, 1775

3.2 ADMINISTRATION

1090. Angelo, Faye, and Nell Ann Pickett. "Technical Writers as Part-Time Teachers in Two-Year Colleges." *JTWC* 18 (1988): 389–392.

Surveys two-year college technical writing teachers, finding that part-time teachers are committed, well-qualified, experienced, and typically employed full-time as writers or editors.

1091. Burgan, Mary. "The Rookie-of-the-Year Syndrome." *BADE* 89 (Spring 1988): 20–23.

Identifies new trends in recruiting faculty and argues against some practices.

1092. Clausen, Christopher. "Part-Timers in the English Department: Some Problems and Some Solutions." *BADE* 90 (Fall 1988): 4–6.

Describes Penn State University's efforts to secure better benefits for part-time teachers by consolidating part-time into full-time lectureships.

1093. Crain, Jeanie C. "A Comment on 'The Wyoming Conference Resolution' [*CE* 49 (March 1987)]." *CE* 50 (January 1988): 96–99.

Responds to the Wyoming Conference Resolution by recounting personal experiences as a temporary English faculty member for 14 years.

1094. Curzon-Brown, Daniel. "The Gripes of Wrath." *TETYC* 15 (October 1988): 195–198.

Details the plight of part-time instructors.

1095. Denham, Robert D. "From the Editor." *BADE* 90 (Fall 1988): 1–3.

Points to the institutionalization of part-time hiring and suggests five ways to fight it.

1096. Estabrook, Marina, and Robert Sommer. "Professors Should Take a Stand on the Issues of Price and Quality of Textbooks." *CHE* 34 (10 February 1988): B2.

Discusses survey findings. Professors seldom consider cost in selecting textbooks. No correlation exists between a book's price and a teacher's opinion of quality.

1097. George, Diana. "Talking to the Boss: A Preface." *WCJ* 9 (Fall-Winter 1988): 37–44.

Explains what writing center directors want English department chairs to know. Originally presented at a meeting of the Midwest Association of Departments of English.

1098. Gillespie, Kim Brian. "Composition and Literature: How Ideology Naturalizes Inequity in English Departments." *WI* 7 (Spring-Summer 1988): 105–114.

The political hierarchy in English departments and inequities among faculty levels help explain the tension created between literature and composition factions.

1099. Hairston, Maxine. "Some Speculations about the Future of Writing Programs." *WPA* 11 (Spring 1988): 9–16.

Considers the relationship between composition studies and literary studies. Argues that, while writing and literature faculty may work together well in liberal arts colleges and urban universities, separate graduate programs in writing and rhetoric may be necessary at research universities.

1100. Jensen, George H. "Bureaucracy and Basic Writing Programs; or, Fallout from the Jan Kemp Trial." *JBW* 7 (Spring 1988): 30–37.

Analyzes reactions to a lawsuit brought by a teacher who was dismissed after complaining about preferential treatment for athletes. Shows "how the *structure* of a literacy program affects its political life."

1101. Kelly, June Bray. "School Administrators: The Relationship between Critical Thinking and Written Communication." *DAI* 48 (March 1988): 2208A.

Studies prospective administrators at two Georgia colleges. Shows that better writers are better thinkers and problem solvers.

1102. Lewis, Karron G., Paul Woodward, and James Bell. "Teaching Business Communication Skills in Large Classes." *JBC* 25 (Winter 1988): 65–86.

Reports on an empirical study. A large class of 58 students using an environmental mode was more effective than smaller classes using lecture and discussion and equally effective as smaller classes using environmental modes.

1103. Martin, Wanda. "Dancing on the Interface: Leadership and the Politics of Collaboration." *WPA* 11 (Spring 1988): 29–40.

Explores the role of the writing program administrator as a catalyst for change. Advocates using portfolio assessment as a means of professional development.

1104. McCleary, Bill. "Two Committees to Implement Wyoming Resolution Begin Their Work." *CompC* 1 (March 1988): 1–3.

Traces the history of the Wyoming Conference Resolution and excerpts related statements by other organizations.

1105. Mitchell, Felicia. "Writing Assignments across the Curriculum: A Study of Faculty Interpretation of a University-Wide Writing Requirement." *DAI* 48 (April 1988): 2527A.

Analyzes questionnaires, syllabuses, writing assignments, writing samples, and teachers' comments collected from nine colleges.

1106. NCTE College Section. *Guidelines for the Workload of the College English Teacher.* Rev. ed. Urbana, Ill.: NCTE, 1987. 3 pages

Newly revised guidelines outline teachers' responsibilities to students, departments, institutions, the community, their profession, and themselves. Also discusses the work load for two-year college teachers.

1107. Perrin, Robert. "Textbook Writers and Textbook Publishers: One Writer's View of the Teaching Canon." *JTW* 7 (Spring-Summer 1988): 67–74.

A textbook writer considers the flexibility of presentation and the inflexibility of content demanded by publishers' market research. Which textbooks teachers order are crucial to changing the canon.

1108. Pfeiffer, William S. "Taking Leave of Your Classes: A Year in Industry for the Technical Writing Teacher." *TWT* 15 (Spring 1988): 111–118.

An analysis of employment and leave-of-absence contracts that facilitate movement between the academy and industry.

1109. Raines, Helen Howell. "Teaching Writing in the Two-Year College." *WPA* 12 (Fall-Winter 1988): 29–37.

Identifies differences between writing programs at two-and four-year colleges. Recommends collaborative projects between university and community college writing faculty to enhance dialogue within the profession.

1110. Selfe, Cynthia. "Computers in English Departments: The Rhetoric of Technopower." *BADE* 90 (Fall 1988): 63–67.

Analyzes the impact of computers on a department as a discourse community and suggests four principles for the use of "technopower."

1111. Thompson, Merle O'Rourke. "The Part-Timer's Wish List." *TETYC* 15 (October 1988): 199.

Professor Fill N. Rescue enumerates some basic needs of part-time instructors, including "the feeling that I belonged."

1112. Trimbur, John, and Barbara Cambridge. "The Wyoming Conference Resolution: A Beginning." *WPA* 12 (Fall-Winter 1988): 13–18.

Argues that the Wyoming Conference Resolution represents an important step forward in the growing political maturity of composition studies. Warns that composition studies risk perpetuating a two-caste system that polarizes teaching and research.

1113. White, Andrea, and Lynn Marie Wright. "Composition and Literature: Re-Viewing the Gap." *WI* 7 (Spring-Summer 1988): 101–104.

Bridging the gap between literature (consumption) and composition (production) remains problematic because the gap is "political as well as pedagogical."

1114. Williams, M. Lee, and Deborah Wiatrek. "Part-Time and Full-Time Faculty Communication Problems in Community Colleges: Analysis and Suggestions." *JT* 22 (Winter 1987): 20–30.

Surveys part-time and full-time instructors of basic speech and English courses to analyze their channels and sources of communication as well as their job satisfaction.

1115. Young, Art. "Quality of Life in Writing Program Administration." Paper presented at the CCCC Convention, St. Louis, March 1988. ERIC ED 294 197. 11 pages

Suggests that writing programs should be integrated with other aspects of English studies.

See also 1045, 1046, 1059, 1170, 1358, 1612, 1729, 1784, 1787, 1796

3.3   SUPPORT SERVICES

1116. Ady, Paul. "Fear and Trembling at the Center: Student Perceptions about the Tutorial." *WLN* 12 (April 1988): 11–12.

Cites ways to improve a writing center's services by eliciting feedback, acknowledging apprehension, being directive when necessary, assisting advanced students, learning to help ESL students, and requiring regular attendance.

1117. Anderson, David. "Writing as Skills, Fine Arts, or Humanities: Implications for the Writing Center." Paper presented at the Midwest Writing Centers Conference, Minneapolis, October 1987. ERIC ED 290 164. 12 pages

Calls for justifying writing as an English department and humanities offering.

1118. Anspach, Marlene. "A Paradoxical Approach to Training Tutors: A Theory of Failure." *WLN* 13 (October 1988): 14–16.

Suggests using reverse psychology, presenting positively 10 bad approaches, to teach tutors good tutoring techniques.

1119. Ashton-Jones, Evelyn. "Asking the Right Questions: A Heuristic for Tutors." *WCJ* 9 (Fall-Winter 1988): 29–36.

Advocates nonprescriptive tutor training. Using a process of self-inquiry, peer tutors

can "generate the kinds of questions which will help tutees make writing decisions."

1120. Asselin, Bonnie, and Nancy Lusignan Schultz. "Optimizing the Writing Center for an Interdisciplinary Course." *WLN* 12 (May 1988): 5–6.

Using faculty-generated newsletters related to specific assignments, lab assistants help tutors work with specialized writing assignments in psychology.

1121. Baker, Tracey. "Critical Thinking and the Writing Center: Possibilities." *WCJ* 8 (Spring-Summer 1988): 37–41.

Argues against treating writing and critical thinking separately and advocates tutors encouraging critical thinking by working with grammar, questioning, and audience analysis.

1122. Barr, Alyce, Winifred Donahue, Anita Podrid, Shari Seelig, Elaine Caputo, Sarah Halloway, Charlotte Rubin, and Lilli Weinger. *Successful College Tutoring: Focusing on the Learning-Disabled Student.* Brooklyn, N.Y.: Long Island University, April 1987. ERIC ED 289 337. 26 pages

Offers suggestions for tutoring learning-disabled students in writing, reading, and study skills.

1123. Battle, Mary Vroman. "Support for the Faculty of Freshman Composition." *CompC* 1 (December 1988): 8–9.

Suggests that regional accreditation associations and faculty-state agreements can help improve substandard teaching conditions.

1124. Beers, Terry. "Decomposing Composing Conventions." Paper presented at the CCCC Convention, St. Louis, March 1988. ERIC ED 294 199. 19 pages

Suggests that the concept of "convention" may be used to rethink the teleological basis of textbooks.

1125. Bilson, Barbara, and Bert Woodruff, eds. *Inside English: Journal of the English*

Council of the California Two-Year Colleges. ERIC ED 288 575. 52 pages

Makes available in ERIC Volume 13 (1985–1986) of the journal of the English Council of the California Two-Year Colleges. Volumes 1–12 are available as ERIC ED 272 238.

1126. Bishop, Wendy. "Opening Lines: Starting the Tutoring Session." *WLN* 13 (November 1988): 1–4.

Cites seven comments students frequently utter at the beginning of tutorials. Suggests appropriate responses and provides an analysis of each situation.

1127. Bishop, Wendy. "Slow Cooking and Fast Foods: Balancing Tutoring Options in the Writing Center." *WLN* 13 (September 1988): 10–12.

Argues that providing brief, one-time tutorials is as important as working with clients regularly over a period of time.

1128. Brown, Alan. "What's an Assistant to Do?" *WLN* 12 (January 1988): 8–9.

An assistant director can benefit a director by reviewing a writing center's holdings, writing instructional materials, collaborating on grant proposals, and providing professional feedback.

1129. Chapman, David. "Out of Dragnet and into the Writing Center." *WLN* 12 (December 1988): 11–12.

Concludes that, although students should have learned grammar in high school, the tutor should teach what students need at the present.

1130. Clark, Irene Lurkis. "Collaboration and Ethics in Writing Center Pedagogy." *WCJ* 9 (Fall-Winter 1988): 3–13.

Some writing center practices may be based on a paranoid fear of plagiarism that disallows imitation and modeling as forms of learning.

1131. Crisp, Sally Chandler. " 'Aerobic' Writing: A Writing Practice Model." *WLN* 12 (May 1988): 9–11.

To gain confidence and proficiency, clients write regularly for a set time, receive positive feedback on content, and revise a few selected pieces.

1132. David, Carol, Margaret Graham, and Anne Richards. "Three Approaches to Proofreading." *WLN* 13 (October 1988): 10–14.

Describes in detail a handout used with walk-in students, a manual for assigned students, and another manual especially designed for ESL students.

1133. Davis, Kevin. "Homemade Pasta, Writing Centers, and the Evolution of Approach: A Call for Research." *WLN* 13 (September 1988): 5–6.

Theorizes that effective writing centers result from experimentation, practice, evaluation, and research.

1134. Davis, Kevin. "Improving Students' Writing Attitude: The Effects of the Writing Center." Paper presented at the East Central Writing Center Association, Youngstown, Ohio, May 1987. ERIC ED 294 183. 12 pages

Reports on the effects of a writing center on students' attitudes toward writing.

1135. Davis, Kevin, Nancy Hayward, Kathleen R. Hunter, and David L. Wallace. "The Function of Talk in the Writing Conference: A Study of Tutorial Conversation." *WCJ* 9 (Fall-Winter 1988): 45–51.

"Tutoring talk has qualities of teaching and non-teaching talk." An analysis of audiotaped conversations suggests that tutors "negotiate," not "seize," positions of control.

1136. DeCiccio, Albert. "The Writing Center and Peer Tutoring." *WLN* 12 (January 1988): 3–5.

Discusses the relationship between peer tutors and collaborative learning, concluding that peer tutoring is "a valuable institutionalized extension of the social nature of learning."

1137. DeLoughry, Thomas J. "Writers, Not Machines, Are Focus of Michigan Tech Computer Center." *CHE* 34 (11 May 1988): A16.

One university's computer writing center uses colorful, nontraditional interior decorations and minimal ground rules to diminish writing anxiety and promote a supportive writing community.

1138. Dillingham, Daniel. "The Outline: A Strategy for Dyslexic Writers." *WLN* 12 (March 1988): 5–6.

To keep dyslexic students on track, suggests taping verbal brainstorming, creating a detailed outline, and checking the writing-in-progress against the outline.

1139. Fish, Stanley. "No Bias, No Merit: The Case against Blind Submission." *PMLA* 103 (October 1988): 739–747.

Argues that, because notions of merit are necessarily interested, a policy of blind submission is implicitly political and thus never blind.

1140. Fitzgerald, Sallyanne H. "Successes and Failures: Facilitating Cooperation across the Curriculum." *WLN* 13 (September 1988): 13–15.

Advocates expanding a writing center's services by presenting lectures to individual classes, providing tutors for specific academic programs, working with individual teachers, and helping with noninstructional projects.

1141. Gills, Paula. "Lab Troubleshooter." *WLN* 13 (December 1988): 7–8.

A new column reports on how to secure and develop tutorial materials with limited funds.

1142. Glassman, Susan. "The English Department Connection." *WLN* 12 (February 1988): 9–10.

Using collaborative learning techniques, a master tutor works with a specific instructor's basic English class to improve students' writing skills.

1143. Greater Pittsburgh Literacy Council. *Tutor Support Systems 1986–1987*. Pittsburgh: Greater Pittsburgh Literacy Council, 1987. ERIC ED 289 063. 33 pages

Discusses four support systems for adult literacy tutors: informal meetings, telephone consultations with specialists, workshops, and mentoring programs.

1144. Green, Sharon, and Mary Gorman. "Tutoring Nontraditional Students: Blending Writing and Informal Counseling." *WLN* 12 (April 1988): 2–3.

Suggests that older people who have experience with children, family, and school make effective tutors for older, returning students.

1145. Harrington, John. "The Idea of a Center for Writing and Speaking." *WLN* 12 (June 1988): 1–3.

Tutors aid students in preparing and delivering oral presentations. Improving oral fluency benefits written work.

1146. Harris, Jeanette, and Joyce Kinkead, eds. *Computers, Computers, Computers*. Lubbock, Tex.: National Writing Centers Association (distributed by NCTE), 1987. 72 pages

Ten essays discuss different ways of using computers in writing centers. Originally published as *The Writing Center Journal* 8 (Fall-Winter 1987).

1147. Harris, Muriel. "Peer Tutoring: How Tutors Learn." *TETYC* 15 (February 1988): 28–33.

Besides increasing their skills in mechanics, peer tutors learn about learning and teaching and polish their problem-solving strategies.

1148. Haynes, Jane. "Triage Tutoring: The Least You Can Do." *WLN* 12 (June 1988): 12–13.

Working with last minute papers, tutors should address only the most severe problems. The burden for improvement should be on the student.

1149. Heller, Scott. " 'A Room of Our Own': Association of Composition Researchers Evolves with the Field." *CHE* 34 (27 April 1988): A7.

In 1949 writing instructors split from the MLA, forming the College Conference on Composition and Communication to discuss issues in teaching writing.

1150. Holbrook, Hilary Taylor. "Issues in the Writing Lab." *EEd* 20 (May 1988): 116–121.

Discusses issues that confront writing center tutors, including writing in content courses and new technology.

1151. Hooks, Rita Daly. "A Delighted Tutor." *WLN* 13 (September 1988): 9.

After working with hostile or disinterested students at state universities, the tutor finds helping appreciative two-year college students a rewarding experience.

1152. Hornibrook, Judy. "Learning from Teaching: A Study of Writing Tutors." *WLN* 12 (January 1988): 7–8.

By working with student writers, tutors learn to be better writers and editors of their own work.

1153. Hubbuch, Susan M. "A Tutor Needs to Know the Subject Matter to Help a Student with a Paper: __Agree __Disagree __Not Sure." *WCJ* 8 (Spring-Summer 1988): 23–30.

Discusses the particular advantages of two categories of tutors, those who are knowledgeable about or ignorant of a field other than writing.

1154. Janangelo, Joseph. "The Polarities of Context in the Writing Center Conference." *WCJ* 8 (Spring-Summer 1988): 31–36.

Discusses two conferences with students, one more positive than the other, to show the effects of a teacher's personal knowledge of students' writing.

1155. Kilborn, Judith. "Lefse, Popovers, and Hot Cross Buns: Observations about Three Tutors." *WLN* 13 (September 1988): 1–4, 12.

Describes successful tutors as self-motivated, curious, flexible, and open. Advocates using the Meyers-Briggs Personality Type Indicator to screen applicants.

1156. Kinkead, Joyce. "The Electronic Writing Tutor." *WLN* 13 (December 1988): 4–5.

On-line tutoring provides services to "an audience that might not ordinarily use the . . . center because of time conflicts, distance problems, second language problems, or shyness."

1157. Klooster, David. "Tutee Training; or, It Takes Two to Collaborate." *WLN* 13 (December 1988): 1–4.

To educate students about the collaborative process, the writing center's director visits classes, offers special-interest workshops, and sends follow-up notes to professors.

1158. Lee, Eleanor. "The Writing Center at Troy State University: A Multiservice Learning Center." *WLN* 13 (October 1988): 1–4.

Presents a detailed description of the center's services: a tutor training program, tutoring, a professional library, instructional materials and equipment, and writing across the curriculum projects.

1159. Masiello, Lea. "Collaborative Pedagogy and Perry's Stages of Cognitive Growth: Some Thoughts on Conferences as Learning Environments." *WLN* 12 (April 1988): 1–2.

Discusses the impact conferences have on tutors and encourages conference participants to be open to new ideas rather than dogmatic in presenting their own.

1160. Masiello, Lea. "Tutor-Instructor Collaboration in the Writing Center and the Classroom." *WLN* 13 (December 1988): 13–15.

Presents three case studies in which a tutor interacts with instructors in technical writing, basic English, and upper-level English classes.

1161. McCleary, Bill. "First-Ever MLA Conference on Right to Literacy Draws Disparate Crowd." *CompC* 1 (October 1988): 1–4.

Reports on a literacy conference held in September 1988 in Columbus, Ohio.

1162. McCleary, Bill. "If It's March, It Must Be Time for 4C's." *CompC* 1 (March 1988): 8–10.

Traces the history of the CCCC convention.

1163. Meyer, Emily, and Louise Z. Smith. *The Practical Tutor*. New York: Oxford University Press, 1988. 368 pages

A guide to tutoring basic writers designed for teachers, tutors, and writing center personnel. Analyzes sample compositions and includes sample dialogues, exercises, and bibliographies.

1164. Molek, Carol. *Tutor Training Packet: Ready-Set-ABE to Ease Students' Transition into ABE Level Studies*. McVeyton, Pa.: Tuscarora Intermediate Unit, 1987. ERIC ED 289 069. 120 pages

Offers suggestions for tutors of adult basic education students. For related documents, see ERIC ED 289 065 through ERIC ED 289 068.

1165. Newbill, Mary Susan. "Speaking Football." *WLN* 12 (March 1988): 7–8.

Having students explain or translate slang expressions helps them generate Standard Edited English required for most writing assignments.

1166. Olson, Gary A., and Evelyn Ashton-Jones. "Writing Center Directors: The Search for Professional Status." *WPA* 12 (Fall-Winter 1988): 19–28.

Reports on a survey of 188 freshman English directors. Finds that writing center directors are viewed largely as administrators and argues that perceptions of writing center directors need to change. Recommends integrating writing centers into writing programs and directors into the academic community.

1167. Patten, Stan. "Peer Professionals." *WLN* 12 (May 1988): 1–4.

Describes the process used to change student tutors into peer professionals during the first four weeks of a semester.

1168. Pendleton, William. "You've Got to Please Yourself; or, Writing Is a Garden Party." *WLN* 12 (January 1988): 1–2.

To solve problems of audience awareness, students should imagine themselves in a particular situation and write to themselves in that situation.

1169. Posey, Evelyn. "Micro Style." *WLN* 13 (November 1988): 8–9.

Argues that computers belong in writing centers because they encourage students to prewrite, revise, and learn an important job skill.

1170. Roberts, David H. "A Study of Writing Center Effectiveness." *WCJ* 9 (Fall-Winter 1988): 53–60.

Results indicate that individuated instruction in a writing center "can be as effective as traditional classroom instruction" at about one-half the instructional cost.

1171. Sartre, Kay, and Valerie Traub. "Nondirective Tutoring Strategies." *WLN* 12 (April 1988): 5–6.

Using open-ended, honest questions and responses, a tutor acts as "explorer and prompter, a companion," not an authority figure, "as she creates and communicates meaning."

1172. Seiger, Karen. "Bumps, Charmers, and Perfect Ones." *WLN* 13 (October 1988): 8–9.

Categorizes clients and discusses the difficulties and advantages of working with each type.

1173. Singley, Carol J., and Holly W. Boucher. "Dialogue in Tutor Training: Creating the Essential Space for Learning." *WCJ* 8 (Spring-Summer 1988): 11–22.

Presents a three-part dialogic method for training tutors (assessment, interpretation, and action) based on theories of Bakhtin and Freire.

1174. Smith, Erin. "A College Try." *WLN* 13 (December 1988): 9–10.

Concludes that writing centers provide an atmosphere that encourages students to succeed rather than fail.

1175. Spellman-Trimble, Lisa. "A Knot of Questions: An Exercise in Training Tutors." *WLN* 12 (May 1988): 7–8.

Describes a study in which eight tutors received a list of 10 frequently used questions and then evaluated their effectiveness in 60 conferences.

1176. Spooner, Michael. "Dictating to the Machine: Voice Activated Computer Technology." *EEd* 20 (May 1988): 109–115.

Describes advances that will enable computers to produce text from oral dictation.

1177. Summerfield, Judith. "Writing Centers: A Long View." *WCJ* 8 (Spring-Summer 1988): 3–9.

Finds that writing centers have value in their second (social) stage. Looks retrospectively at the emergence and influence of the writing center at City University of New York.

1178. Taylor, David. "A Counseling Approach to Writing Conferences." *WLN* 12 (January 1988): 10–11.

Suggests adapting the five stages of the counseling session to the tutorial so that students can understand their problems and gain control of their writing.

1179. Taylor, David. "Listening Skills for the Writing Center." *WLN* 12 (March 1988): 1–3.

Five listening skills—paraphrasing, perception checking, indirect leading, interpreting, and summarizing—enable tutors to interact with clients.

1180. Taylor, Mandy. " 'Twas a Semester at the Writing Center." *WLN* 13 (December 1988): 9.

A parody of " 'Twas the Night Before Christmas." Expresses feelings about completing a semester's work and anticipating the next.

1181. Thompson, Melinda Rainey. "Imitation and Explanation." *WLN* 13 (October 1988): 5–7.

Explains the techniques of reformulation, controlled composition, and traditional drills. Suggests that tutors combine strategies to meet the specific needs of individual ESL students.

1182. Trimmer, Joseph F. "Story Time: All about Writing Centers." *Focuses* 1 (Fall 1988): 27–35.

Brief personal histories narrate the development of the writing workshop/laboratory/clinic/center from about 1960 to 1990.

1183. Vaughan, Elinor Folger. *An Examination of the Library Involvement in the Literacy Programs of the North Carolina Community College System: A Perceptual Analysis.* Chapel Hill, N.C.: University of North Carolina, 1986. ERIC ED 288 563. 265 pages

A dissertation exploring the involvment of libraries in literacy programs at North Carolina's 58 two-year colleges.

1184. Veinot, Cynthia. "What Is a Peer Tutor?" *WLN* 13 (November 1988): 7.

Defines "peer tutor" and describes the tutor's role in helping clients develop ways "to refine and improve writing abilities."

1185. Waggoner, Tim. "We Used to Help Them with Writing." *WLN* 12 (April 1988): 7.

A tutor, writing at some time in the future, recalls helping various types of students learn to write during the good old days.

1186. Wallace, Ray. "Towards Heuristic Use Later in the Writing Process: The Role of the Writing Center Tutor." *Focuses* 1 (Fall 1988): 19–26.

Urges broader use of discovery techniques in revision as writing moves from writer- to reader-based concerns.

1187. Wallace, Ray. "The Writing Center's Role in the Writing across the Curriculum Program: Theory and Practice." *WCJ* 8 (Spring-Summer 1988): 43–48.

Describes an institution's coordination of a writing across the curriculum program through its writing center.

1188. Zimmerman, Nancy. "Foiling Your Tutor: A Process Analysis for Tutees." *WLN* 12 (February 1988): 7–8.

Presents tongue-in-cheek advice to students on how to thwart tutorial sessions and frustrate tutors.

See also 7, 1055, 1097, 1264, 1330, 1340, 1636, 1734

3.4   ROLE IN SOCIETY

1189. Bruffee, Kenneth A. "On Not Listening in Order to Hear: Collaborative Learning and the Rewards of Classroom Research." *JBW* 7 (Spring 1988): 3–12.

Keynote address to the Community College Humanities Association. Traces the speaker's intellectual history and encourages teachers to document cultural (including political and social) aspects of American life.

1190. Bryant, Napoleon. "Sons, Daughters, Where Are Your Books?" *JCST* 17 (March–April 1988): 344–347.

If black students are to succeed, teachers and the community must alter their attitudes and provide more concrete support for reading and writing.

1191. Cadegan, Una M. "All Good Books Are Catholic Books: Literature, Censorship, and the Americanization of Catholics, 1920–1960." *DAI* 49 (August 1988): 283A.

Addresses the question of why American Catholics are virtually absent from the canon of American authors.

1192. Chaplin, Miriam T. "Issues, Perspectives, and Possibilities." *CCC* 39 (February 1989): 52–62.

Inventories some concerns of writing teachers in the 1980s: social, economic, and political issues; changing student populations; curricular goals; teacher preparation; and standardized testing.

1193. Cioffi, Frank L. "The Audience within the Object: The Implied Teacher in Composition Textbook Advertisements." *WC* 5 (July 1988): 277–305.

Examines a series of composition textbook advertisements from 1982 to 1987. Concludes that "the audience projected by the ads are wrong—patronizing, sexist, authoritarian, passe."

1194. Davis, James E., and Hazel K. Davis, eds. *Collaboration between College English Departments and Secondary Schools*. Athens, Ohio: Southeastern Ohio Council of Teachers of English (distributed by NCTE), 1988. 56 pages

Twenty-three essays discuss ways in which colleges and universities can help secondary English teachers. Offers suggestions for stimulating and organizing collaboration. Includes bibliography. Originally published as *Focus* (Winter 1988).

1195. Delpit, Lisa D. "The Silenced Dialogue: Power and Pedagogy in Educating Other People's Children." *HER* 58 (August 1988): 280–298.

The debate over process-oriented versus skill-oriented writing instruction serves as the starting point for examining society's culture of power. Analyzes five complex rules of power that influence the debate.

1196. Gerson, Mark. "Anti-Pornography Legislation Pending in Canada Is Opposed as 'Puritanical' by Professors' Group." *CHE* 34 (13 January 1988): A44.

A Canadian association of academics charges that a pending bill meant to outlaw pornography could prevent the study of great literary works.

1197. Greenman, Nancy P. "American Education: Emerging Contexts for a Model of the Future." *DAI* 49 (September 1988): 476A.

Addresses the issue of reality prevalent in Western education; reviews existing models; examines their sociocultural, philosophical, and human contexts; and proposes another model for education.

1198. Heller, Scott. "Experts Convened by Endowment Head Are Divided in Assessing the Health of the Humanities." *CHE* 34 (9 March 1988): A4, A11-A12.

Panelists from universities expressed support for humanities teaching, while participants from outside the academy protested esoteric research and diminished standards.

1199. Knoblauch, C. H. "Some Observations on Freire's *Pedagogy of the Oppressed*." *JAC* 8 (1988): 50–54.

Argues that, since Freire's work is genuinely subversive of both state and academy, its "iconic stature" in composition is ironic and rests on "trivialized reading."

1200. Kramer, Melinda G. "*Caveat Vendor:* Packaging Rhetoric for the Corporate Marketplace." *JBTC* 2 (September 1988): 71–77.

Warns potential writing consultants that job efficiency or productivity is the primary measure of their success. Since corporate "writing problems" may be problems of management, production, or personnel, consultants must be prepared to identify and solve hidden problems.

1201. Levitt, Paul M. "Why Are Students Unprepared for College? That's the Way Our Society Wants Them to Be." *CHE* 34 (4 May 1988): B3.

Society wants students ignorant for several reasons: anti-intellectualism, antipathy for moral and intellectual subtleties, and fears

about children surpassing their elders in sophistication.

1202. Long, Maxine. "Composition Teachers Can Become Writing Consultants Too." *CompC* 1 (November 1988): 1–2.

Describes consulting as a natural extension of teaching.

1203. Lyon, Arabella. "Paideia to Pedantry: The Dissolving Relationship of the Humanities and Society." *JTWC* 18 (1988): 55–62.

English departments resist teaching applied writing because they are isolated from the practical concerns of society. Technical communication can help reengage them.

1204. Mooney, Carolyn J. "A New Book Excoriates Professors for the 'Demise' of Higher Education." *CHE* 35 (2 November 1988): A1, A14.

Charles Sykes's book *ProfScam* argues that academics are underworked, overpaid, and get away with "atrocious" behavior because of tenure.

1205. Savage, Mary C. "Can Ethnographic Narrative Be a Neighborly Act?" *A&E* 19 (March 1988): 3–19.

Finds that critical ethnography facilitates communication between universities and schools and universities and civic communities in the interest of common educational goals.

1206. Steinle, Pamela L. "If a Body Catch a Body: J. D. Salinger's *The Catcher in the Rye* and Post-World War II American Culture." *DAI* 49 (July 1988): 107A.

Examines censorship controversies surrounding *The Catcher in the Rye*, regarding them as a cultural debate.

1207. Treadwell, D. F. "A New Role for Technical Communication." *JTWC* 18 (1988): 263–268.

Increasing public involvement in science and technology suggests that technical communicators may have to develop the skills necessary to help facilitate the audiences' own information searches.

1208. Walker, David. "Have You Heard the One about the British Structuralist and Chaucerian Imagery?" *CHE* 34 (3 February 1988): A42.

British television's popular comedy based on *Small World,* fiction by professor and novelist David Lodge, satirizes professors and English department specialties.

See also 394

4

Curriculum

4.1 GENERAL DISCUSSIONS

1209. Armon, Jan. "Functions of the Personal, Reflective Essay as Academic Writing." *DAI* 49 (November 1988): 1080A.

Examines the theory and practice of using personal writing as a supplement or alternative to expository writing in the composition classroom.

1210. Atkins, Elaine. "Reframing Curriculum Theory in Terms of Interpretation and Practice: A Hermeneutical Approach." *JCS* 20 (September–October 1988): 437–448.

Presents the hermeneutic tradition as a metaphor for conceptualizing needed curriculum changes. Points to a reframing of theory based on interpretation, community, and language.

1211. Babich, Roger M. "Dialects in the Classroom: Their Functions, Some Potential Problems, and Guidelines for Teachers." *JT* 22 (Winter 1987): 89–94.

Explains the nature of dialects, classroom problems associated with them, and relevant ways in which dialects should be acquired and used in classrooms.

1212. Baer, Vicki. "Computers as Composition Tools: A Case Study of Student Attitudes." *JCBI* 15 (Autumn 1988): 144–148.

A study of 58 seventh graders shows that most students enjoyed writing more when using a word processor.

1213. Barrett, Edward, and James Paradis. "Teaching Writing in an On-Line Classroom." *HER* 58 (May 1988): 154–171.

Documents an experimental writing course that uses electronic networks to create an on-line classroom for writing instruction. Describes a typical class meeting, examining its challenges and results.

1214. Benjamin, Ludy T., Jr. "A History of Teaching Machines." *AmP* 43 (September 1988): 703–712.

Gives an overview of self-instruction via teaching machines from 1866 to the 1960s and via classroom computers in the 1970s and 1980s.

1215. Berlin, James. "Rhetoric and Ideology in the Writing Class." *CE* 50 (September 1988): 477–494.

Given three classroom ideologies—cognitive psychology, expressionism, and social-epistemic—the third is superior because it incorporates economic, social, political, and cultural spheres of experience.

1216. Biggs, John. "Students' Approaches to Essay Writing and the Quality of the Written Product." Paper presented at the AERA, New Orleans, April 1988. ERIC ED 293 145. 17 pages

Students from eleventh grade through graduate school get better grades and write in an appropriate genre when focusing on ideational levels during the composing process.

1217. Bishop, Wendy. "Helping Peer Writing Groups Succeed." *TETYC* 15 (May 1988): 120–125.

Reviews research on peer groups and suggests methods for preparing teachers, training students, and evaluating groups.

1218. Braaten, Jennifer Lou. "An Overview of Several Implementations of the Educational Philosophy of Paulo Freire within the U.S. from 1967 to 1987." *DAI* 48 (February 1988): 2013A.

Considers the uses and appropriateness of Freire's pedagogy and literacy design for adult, secondary, and higher education.

1219. Brooke, Robert. "Modeling a Writer's Identity: Reading and Imitation in the Writing Classroom." *CCC* 39 (February 1988): 23–41.

Advocates using readings so that students can imitate those writers' reasons for writing, rather than imitating the writers' processes or forms.

1220. Burns, Gerald T. "Tradition and Revolution in the American Secondary Curriculum: The Cambridge High School Case." *JCS* 20 (March–April 1988): 99–118.

A historical review of two early curricular traditions, "classics" and "English Department." Traces their influence from the mid-nineteenth century to 1984 college entrance requirements.

1221. Burton, Dolores M. "Paperchase: A Flexible Program for Composition Class." *CollM* 6 (February 1988): 45–50.

Reviews a computer program designed to maximize the utility of comments made on papers. Finds the program useful in guiding long-term revision.

1222. Cherryholmes, Cleo H. "An Exploration of Meaning and the Dialogue between Textbooks and Teaching." *JCS* 20 (January–March 1988): 1–21.

Discusses the relationship between meaning theories (truth-conditional semantics, speech-act theory, discourse theory, and deconstructionism) and teaching that moves "behind and beyond the text through language."

1223. Ciske, Mary Desjarlais. "An Error Analysis of Standard English Verb Use by Speakers of a Nonstandard Black Dialect." *DAI* 48 (April 1988): 2615A.

Demonstrates one method of analyzing verb use in speech, free writing, and edited writing. Suggests strategies for solving verb problems.

1224. Clark, Charles. "The Necessity of Curricular Objectives." *JCS* 20 (July–August 1988): 339–349.

Discusses process versus product models of curriculum design, accomodating arguments for both in terms of teaching practice.

1225. Coles, William E., Jr. *The Plural I— And After*. Portsmouth, N.H.: Boynton/Cook, 1988. 320 pages

Reissues Coles's *The Plural I* (1979). Two accompanying essays review the importance of the original work in the author's life and discuss the value of literacy.

1226. Collins, James L. "A Nonlinear Alternative to Outlining." *CompC* 1 (October 1988): 6–7.

Advocates algorithm-style planning derived from computer programming as a model for writers.

1227. Collins, Terence, Nancy Engen-Wedin, and William Margolis. "Persistence and Course Completion." *CC* 6 (November 1988): 27–32.

Students enrolled in microcomputer sections completed two writing courses at higher rates than those enrolled in other sections.

1228. Comprone, Joseph. "The Function of Text in a Dialogic Writing Course." Paper presented at the Kentucky Philological Association, Louisville, Ky., March 1987. ERIC ED 284 239. 29 pages

Applies concepts of dialogic discourse and textuality to S. J. Gould's scientific writing. Gives associated classroom activities for learning collaboratively about reader-writer relationships.

1229. Conti, Gary J., and Robert A. Fellenz. "From Theory to Practice: Stimulating Discussion with Agree-Disagree Statements and Expanding Groups." *AdLBEd* 12 (1988).

Offers a model for discussion, a mechanism for stimulating free contributions from everyone in a nonthreatening manner.

1230. Crew, Louie. "Software for the Gullible." *CollM* 6 (February 1988): 43–44.

Evaluates The Writer, a multifunction writing program. Concludes that the program is inferior in speed, flexibility, and effectiveness in transferring skills.

1231. Crew, Louie. "The Style-Checker as Tonic, Not Tranquilizer." *JAC* 8 (1988): 66–70.

Illustrates and defends the use of style-checking software under the author's control.

1232. Crowley, Sharon. "Derrida, Deconstruction, and Our Scene of Teaching." *Pre/Text* 8 (Fall-Winter 1987): 169–183.

Sees deconstruction as the basis for a revisionist pedagogy. Demonstrates the logocentrism of expository discourse.

1233. Dahl, Karin L. "Writers Teaching Writers: What Children Learn in Peer Conferences." *EQ* 21 (1988): 164–173.

An ethnographic study of peer conferences, finding that 38 percent of the interactions addressed revision and that 46 percent of the suggested revisions were made.

1234. Davis, James E. "No Apologies, Phyllis, Journal Writing Is Here to Stay." *ET* 19 (Spring 1988): 7–8.

Uses students' support for journal writing to counter Phyllis Schlafly's belief that journals are ineffective.

1235. Davis, Ken, ed. *Literacy and Locality*. Elizabethtown, Ky.: Kentucky Council of Teachers of English/Language Arts (distributed by NCTE), 1986. 72 pages

Six essays offer models that use regional history and language patterns in Kentucky to teach literacy. Discusses guidelines for teaching dialect speakers. Originally published as *Kentucky English Bulletin* (Fall 1986).

1236. Day, John T. "Writer's Workbench: A Useful Aid But Not a Cure-All." *CC* 6 (November 1988): 64–78.

A study at St. Olaf College concludes that the program is viewed by faculty and students as neither a cure-all nor a technological gimmick.

1237. DeCiccio, Albert C. "Social Constructionism and Collaborative Learning: Recommendations for Teaching Writing." Paper presented at the CCCC Convention, St. Louis, March 1988. ERIC ED 294 201. 15 pages

Discusses the importance of establishing a sense of community in collaborative classrooms.

1238. DeLoughry, Thomas J. "For Many Writing Instructors, Computers Have Become a Key Tool." *CHE* 34 (11 May 1988): A9, A16.

Many schools such as Michigan Technological University offer writing instruction with computers. Most students prefer word processing classes to classes using traditional methods of teaching.

1239. Dickinson, Barbara Ann. "Imitation in the Writing Process: Origins, Implications, Applications." *DAI* 49 (November 1988): 1081A.

A historical survey of imitation as a theoretical and practical tool in the composition classroom.

1240. Dillon, J. T. "The Remedial Status of Student Questioning." *JCS* 20 (May–June 1988): 197–210.

An observational study of 27 classrooms. Relates students' question-asking behavior to curriculum materials, pedagogy, the teacher's reaction, and the assumptions about transmitting knowledge or establishing an atmosphere of inquiry.

1241. DiPardo, Anne, and Sarah Warshauer Freedman. "Peer Response Groups in the Writing Classroom: Theoretic Foundations and New Directions." *RER* 58 (Summer 1988): 119–149.

Examines research and theoretical and pedagogical literature. Suggests a reconceptualization of peer response.

1242. Duin, Ann Hill. "Computer-Assisted Instructional Displays: Effects on Students' Computing Behaviors, Prewriting, and Attitudes." *JCBI* 15 (Spring 1988): 48–56.

Finds that well-designed computer displays enhanced students' computing behaviors, prewriting, and attitudes. Poorly designed displays did not.

1243. Durfee, Mary. "Writing with the Students: Becoming a Community of Learners." *CollT* 36 (Winter 1988): 12–15.

Presents a teacher's experiences with collaboration in the writing process.

1244. Ellington, Henry. *Educational Objectives.* Teaching and Learning in Higher Education, no. 1. Aberdeen, Scotland: Scottish Central Institutions Committee for Educational Development, 1984. ERIC ED 289 484. 17 pages

Indicates for teachers the role of educational objectives and offers suggestions based on Bloom's taxonomy for writing them.

1245. Fenlon, Katherine F. "Campus Visit: Jefferson Community College." *CompC* 1 (February 1988): 8–9.

Describes the writing program of a college in Watertown, N.Y.

1246. Flynn, Elizabeth. "Campus Visit: Michigan Technological University." *CompC* 1 (April 1988): 8–9.

Describes the writing program of a college in Houghton, Michigan.

1247. Flynn, Elizabeth. "Composing as a Woman." *CCC* 39 (December 1988): 423–435.

Analyzes four students' papers for gender differences. Recommends a curriculum that explores how gender affects language use.

1248. Fordham, Signithia. "Racelessness as a Factor in Black Students' School Success: Pragmatic Strategy or Pyrrhic Victory?" *HER* 58 (February 1988): 54–84.

Examines the tensions six high-achieving black students experience. Finds that students caught between "making it" and solidarity with black culture opt for racelessness as a strategy.

1249. Foster, Myrna Lynn. "Learning How to Communicate with Computers: An Analysis of Three Basic Forms of Computer Instruction." *DAI* 48 (April 1988): 2487A.

> Studies three methods—documentation, lecture, and group interaction—for effectively teaching the use of computers in the classroom.

1250. Fulkerson, Richard. "Technical Logic, Comp-Logic, and the Teaching of Writing." *CCC* 39 (December 1988): 436–452.

> Discusses the shortcomings of teaching induction, deduction, fallacy recognition, and Toulmin's model of argument in the writing class. Recommends teaching *stasis* theory instead.

1251. Gallehr, Donald R. "A Bright Idea Does Not Enlightenment Make [response to Graves, *Focuses* 1 (Spring 1988)]." *Focuses* 1 (Fall 1988): 36–40.

> Agrees that connecting meditation with writing is useful but argues that a writer's breakthrough amounts to more than Zen satori.

1252. Gardner, Ruth, and Jo McGinnis. *Computers in College Composition: A Comparative Study of Ten Schools.* Alexandria, Va.: ERIC Document Reproduction Service, 1986. ERIC ED 284 241. 131 pages

> Surveys the use of computers in composition courses and labs at representative universities.

1253. Golub, Jeff, and NCTE Committee on Classroom Practices, eds. *Focus on Collaborative Learning.* Classroom Practices in Teaching English. Urbana, Ill.: NCTE, 1988. 170 pages

> Twenty-three essays discuss the benefits of teaching students to work with each other on composition and literary studies. Suggests ways of teaching students the skills necessary for collaborative projects.

1254. Gorrell, Donna. "Writing Assessment and the New Approaches." Paper presented at the CCCC Convention, St. Louis, March 1988. ERIC ED 296 334. 12 pages

> Studies the relationship of writing instruction to assessment.

1255. Grant, Grace E. *Teaching Critical Thinking.* New York City: Praeger, 1988. 148 pages

> A case-study analysis of four teachers who conveyed their understanding of content in four disciplines through tasks involving critical thinking.

1256. Graves, Richard L. "Breakthrough: The Satori Experience in the Composition Classroom." *Focuses* 1 (Spring 1988): 20–28.

> Extends Rohman's concept of the role meditation can play in the teaching of writing.

1257. Halpern, Jeanne W. "Responding in and to Journals." Paper presented at the CCCC Convention, St. Louis, March 1988. ERIC ED 295 162. 12 pages

> Explains how to respond to journals, given Bakhtin's speech-genre theory.

1258. Hamilton-Wieler, Sharon. "Empty Echoes of Dartmouth: Dissonance between the Rhetoric and the Reality." *WI* 8 (Fall 1988): 28–41.

> Argues that the rhetoric of a paradigm shift does not match pedagogic reality in North American and British schools. Illustrates several forces that influence change.

1259. Harris, Joseph. "Rethinking the Pedagogy of Problem Solving." *JTW* 7 (Fall-Winter 1988): 157–165.

> Cautions that moving from writer- to reader-based prose can distort the writer's meaning. Analyzes the limits of cognitive theory and warns against teaching exclusionary prose.

1260. Hasenauer, Jim. "Using Ethnic Humor to Expose Ethnocentrism: Those Dirty DEGs." *ETC* 45 (Winter 1988): 351–357.

> Describes a technique to help students examine their own biases and linguistic prejudices using generic ethnic humor.

1261. Hawisher, Gail E. "Research Update: Writing and Word Processing." *CC* 5 (April 1988): 7–27.

Concludes from 16 studies published in 1987 that students who write with computers create fewer errors, compose longer texts, hold more positive attitudes, and among basic writers, improve their writing.

1262. Heyda, John. "A Recipe for Writerly Relations: Writing the Satiric Sketch." *WI* 7 (Spring-Summer 1988): 145–155.

Writing assignments that "originate in students' reading literary texts—then writing their own texts" promotes both writing ability and cultural literacy. Presents a sample assignment.

1263. Hibbs, Morrow Daniel. "Black American English Style Shifting and Writing Error." *RTE* 22 (October 1988): 326–340.

Analyzes the Black American English style of four college freshmen. Suggests that an inverse relationship exists between style shifting rates and writing error.

1264. Horner, Winifred Bryan. "Dialectic as Invention: Dialogue in the Writing Center." *Focuses* 1 (Spring 1988): 11–19.

Examines how dialectic might be used in the classroom, in responding to papers, and in writing center conferences.

1265. Huff, Roland, and Charles R. Kline, Jr. *The Contemporary Writing Curriculum: Rehearsing, Composing, and Valuing.* New York: Teachers College, Columbia University, 1987. 202 pages

Advances simultaneously a curriculum, a pedagogy based on research, and a rhetorically grounded theory of composition. Includes chapters on using journals; integrating predrafting, drafting, and revision into the curriculum; using peer groups; and integrating evaluation into the composing process.

1266. Hull, Glynda Ann. "Literacy, Technology, and the Underprepared: Notes toward a Framework for Action." *CSWQ* 10 (July 1988): 1–3, 16–23.

Reflects on the role of technology in a liberatory pedagogy and offers ideas about using new information tools in literacy instruction, particularly writing.

1267. Hult, Christine A. "The Computer and the Inexperienced Writer." *CC* 5 (April 1988): 29–38.

Students need careful instruction in using word processing effectively, especially to prevent the ineffectual revision processes that text-analysis programs seem to engender.

1268. Hunter, Susan M. "Yes, There Are Texts in This Writing Class! The New Synthesis of Composition and Literature." *WI* 7 (Spring-Summer 1988): 138–144.

A survey of anthologies for composition courses. Cautions that a lingering emphasis on reading processes over writing processes may "imprison" students in a "solopsistic world of writer-based prose."

1269. Hurlbert, C. Mark. "Ideology, Process, and Subjectivity: The Role of Hermeneutics in the Writing Conference." Paper presented at the CCCC Convention, Atlanta, March 1987. ERIC ED 289 161. 15 pages

Analyzes the social and institutional interplay of the writing conference.

1270. Hurlbert, C. Mark. "Rhetoric, Possessive Individualism, and Beyond." *WI* 8 (Fall 1988): 8–16.

Argues that all curricula make ideological statements. Both product and process approaches are based on "possessive individualism," an ideology that should be replaced by "social individualism."

1271. Jasen, Patricia Jane. "The English-Canadian Liberal Arts Curriculum: An Intellectual History, 1800–1950." *DAI* 48 (February 1988): 2003A.

Analyzes the development of the liberal arts curriculum and explores why unifying principles remain unfounded in the twentieth century.

1272. Johnson, Michael L. "Hell Is the Place We Don't Know We're In: The Control-Dictions of Cultural Literacy, Strong Reading, and Poetry." *CE* 50 (March 1988): 309–317.

Divides the reading experience into three levels, stressing that poetry engenders the highest level and should have a prominent role in English and language arts curricula.

1273. Juncker, Clara. "Writing (with) Cixous." *CE* 50 (April 1988): 424–435.

Examines French feminist theory, particularly Helen Cixous's work, and discusses feminist teaching strategies that encourage multiple kinds of writing.

1274. Kelly, Patricia P., and Robert C. Small, Jr., eds. *Language, the Forgotten Content.* Blacksburg, Va.: Virginia Association of Teachers of the English Language Arts (distributed by NCTE), 1987. 158 pages

Thirty-one essays discuss ways to give students a substantial knowledge of language that makes them aware of the vital human dynamics involved in the history, forms, and uses of language. Originally published as *Virginia English Bulletin* 37 (Spring 1987).

1275. "The Kingman Report." *EngT* 4 (October 1988): 15–16.

Presents extracts from and reactions to the March 1988 Report of the Committee of Inquiry into the Teaching of English Language.

1276. Knudson, Ruth E. "The Effects of Highly Structured Versus Less Structured Lessons on Student Writing." *JEdR* 81 (July–August 1988): 365–368.

Frequent teacher intervention in the writing process of primary students may lead to inferior written products.

1277. Krieger, Barbara Jo. "Process and Form in the Teaching of College-Level Writing:

From Polarization to Synthesis." *DAI* 49 (December 1988): 1394A.

Articulates the relationship between form and process. Suggests that a "formative process" approach to instruction works best.

1278. Lauer, Janice M. "Instructional Practices: Toward an Integration." *Focuses* 1 (Spring 1988): 3–10.

Suggests that writing be taught as an art as well as a natural process, using the best features of imitation and practice.

1279. Lemon, Hallie S. "Collaborative Strategies for Teaching Composition: Theory and Practice." Paper presented at the CCCC Convention, St. Louis, March 1988. ERIC ED 294 221. 14 pages

Studies writing teachers at various educational levels to determine which teachers use collaborative writing and when.

1280. Lightfoot, Martin, and Nancy Martin, eds. *The Word for Teaching Is Learning: Essays for James Britton.* Portsmouth, N.H.: Boynton/Cook, 1988. 320 pages

Sixteen essays, commissioned to honor James Britton, are grouped under the following four headings: Teaching the Mother Tongue as a Model for Education, Literacy and the Growth of Consciousness, Coming to Terms with the World, and Implementing Change.

1281. Littler, Frank Anthony. "The Impact of the Golden Rule on Student Writing in Florida Colleges and Universities." *DAI* 48 (March 1988): 2264A.

Shows that curricular reform, requiring 12 hours of English for all students in the higher education system, improved undergraduate students' writing.

1282. Mackler, Tobi. "Group Produced Documents: An Exploratory Study of Collaborative Writing Processes." *DAI* 49 (July 1988): 52A.

Using an open-ended questionnaire, investigates "the process by which small task groups produce documents."

1283. Marshall, Thomas A. "Some Political Implications of Teaching Institutional Discourse." Paper presented at the CCCC Convention, St. Louis, March 1988. ERIC ED 294 206. 8 pages

Discusses the effects of learning to write institutional discourse before learning to write for personal expression.

1284. Martin, David. "Terminal English." *ET* 19 (Spring 1988): 26–28.

A personal and humorous look at different types of English classes.

1285. Marting, Janet. "The Disenfranchisement of Composition Students." *TETYC* 15 (October 1988): 157–164.

Despite new theories in composition, instructors remain unwilling to give up control of classrooms.

1286. McGuinness, Kathleen, ed. *Nontraditional and Interdisciplinary Programs: Selected Papers from the Fifth Annual Conference.* Fairfax, Va.: George Mason University, 1987. ERIC ED 289 403. 113 pages

Offers 113 papers from an annual conference. Many papers discuss writing across the curriculum. Authors are not indexed separately in this volume.

1287. Moffett, James. *Coming on Center: Essays in English Education.* 2d ed. Portsmouth, N.H.: Boynton/Cook, 1988. 224 pages

Analyzes the cultural and political forces shaping instruction in basic skills, composition, and thinking. Contains seven talks and articles written since the first edition appeared in 1979.

1288. Morgan, Bobbette. "Cooperative Learning: Teacher Use, Classroom Life, Social Integration, and Student Achievement." *DAI* 48 (June 1988): 3043A.

Classes that make greater use of cooperative learning strategies show improved classroom life and greater achievement than classes that only minimally use cooperative work.

1289. Mullins, Carolyn J. "Teaching Technical Writing with PCs." *TWT* 15 (Winter 1988): 64–72.

Experimental results indicate that using word processing tools had a positive effect on the quality of freshmen and advanced students' writing.

1290. Newman, Judith M. "Sharing Journals: Conversational Mirrors for Seeing Ourselves as Learners, Writers, and Teachers." *EEd* 20 (October 1988): 134–156.

Finds value in journal writing for both the reader and the teacher. Provides journal entries to support topics from both students and the instructor.

1291. Noe, Marcia. "Some Heretical Thoughts on the Teaching of Writing." *TETYC* 15 (October 1988): 175–179.

"Just Because They Write It Doesn't Mean We Have to Read It . . . Just Because We Read It Doesn't Mean We Have to Evaluate It . . . Just Because We Evaluate It Doesn't Mean They're Going to Benefit by Our Efforts."

1292. Odoroff, Elizabeth. "The Influence of Writers' Perceptions of Audience on Texts: A Study of the Writing Teacher as Primary and Secondary Audience." *DAI* 49 (July 1988): 52A.

Investigates whether students could adapt their texts to audiences differently perceived.

1293. Orr, Claudia Lynn. "A Comparison of Achievement and Attitudes of Postsecondary Students Taught by Two Methods of Instruction in Word Processing." *DAI* 49 (December 1988): 1352A.

Finds no significant differences between groups that use textbooks as computer guides and those that use computer-based tutorials.

1294. Perrin, Robert. "What Handbooks Tell Us about Teaching Writing with Word-Processing Programs." *CC* 6 (November 1988): 15–26.

Examines what 10 current handbooks say about using word processing for writing.

1295. Perron, John A. "Campus Visit: St. Edward's University." *CompC* 1 (September 1988): 8–10.

Describes the writing program of a college in Austin, Texas.

1296. Peterson, Alan J. "Grandfather and Computers." *CC* 5 (April 1988): 71–73.

Believes that teachers should relinquish past methods of teaching courses because of the continuing effect of computer literacy.

1297. Petry, John R. "The Revival of General Education Programs in American Colleges and Universities." Paper presented at the AERA, Chicago, November 1987. ERIC ED 288 439. 25 pages

Notes the features of general education programs, including writing across the curriculum programs.

1298. Prest, Peter, and Julie Prest. "Theory into Practice: Clarifying Our Intentions: Some Thoughts on the Application of Rosenblatt's Transactional Theory of Reading in the Classroom." *EQ* 21 (1988): 127–133.

Recommends clarifying purposes to avoid the dilemma of having to choose individual responses to a text over literal interpretations of a text.

1299. Pytlik, Betty. "Designing Effective Writing Assignments: What Do We Know?" Paper presented at the CCCC Convention, New Orleans, March 1986. ERIC ED 291 107. 14 pages

Categorizes research questions about designing topics and recommends Lindemann's and Larson's work on designing assignments.

1300. Pytlik, Betty. "Sequenced Writing Assignments: What's Been Done and Why?" Paper presented at the CCCC Convention, St. Louis, March 1988. ERIC ED 294 202. 15 pages

Discusses sequenced writing assignments and their goals and effects.

1301. Quinn, Karen Beryl. "Researching the Relationship between Reading and Writing: The Generation and Elaboration of Ideas from Reading Informational Prose to Writing Argument." *DAI* 48 (March 1988): 2265A.

Studies the effects of analogies in a text and of varying information available to students who are writing about a text.

1302. Reed, W. Michael, and John K. Burton, eds. *Educational Computing and Problem Solving*. Computers in the Schools, vol. 4. New York: Haworth Press, 1988. 210 pages

Treats current issues in problem-solving theory and computer research. Reviews software, including writing theory and composing process software.

1303. Russell, David R. "The Search for Tradition." *CE* 50 (April 1988): 437–443.

Reviews four books discussing traditions of teaching, finding Berlin's and Brereton's historical approach more useful than Coles and Vopat's or Macrorie's romantic approach.

1304. Schwartz, Helen J. "The Student as Producer and Consumer of Text: Computer Uses in English Studies." *JTW* 7 (Spring-Summer 1988): 57–66.

Students with computers tailor "expert knowledge to individual needs." Advocates using programs in imaginative and expository writing to "analyze models and generate ideas."

1305. Simon, Linda. "The Papers We Want to Read." *CollT* 36 (Winter 1988): 6–8.

Proposes that writing teachers focus on essay assignments by providing students with information regarding audience expectations and relevant sources.

1306. Smye, Randy. "Style and Usage Software: Mentor, Not Judge." *CC* 6 (November 1988): 47–61.

Discusses how some present style and usage checkers can be developed to encourage among students a recursive pattern of revision.

1307. Spear, Karen. *Sharing Writing: Peer Response in English Classes*. Portsmouth, N.H.: Boynton/Cook, 1988. 192 pages

Both a theoretical discussion of and a practical guide to using peer response groups in English classes.

1308. Stang, Sandra J., and Robert Wiltenbert, eds. *Collective Wisdom: A Sourcebook of Lessons for Writing Teachers*. New York: Random House, 1988. 365 pages

An anthology of 71 lessons and assignments grouped into five sections: first principles, observation to essay, critical reading, argument, and opening out. Instructors describe each lesson's goal, the materials used, the execution of the lesson, and how it results in a writing assignment. Individual contributors are not indexed separately in this volume.

1309. Stewart, Donald. "Collaborative Learning and Composition: Boon or Bane?" *RR* 7 (Fall 1988): 58–83.

Defines collaborative learning, gives a brief history, and explains its theoretical and philosophical bases, as well as its usefulness. Cautions against its limitations, its "moral relativism," and its "unsound" psychology.

1310. Styne, Marlis M. "Computers for College Writing: A Promising Beginning." Paper presented at the Chicago Universities Consortium, Cultural and Cognitive Approaches to Teaching Writing and Mathematics, Chicago, April 1987. ERIC ED 289 173. 22 pages

Enumerates the advantages and disadvantages of word processing. Includes an annotated bibliography.

1311. Tanner, Clarabel Weir. "The Criteria for Judging the Suitability of a Story for Telling." *DAI* 49 (December 1988): 1545A.

Uses the Delphi technique to identify the factors 100 selected experts considered essential for good stories and good storytellers.

1312. Tarnove, Elizabeth. "Journal Keeping Bridges Gap between Theory, Experience." *JourEd* 42 (Autumn 1988): 24–27.

Reviews the purposes of keeping journals and discusses common pitfalls.

1313. Tchudi, Stephen N. *Teaching Writing in the Content Areas: College Level*. West Haven, Conn.: NEA Professional Library, 1986. ERIC ED 296 648. 131 pages

An overview of writing across the curriculum and writing in the content areas for college teachers.

1314. Trimbur, John. "Cultural Studies and Teaching Writing." *Focuses* 1 (Fall 1988): 5–18.

Examines the "new political sensibility" in composition studies, speculating about the possibility of realizing a "literate democracy, as a popular, not an academic goal."

1315. Tuman, Myron C. "Class, Codes, and Composition: Basil Bernstein and the Critique of Pedagogy." *CCC* 39 (February 1988): 42–51.

Argues that pedagogies designed to empower disadvantaged students, without disempowering the advantaged, only sustain the existing social class structure.

1316. Turner, Judith Axler. "Books Versus Computers: The Message, Not the Medium, Is Said to Be Important for Students." *CHE* 35 (5 October 1988): A22.

Studies comparing the effectiveness of computers and workbooks are inconclusive because of the quality of the compositions, not the quality of the medium.

1317. Wahlquist, Elizabeth. "Letters: Value to Self and Society." Paper presented at the CCCC Convention, St. Louis, March 1988. ERIC ED 294 207. 18 pages

Discusses the role of letter writing in college composition courses.

1318. Warren, Thomas. "Cognitive Psychology and Instructions: New Schemes for Old Ways." Paper presented at the NCTE Convention, Los Angeles, November 1987. ERIC ED 292 104. 10 pages

Proposes using directly information from cognitive psychology about psycholinguistic processing.

1319. Watkins, Beverly T. "Endowment Chief Faults Teaching of Humanities." *CHE* 35 (21 September 1988): A1, A16-A23.

Contains the full text of NEH chief Lynn V. Cheney's address on the state of the humanities in America.

1320. Wauters, Joan K. "Non-Confrontational Critiquing Pairs: An Alternative to Verbal Peer-Response Groups." *WI* 7 (Spring-Summer 1988): 156–166.

Presents a method of responding to papers. Student authors are not present during the discussion of their papers. Written comments prompt authors to ask peer editors for a verbal clarification of the written critique.

1321. Wilson, Edward E., ed. *Creativity*. Abilene, Tex.: Texas Joint Council of Teachers of English (distributed by NCTE), 1986. 44 pages

Nine essays discuss ways of using students' own backgrounds and memories, natural speaking skills, and popular culture to develop creativity in the classroom and an interest in writing and reading fiction. Originally published as *English in Texas* 17 (Spring 1986).

1322. Wilson, Robin. "Bennett: Colleges' Trendy Lightweights Replace Classics with Nonsense." *CHE* 34 (10 February 1988): A19, A27.

Former Education Secretary William Bennett, in a speech to an association of independent colleges, complained that professors were assigning "nonsense" in lieu of classics.

1323. Winterowd, W. Ross. "Rediscovering the Essay." *JAC* 8 (1988): 146–157.

Advocates stressing the informal essay (prose lyric) in classes. Analyzes the non-hierarchical structure of essays by Didion, Thomas, and Eiseley.

See also 23, 66, 210, 216, 217, 218, 219, 254, 722, 1558

4.2   HIGHER EDUCATION

4.2.1 DEVELOPMENTAL WRITING

1324. Armstrong, Cheryl. "Reexamining Basic Writing: Lessons from Harvard's Basic Writers." *JBW* 7 (Fall 1988): 68–80.

Argues that "basic writers' problems are basic to writing." Identifies nine problems and finds useful a pedagogy focusing on meaning, fluency, revision, and confidence building.

1325. Baxter, Barbara. "Basic Writing: Breaking through the Barriers of Apathy and Fear." Paper presented at the Annual Meeting of the Southeastern Conference on English in the Two-Year College, Jackson, Miss., February 1987. ERIC ED 286 202. 13 pages

Recommends methods for improving the motivation and self-esteem of students who have difficulty writing.

1326. Bernhardt, Stephen A. "Text Revisions by Basic Writers: From Impromptu First Draft to Take-Home Revision." *RTE* 22 (October 1988): 266–280.

Finds that many basic writers can revise and improve their writing when given enough time to do so.

1327. Capossela, Toni-Lee. "Old Saws and New Perspectives." *ArEB* 30 (Winter 1988): 35–36.

Describes an assignment in which basic writers uncover inherent narratives in aphorisms.

1328. Carino, Peter. "Introducing Basic Writers to Source Writing: A Three-Step Method in Three Lessons." *ExEx* 33 (Spring 1988): 39–42.

Provides strategies that help students bridge the gap between personal and academic writing.

1329. Collins, James L., and Joanne Bakker. "Organizing Severe Writing Problems for Instruction." *CompC* 1 (February 1988): 6–7.

Advises distinguishing among problems in content, form, sentences, and words.

1330. Comer, James P. "Educating Poor Minority Children." *SAm* 259 (November 1988): 42–48.

Describes a model curriculum in which parents and teachers collaborate to improve the reading, writing, and math skills of economically disadvantaged minority students.

1331. Crain, Jeanie, Jane Frick, Karen Fulton, and Christa McCay. "Revised Development Program at Missouri Western State College Receives Praise, Shows Good Results." *CompC* 1 (September 1988): 5–6.

New methodologies benefited high-risk students in the authors' classes.

1332. Cross, Geoffrey A. "What Are They Really Doing? Observations of Basic and Professional Writers Using Word Processing." Paper presented at the CCCC Convention, St. Louis, March 1988. ERIC ED 295 180. 19 pages

Reports on two qualitative studies of basic and professional writers as they write on word processors.

1333. Cullen, Robert. "Computer-Assisted Composition: A Case Study of Six Developmental Writers." *CollM* 6 (August 1988): 202–212.

Describes the planning, drafting, and revising strategies of first-year developmental writers composing with Wandah, a word-processing package that includes computerized prewriting and revising aids.

1334. Deem, James M., and Sandra A. Engel. "Developing Literacy through Transcription." *JBW* 7 (Fall 1988): 99–107.

Advocates a holistic approach to teaching basic writing and developmental reading. Explains two transcription projects, an oral history and a newsletter, that place students' writing at the center of a course.

1335. Deem, James M., and Sandra A. Engel. "The Educational Oral History: An Approach to Teaching Basic English." *TETYC* 15 (May 1988): 105–109.

Students in a team-taught developmental reading and writing course wrote their own and their teachers' educational histories.

1336. DeMario, Marilyn Bohman. "Tea and Literacy: An Ethnographic Inquiry into the Social Constructions of Literacy by Basic Reading and Writing Students." *DAI* 49 (November 1988): 1080A.

Examines how a small group of basic writing students developed and "enacted their own versions of academic literacy."

1337. Deutsch, Lucille. "Word Processing: A Motivational Force in Developmental English: A Comparison of Two Developmental English Classes." Paper presented at the National Association for Developmental Education, Orlando, March 1988. ERIC ED 295 702. 47 pages

Studies how word processing motivates students in developmental composition courses.

1338. Dobie, Ann B. "Orthography Revisited: A Response to Kristine Anderson [*JBW* 6 (Fall 1987)]." *JBW* 7 (Spring 1988): 82–83.

Lists major points of agreement between Dobie and Anderson on spelling instruction. Re-emphasizes the importance of using inductive, efficient, and productive approaches to spelling improvement.

1339. Dobler, Judith M., and William J. Amorielle. "Comments on Writing: Features That Affect Student Performance." *JR* 32 (December 1988): 214–223.

Studies the correlation between high school students' success in writing and tutors' comments on the writing.

1340. Enright, Gwyn. "Developmental Education and the Liberal Arts: An Interview with Arthur M. Cohen." *JDEd* 12 (November 1988): 16–18.

Asserts that remediation and learning assistance are central to the mission of a college.

1341. Fitzgerald, Sallyanne H. "Relationships between Conferencing and Movement between General and Specific in Basic Writers' Compositions." *DAI* 48 (June 1988): 3040A.

Finds no significant difference between writing samples that move from general to specific after comparing conferenced with nonconferenced essays.

1342. Greenberg, Karen Joy. "Ethical Dimensions in Instructor's Manuals for the Basic Course in Communication." *DAI* 48 (March 1988): 2193A.

Assesses idealized and realized depictions of ethical accountability in instructor's manuals for basic communication courses. Sees ideological conflicts.

1343. Hashimoto, Irvin. "Pain and Suffering: Apostrophes and Academic Life." *JBW* 7 (Fall 1988): 91–98.

Shows what happens as students and teachers "wade into the wonderful sea of arbitrary punctuation." Encourages teachers to be more tolerant of punctuation errors.

1344. House, Elizabeth, William M. Dodd, and John W. Presley. "Problem Solving: A Link between Developmental Writing and Reading." *TETYC* 15 (May 1988): 81–87.

Presents strategies for helping students integrate approaches to reading and writing.

1345. Huot, Brian. "Reading-Writing Connections on the College Level." *TETYC* 15 (May 1988): 90–98.

Advocates reintegrating reading and writing instruction.

1346. Huot, Brian. "Working with Charlotte: A Close Look at Tutoring the Special Learner." *WLN* 13 (November 1988): 9–12.

Describes extensive work with a special learner. Concludes that such students can succeed but need structure, time, and constant encouragement.

1347. James, Deborah J. "A Distant Place, an Uncertain People: A Participant Observation of a Basic Writing Class." *DAI* 48 (February 1988): 2008A.

Examines what kinds of students make up a basic writing population and what contexts they encounter in basic writing courses.

1348. Kelly, William Jude. "Personality Differences between Basic and Standard Writers." *DAI* 49 (October 1988): 753A.

Using the Myers-Briggs Type Indicator, this study finds that basic writers displayed significant differences in personality types. Proposes strategies for accomodating them.

1349. Liebman, JoAnne. "Contrastive Rhetoric: Students as Ethnographers." *JBW* 7 (Fall 1988): 6–27.

Describes a project involving basic writers as co-researchers. Advocates investigating further "how writing purposes and processes might differ across cultures."

1350. Martinez, Joseph, and Nancy Martinez. "Are Basic Writers Cognitively Deficient?" Paper presented at the Western College Reading and Learning Association, Albuquerque, N.M., April 1987. ERIC ED 285 179. 12 pages

Two controlled studies of basic writers suggest that they are unfamiliar with writing tasks and conventions rather than cognitively immature.

1351. McAllister, Carole, and Richard Louth. "The Effect of Word Processing on the Quality of Basic Writers' Revisions." *RTE* 22 (December 1988): 417–427.

In this comparison of three groups of college writers, results indicate that word processing positively affected the quality of revision in basic writers.

1352. Mercadante, Richard A. "Classical Dialectic and Philosophy in the English Classroom." *Leaflet* 87 (Fall 1988): 22–31.

Describes the principles of Socratic dialectic and how to guide students in writing such dialogues.

1353. Plummer, Joseph. "Curing Students of Passive Voice." *JourEd* 42 (Winter 1988): 33–36.

Discusses the purposes of active and passive voice, giving suggestions to help writers minimize the use of passive voice.

1354. Puangmali, Suraprom. "Effects of Modal Instruction on Recall from Reading Informative Discourse." *DAI* 49 (September 1988): 471A.

Examines how instruction in three modes of text organization—classification, description, and narration—affected college readers' written recall.

1355. Ricker, Curtis Eugene. "Teaching Writing through Conferencing: A Survey and a Study of Its Effect on Basic Writers." *DAI* 49 (September 1988): 450A.

Attempts to verify the usefulness of teacher-student conferences in basic writing instruction.

1356. Robertson, Elizabeth. "Moving from Expressive Writing to Academic Discourse." *WCJ* 9 (Fall-Winter 1988): 21–28.

Describes a case study in which a student's confidence in writing increased as she constructed formal essays based on expressive observations from her reading journals.

1357. Rosenberg, Ruth Herzberger. "Text Mapping as Procedural Facilitation for Teaching Argument to Basic Writers in a Community College." *DAI* 49 (September 1988): 423A.

Adapts a mapping procedure, based on Comprone's wheel and taught to 36 basic writers, to argumentative writing.

1358. Roskelly, Hephzibah, ed. "Survival of the Fittest: Ten Years in a Basic Writing Program." *JBW* 7 (Spring 1988): 13–29.

Traces the evolution of the University of Louisville's program from 1976 to 1987 through personal accounts by the program's first seven directors.

1359. Rothstein-Vandergriff, Joan, and Joan Tedrow Gilson. "Collaboration with Basic Writers in the Composition Classroom." Paper presented at the CCCC Convention, St. Louis, March 1988. ERIC ED 294 220. 16 pages

Studies two college composition classes to determine why collaborative writing often fails.

1360. Royar, Robert D. "Designing Software and Using Computer Networks to Teach Basic Writing." *DAI* 48 (May 1988): 2825A.

Describes a way to use computers that emphasizes their strengths and allows the teacher to adapt the computer to the classroom.

1361. Schatzberg-Smith, Kathleen. "Effects of Dialogue Journal Writing on Study Habits and Attitudes of Underprepared College Students." Paper presented at the Annual Symposium on Developmental/Remedial Education, Glenville, N.Y., April 1988. ERIC ED 296 755. 45 pages

Explores the effects of structured dialogue journal writing on the study habits and attitudes of underprepared college students.

1362. Smith, Lois, and Greg Smith. "A Multivariate Analysis of Remediation Efforts with Developmental Students." *TETYC* 15 (February 1988): 45–52.

Remedial students completing a grammar course with tutoring had higher grades in freshman composition than students who had passed the placement test. The grammar course without tutoring was less successful.

1363. Sollisch, James. "Collaborative Learning: At the Intersection of Reading, Writing, and Response." *TETYC* 15 (May 1988): 99–104.

Collaborative learning offers both reading and writing practice for developmental students. Includes suggestions for encouraging active reading.

1364. Stumhofer, Nancy. *The Impact of Computer-Assisted Instruction on Students' Knowledge of Basic Writing Skills*. Schuylkill Haven, Pa.: Pennsylvania State University, 1988. ERIC ED 293 600. 25 pages

Reports on how a state college uses CAI to teach grammar and usage in basic writing.

1365. Stygall, Gail. "Politics and Proof in Basic Writing." *JBW* 7 (Fall 1988): 28–41.

Describes curricular changes involved in a "program-wide shift from a traditional product-centered course to a process course." Presents statistical proof of the latter's effectiveness.

1366. Swope, John W. "Improvisation: Creating a Context for Shakespeare." *Leaflet* 87 (Spring 1988): 13–18.

Describes improvisation as a strategy for aiding comprehension because it activates students' prior knowledge and provides a cultural context.

1367. Thompson, Diane P. "Conversational Networking: Why the Teacher Gets Most of the Lines." *CollM* 6 (August 1988): 193–201.

A study focusing on the benefits of teacher-centered discourse for computer conferencing in writing classes.

See also 111, 112, 130, 879, 946, 1100, 1131,

1142, 1378, 1393, 1403, 1405, 1408, 1572, 1739, 1748, 1763, 1779, 1789

4.2.2 FRESHMAN COMPOSITION

1368. Arms, Valarie Meliotes. "The Right Answer to the Wrong Question." *CC* 6 (November 1988): 33–46.

Discusses a first-year composition course seeking to meld creativity and visualization with writing on a Macintosh. Contrasts the course with advanced courses for engineers.

1369. Bailey, Richard E. "Case Writing in the Composition Class." *Issues* 1 (Fall 1988): 50–63.

Questions the usefulness of expressive writing in composition courses. Argues that responding to cases helps students overcome problems of voice and audience.

1370. Balester, Valerie. "The Development of the Writer's *Ethos* in Collaborative Learning." Paper presented at the CCCC Convention, St. Louis, March 1988. ERIC ED 294 230. 13 pages

Studies how student writers developed ethical approaches to argument through collaborative learning.

1371. Barker, Ian Churchill. "The College-Level Academic Skills Test and a Computer-Based Writing Course." *DAI* 49 (September 1988): 448A.

A case study of seven community college students enrolled in freshman composition. Assesses the word processing and composing strategies of inexperienced writers.

1372. Bergdahl, David. "A Sequence of Assignments Focusing on Language Use." *ExEx* 33 (Spring 1988): 28–31.

Provides nine writing assignments that require students to observe language around them.

1373. Black, Kathleen Marie Kiel. "An Investigation of the Relationship between the Ability to Analyze Audiences and the Ability to Adapt Discourse to the Audience in the Persuasive

Writing of College Students." *DAI* 48 (February 1988): 2005A.

Examines audience awareness and its effect on persuasive writing.

1374. Blanchard, Lydia. "Freshman English and the Academy: Preparing Students for Writing in the Disciplines." Paper presented at the CCCC Convention, Atlanta, March 1987. ERIC ED 292 092. 14 pages

Provides an alternative curriculum for freshman composition by sequencing increasingly more complex, school-based writing tasks.

1375. Bridges, Jean B. "Honors Composition in the Two-Year College." *TETYC* 15 (February 1988): 38–44.

Describes an honors course in freshman composition based on Moffett's modes of discourse.

1376. Burghdurf, Cheryl J. "Conversing in Communities: An Approach to Teaching Writing." *DAI* 48 (May 1988): 2823A.

Concludes that classroom conversation in a supportive environment improved freshman composition students' attitudes, confidence, and desire to improve.

1377. Chase, Dennis. "Pass the Peek Freans, Please: Some Food for Thought in Composition Class." *CLAJ* 31 (March 1988): 309–323.

Recounts using food-based freewritings, themes, and peer-analysis assignments, offering several examples. Brainstorming, creativity, motivation, and the use of details are among the benefits.

1378. Cheney, Fred. "If It Isn't a Dialog, It Isn't Communication." *JTW* 7 (Spring-Summer 1988): 51–55.

Suggests ways to continue a dialogue about written products even after they are submitted for grading: avoiding long papers, using open-ended questions, and accepting papers from other disciplines.

1379. Comprone, Joseph J. "Classical 'Elementary Exercises' and In-Process Composing." *FEN* 17 (Fall 1988): 5–13.

Describes Renaissance rhetorical exercises that support a contemporary composition unit when modified by purpose, context, and community.

1380. Connors, Patricia. "Making Private Writing Public: Teaching Expressive Writing in the Composition Class." *TETYC* 15 (February 1988): 25–27.

Discusses expressive writing taught via students' journals.

1381. Cornell, Cynthia, and Robert Newton. "Collaborative Revision on a Computer." Paper presented at the CCCC Convention, St. Louis, March 1988. ERIC ED 295 155. 27 pages

Investigates the effects of large screen computer instruction on revision in a college composition course.

1382. Cox, Diana. "Developing Software for Freshman Composition: Sentence Patterns." *CollM* 6 (May 1988): 161–164.

Describes Sentence Patterns, software developed to instruct students in using sentences.

1383. Davis, Kevin, Wendy Bishop, and Penny Smith. "Composing at the Word Processor: Confessions and Comments." *TETYC* 15 (May 1988): 110–114.

Three writing teachers examine their own use of word processing and make suggestions for computer-oriented classes.

1384. Davis, M. Francine. "Asking the 'Irresistible Question' and Other Virtues of Interview Assignments." Paper presented at the CCCC Convention, St. Louis, March 1988. ERIC ED 296 349. 10 pages

Discusses the value of interviewing in a college composition course.

1385. Davis, Wesley K. "The Effects of Process-Centered and Form-Centered Instruction on the Writing of College Freshmen." *DAI* 49 (October 1988): 752A.

Compares two approaches as they influenced writing growth among 97 freshmen.

Indicates that techniques from both approaches can benefit students.

1386. Deming, Mary Penelope. "The Effects of Word Processing on Basic College Writers' Revision Strategies, Writing Apprehension, and Writing Quality while Composing in the Expository Mode." *DAI* 48 (March 1988): 2263A.

Suggests that word processing facilitates microstructure revisions but does not improve writing quality or lower apprehension.

1387. Devet, Bonnie. "Figurative Language in Students' Writing." *FEN* 17 (Fall 1988): 24–26.

Examines students' writings for figurative language and advocates teaching some figures of speech to build on available strategies.

1388. Devet, Bonnie. "Rewriting Classical Persuasion as Rogerian Argument." *ExEx* 33 (Spring 1988): 8–10.

Presents an assignment that requires students to write a persuasion paper using the arrangement and style of classical rhetoric and then revise it into a Rogerian argument.

1389. Droll, Belinda Wood. "Teaching College Composition Freshmen to Structure Discourse: The Effects of Summarizing Versus Sentence Outlining." *DAI* 48 (March 1988): 2263A.

Indicates that summarizing texts is more effective than sentence outlining and can improve the overall quality of students' essays.

1390. Garrett-Petts, W. F. "Developing a Community of Readers: Computer Networking in the Freshman Literature Classroom." *EQ* 21 (1988): 29–40.

Argues that we need to concentrate on using the computer to encourage interactive, collaborative learning.

1391. Gray, Dabney. "Flux: The Shifting Role of the Composition Teacher." *FEN* 17 (Fall 1988): 29–33.

A personal essay exploring the author's movement from a traditional evaluative stance to one that gives more control to the student.

1392. Hamilton-Wieler, Sharon. "Writing as a Thought Process: Site of a Struggle." *JTW* 7 (Fall-Winter 1988): 167–179.

Writing is a mode of inquiry that dialectically incorporates convention and choice. Analyzes student writers and composition classrooms to confirm the interrelationship.

1393. Harris, Jeane. "Risky Business: Malcolm X, Student-Centered Learning and Teacher *Ethos*." *JTW* 7 (Spring-Summer 1988): 19–25.

Uses a compelling *ethos* to motivate students' taking responsibility for their own learning. Gives an assignment featuring Malcolm X in a text and in rap music.

1394. Harris, Jeanette. "Rethinking Invention." *FEN* 17 (Fall 1988): 13–16.

Suggests that the teaching of invention should include using both introspection and exploration of subjects.

1395. Herbert, Kathleen. "Collaborative Learning: Magic in the Classroom." *ExEx* 34 (Fall 1988): 24–28.

Provides four bibliographic references to research on collaborative learning and explains how to plan and execute collaborative activities in the classroom.

1396. Hesse, Douglas D. "Insiders and Outsiders: A Writing Course Heuristic." *WI* 7 (Winter 1988): 85–94.

Describes a writing course in which the class operates as a discourse community to investigate the subject of discourse communities.

1397. Hillbrink, Lucinda. "Teaching for the University: Is 'Good Writing' Relative?" *CalE* 24 (May–June 1988): 12.

Concludes that freshmen writers should be advised to "know your audience."

1398. Holladay, Sylvia. "Integrating Reading and Writing." *TETYC* 15 (October 1988): 187–194.

Discusses the relationship between reading and writing skills, offering classroom suggestions.

1399. Holtz, Daniel James. "Interrelationships between the Reading Comprehension and Writing Achievement of College Freshmen and Their Abilities to Reconstruct Scrambled Expository Paragraphs." *DAI* 48 (January 1988): 1680A.

Studies 60 students to determine if extended practice in reconstructing scrambled paragraphs is warranted.

1400. Hopper, Jeane. "Sense-ational Writing for Learning." *ExEx* 34 (Fall 1988): 29–33.

Describes a series of activities designed to enhance students' understanding of the five senses and to strengthen the use of detail in writing.

1401. Hunt, Maurice. "*Imitatio* Revived: A Curriculum Based upon Mimesis." *FEN* 17 (Fall 1988): 16–19.

A brief review of classical *imitatio* leads to a pedagogical tactic, imitating model student essays.

1402. Ivy, Diana Kay. "Communication in the Socialization Process of Nontraditional College Students." *DAI* 48 (February 1988): 1929A.

A study of the socialization processes of 24 traditional and nontraditional students during one college semester.

1403. Jackson, Robert M. "Writing: A Line of Reasoning." *JTW* 7 (Spring-Summer 1988): 9–17.

Provides activities to encourage students' awareness of evaluative measures and of the writing process. Suggests strategies for monitoring the writing process.

1404. Janda, Mary Ann. "Smell the Roses or Smell the Coffee: Reflective Writing on Expressive Expository Writing, and This Thing We Call Mechanics." *JTW* 7 (Fall-Winter 1988): 187–192.

Models thinking aloud about expressive writing in an expressive essay.

1405. Jenkinson, Edward B. "Learning to Write/Writing to Learn." *PhiDK* 69 (June 1988): 712–717.

Discusses the prevalence of grammar and workbook exercises in English classes. Suggests specific writing activities for average students and explains how these experiences enhance learning.

1406. Johnson, Diane B. "Show Me What You Mean: Student Posters Teach Lengthy/Wordy Material." *ExEx* 34 (Fall 1988): 44–46.

In this assignment, designing posters teaches students reasoning fallacies.

1407. Knox, William L. "First Semester Composition in the Life-Worlds of University Students." *DAI* 48 (May 1988): 2798A.

Explains how student writing networks that extend beyond the classroom can help advance literacy.

1408. Krest, Margie. "Monitoring Student Writing: How Not to Avoid the Draft." *JTW* 7 (Spring-Summer 1988): 27–39.

Provides a rationale for reacting to drafts, gives three examples of monitoring freshman composition students, and offers four general suggestions for monitoring.

1409. Lawton, David L. "Composition Courses for College Freshmen Are Ineffective: They Should Be Abolished." *CHE* 35 (21 September 1988): B1-B2.

Argues that research shows college writing courses to be ineffective. Advocates dropping the classes and using the funds for writing instruction in high schools and elementary classrooms.

1410. Looper, Travis. "Exploratory Discourse: From a Peak in Darien." *ET* 19 (Spring 1988): 9–12.

Advocates teaching exploratory thinking and writing. Gives several suggestions for composition and literature courses.

1411. MacKenzie, Nancy. "Prewriting with Writer-Based Drawings." *ExEx* 33 (Spring 1988): 3–5.

Presents an "idea-sketching" exercise and provides example drawings.

1412. Maimon, Elaine P. "Cultivating the Prose Garden." *PhiDK* 69 (June 1988): 734–739.

Urges encouragement and "careful cultivation" of ideas in students' essays to develop students' confidence and potential.

1413. McClish, Glen. "Controversy in the Composition Classroom: Debate as a Mode of Prewriting." Paper presented at the CCCC Convention, St. Louis, March 1988. ERIC ED 295 189. 13 pages

Discusses how controversy and debate can be used as a prewriting technique in college composition classes.

1414. McDaid, John. "Getting Down to Nets and Bytes." *CompC* 1 (May 1988): 4–6.

Offers advice on "getting started in computers and composition."

1415. Meyer, James William. "Paragraphs in Process: What Student Writers Really Do." *DAI* 48 (March 1988): 2264A.

Concludes that students are more aware of paragraphing in revision than they are in initial drafting.

1416. Miccinati, Jeannette L. "Mapping the Terrain: Connecting Reading with Academic Writing." *JR* 31 (March 1988): 542–552.

Uses graphic pictures to enhance metacognitive skills, to illustrate relationships between ideas, and to help students write more cohesive papers.

1417. O'Friel, Patricia. "Getting to Know 'The Watcher at the Gates': A Writing Exercise." *ExEx* 34 (Fall 1988): 19–21.

Explains a writing assignment that encourages students to personify the inner critics or "watchers" of their own writing.

1418. Owen, William Davis. "The Effects of Learning Comma Usage through Instruction in Intonation Cues." *DAI* 48 (May 1988): 2824A.

Presents research findings and teaching techniques.

1419. Pixton, William H. "Toward Demystifying Voice: An Approach for Novice Writers." *RSQ* 18 (Summer 1988): 31–47.

Reviews current discussions of voice and provides methods for promoting personal voice in students' texts.

1420. Ranieri, Paul H. " 'A Very Dull Meat-Ax': Sacrificing Composition and the Humanities to the Great Competency Gods." *JGE* 39 (1987): 54–68.

Integrates the work of Isocrates and Ernest Boyer in creating a writing course that the author calls a humanistic "cultural workshop."

1421. Reynolds, John Frederick. "The Effect of Collaborative Peer Revision Groups on Audience-Consciousness in the Writing of College Freshmen." *DAI* 48 (June 1988): 3065A.

Finds that audience consciousness is greater among students who revise in collaborative groups than among those who revise on their own.

1422. Risk, Tracy A. "Understanding Math through Language." *ExEx* 34 (Fall 1988): 34–36.

Explains how assigning a problem of the week can enable students to observe and comment on their own approach to problem solving.

1423. Rocha, Mark. "The Unsurprising Case against Television Literacy." *FEN* 17 (Fall 1988): 27–29.

Critiques Mano's research [*WI* 5 (Spring 1986)] on the usefulness of television in improving literacy, contending that composition demands an active rhetoric.

1424. Roen, Duane H., and R. J. Willey. "The Effects of Audience Awareness on Drafting and Revising." *RTE* 22 (February 1988): 75–88.

A three-treatment study of 60 freshmen. Concludes that students with instruction in audience improved their holistically scored essays most when attention was focused on audience during revising.

1425. Ross, Donald. "Computer-Based Writing Assignments." *CAC* 3 (Summer 1988): 31–42.

Reviews theories of communication and discusses how Access or a similar computer program can guide students into developing their ideas.

1426. Slater, Wayne H., Michael F. Graves, Sherry B. Scott, and Teresa M. Redd-Boyd. "Discourse Structure and College Freshmen's Recall and Production of Expository Text." *RTE* 22 (February 1988): 45–61.

A three-treatment study of 126 freshmen. The experimental group with instruction in discourse structures achieved higher scores on posttest writing assignments.

1427. Snipes, Wilson. "A Modest Proposal: In Defense of Digressive Writing." *FEN* 17 (Fall 1988): 19–24.

Explores the importance of digression for student writers by questioning the value of uncritically accepting set patterns or forms of writing.

1428. Sosville, Jerri Knowlton. "The Ethical Appeal of Teaching Ethical Appeal." *ExEx* 34 (Fall 1988): 7–10.

Helps students understand that a writer's ethical appeal includes carefully presenting and treating the topic, research sources, and mechanics.

1429. Steedman, Carol S. "Reasoning and Decision Making: The Development of a Short Text for the Adult Learner." *DAI* 48 (June 1988): 3034A.

Using Aristotle's rhetoric to teach critical thinking and dialogical reasoning improved decision making among freshmen.

1430. Stracke, Richard. "The Effect of a Full-Service Computer Room on Student Writing." *CC* 5 (April 1988): 51–56.

Describes setting up a first-year composition course in a room that became a supportive environment because both the computers and full-service support were located there.

1431. Stroble, Elizabeth, and Paul E. Stroble. "Simulated Garbage: Leaps of Inference from Artifacts." *ExEx* 34 (Fall 1988): 3–6.

Describes an archeological writing exercise based on a list of items and designed to elicit student inferences about a culture's religion.

1432. Tebeaux, Elizabeth. "The Trouble with Employees' Writing May Be Freshman Composition." *TETYC* 15 (February 1988): 9–19.

Composition courses fail to prepare students for writing in later careers. Such courses emphasize essays while neglecting to teach visual design strategies and deductive organization.

1433. Vockell, Edward L., and Eileen Schwartz. "Microcomputers to Teach English Composition." *CollM* 6 (May 1988): 148–154.

Concludes that college students using microcomputers wrote more coherent, unified papers than control students because the computer allowed more time for higher-level activities, not just mechanical ones.

1434. Werner, Charles Dantzler. "Responses of College Readers with Different Cultural Backgrounds to a Short Story." *DAI* 48 (March 1988): 2266A.

Concludes that written responses to a text were a product more of personal style and classroom experience than of cultural background.

1435. Weston, James Thomas. "Toward a Contextual Approach to Cliches." *DAI* 49 (August 1988): 248A.

Gives a model to determine whether using cliches is legitimate, arguing that traditional evaluations dismiss the validity of cliches in composition.

1436. Whitaker, Elaine E. "Creating an Essay by Committee (with or without Computer)." *ExEx* 34 (Fall 1988): 22–23.

An assignment with the object of alerting students to the importance of a thesis, supporting evidence, and collaboration in constructing a five-paragraph essay. The assignment also demonstrates the benefits of word processing.

See also 1333, 1343, 1446, 1447, 1450, 1511, 1572

4.2.3 ADVANCED COMPOSITION

1437. Brozo, William G. "Applying a Reader Response Heuristic to Expository Text." *JR* 32 (November 1988): 140–145.

Describes using written responses to a text, then moving to personal narratives.

1438. Carroll, Jeffrey. "The Vulgar Canon and Its Uses in the Classroom." Paper presented at the CCCC Convention, St. Louis, March 1988. ERIC ED 294 194. 12 pages

Using the theories of Bakhtin, suggests ways of using argumentative literature in the writing classroom.

1439. Covino, William. "Defining Advanced Composition: Contributions from the History of Rhetoric." *JAC* 8 (1988): 113–122.

Modern interpretations notwithstanding, classical theorists posit advanced thinking and writing as nonformulaic, tolerating intellectual ambiguity.

1440. Davis, Kevin. "The Dimensions of Talk in Peer Groups Negotiating Control in Writing Group Conversation." Paper presented at the CCCC Convention, St. Louis, March 1988. ERIC ED 294 232. 15 pages

Studies five college freshmen in peer group activities, revealing how peer group conversation resembles nonteaching conversation.

1441. Dickerson, Mary Jane. "A Voice of One's Own: Creating Writing Identities." Paper presented at the CCCC Convention, St. Louis, March 1988. ERIC ED 294 178. 11 pages

Examines the role that autobiographical writing can play in the composition class.

1442. Gaunder, Eleanor Parks. "Case Studies of Re-Entering Students in Advanced Composition: Composing Using the Word Processor." Paper presented at the CCCC Convention, St. Louis, March 1988. ERIC ED 296 342. 15 pages

Examines how re-entering students revise on the word processor.

1443. Hollis, Karyn. "Building a Context for Critical Literacy: Student Writers as Critical Theorists." *WI* 7 (Spring-Summer 1988): 122–130.

Uses Raymond Geuss's *The Idea of a Critical Theory: Habermas and the Frankfurt School* to focus on context and to develop a means for its critique.

1444. Logan, Shirley W. "A Study of Four Undergraduate Computer-Writers." *CollM* 6 (May 1988): 135–146.

Studies the "meaning assigned to the activities of writing at a computer" by analyzing advanced composition students' attitudes, writing strategies, and documents.

1445. Redd-Boyd, Teresa Marie Camper. "The Effects of Audience Specifications on the Quality of Undergraduate Writing." *DAI* 48 (February 1988): 2009A.

Examines the effects of real and imaginary teacher-specified audiences in an advanced composition course.

1446. Schweibert, John. "Learning about Writing on the Job." *ExEx* 33 (Spring 1988): 6–7.

Presents an assignment that requires students to conduct interviews with professionals about the kinds of writing they do.

1447. Scriven, Karen. "Composition as Content: Clarifying the Limits of Literature in the Writing Classroom." *WI* 7 (Spring-Summer 1988): 115–121.

Posits that writing assignments based on literature can be used to enhance exposition because they "emphasize cognitive and writing skills relevant to any discipline."

1448. Simpson, Jeanne. "Word Processing in Freshman Composition." *CAC* 3 (Summer 1988): 11–17.

Finds that CAI does not affect t-unit length but does cause students to write longer, more coherent essays.

1449. Sullivan, Patricia. "Desktop Publishing: A Powerful Tool for Advanced Composition Courses." *CCC* 39 (October 1988): 344–347.

Defines desktop publishing and recommends it for spurring creativity, increasing sensitivity to layout, encouraging collaboration, and providing students with a useful skill.

1450. Thaden, Barbara Z. "Derrida in the Composition Class: Deconstructing Arguments." *WI* 7 (Spring-Summer 1988): 131–137.

Uses binary opposition as a questioning heuristic to examine arguments for weaknesses and unstated premises.

See also 1377, 1492

4.2.4 BUSINESS COMMUNICATION

1451. Arnold, Vanessa Dean, and John C. Malley. "Communication: The Missing Link in the Challenger Disaster." *BABC* 51 (December 1988): 12–14.

Argues that management and technical personnel need to practice improved communication to avoid disasters in technical projects.

1452. Banset, Elizabeth A., and Gerald M. Parsons. "Understanding Criteria Development:

A Rationale and Method for Instruction." *JTWC* 18 (1988): 63–73.

One way to develop students' problem-solving skills is to teach them to develop criteria for evaluating the merits of potential solutions to problems.

1453. Barbour, Dennis H. "The Word Processing Lab in the Business Writing Course." *BABC* 51 (September 1988): 19–20.

Explains how students benefit from time in a word-processing lab.

1454. Beach, Richard, and Chris M. Anson. "The Pragmatics of Memo Writing: Developmental Differences in the Use of Rhetorical Strategies." *WC* 5 (April 1988): 157–183.

Compares rhetorical strategies used by adolescents and adults in writing memos during a roleplaying session.

1455. Becker, Susan, and Edwina Jordan. "Will the Real Job Applicant Please Stand Up?" *BABC* 51 (December 1988): 22–26.

Suggests ways in which female job applicants can write successful resumes.

1456. Bennett, Kaye, and Steven C. Rhodes. "Writing Apprehension and Writing Intensity in Business and Industry." *JBC* 25 (Winter 1988): 25–39.

Discusses results of a questionnaire developed to measure the writing intensity of a particular job. Correlations with Daly's measure of anxiety show that the most anxious writers are in the lowest intensity jobs.

1457. Blyler, Nancy Roundy. "The Components of Purpose and Professional Communication Pedagogy." *JTWC* 18 (1988): 23–33.

Discusses four components of purpose in professional writing: the writer's viewpoint, the writing situation, the reader's viewpoint, and purpose related to discourse type.

1458. Bosley, Deborah. "Writing Internships: Building Bridges between Academia and Business." *JBTC* 2 (January 1988): 103–113.

Chronicles the development of the undergraduate internship program at Millikin University. Internships can increase curriculum visibility for English departments and enhance job prospects for liberal arts majors.

1459. Connor, Jennifer J. "Research in Business Communication: A Plea for Originality and Relevance in Pedagogic Examples." *BABC* 51 (September 1988): 21–24.

Explains why business communication textbooks need to use fresh examples of communication principles. Based on qualitative research.

1460. Cosgrove, Cornelius. "A Unique Perspective: Two-Year College English Faculty and Our Students' Future Writing." *TETYC* 15 (October 1988): 180–186.

Research into job-related writing encourages teachers to "expand our notion of relevance."

1461. Crow, Peter. "Plain English: What Counts besides Readability?" *JBC* 25 (Winter 1988): 87–95.

Argues that plain English is not measurable by stylistic features but is a function of company attitudes and values.

1462. Douglas, George H., ed. *Teaching Business Communication Two*. Urbana, Ill.: Association for Business Communication, 1988. 300 pages

A collection of 38 essays grouped into five categories: a word to the teacher, course curricula and content, teaching methods and techniques, grading practices, and teaching aids.

1463. Dukes, Thomas. "I Was a Victim of the Process Approach." *TWT* 15 (Fall 1988): 78–83.

Advocates a mixture of product and process approaches to instruction in business and technical writing classes.

1464. Dukes, Thomas. *"The Wall Street Journal* in the Business Writing Classroom." *BABC* 51 (March 1988): 25–26.

Describes an assignment in critical reading and writing, using the *Wall Street Journal*.

1465. Dukes, Thomas. "Writing and Responsibility: A New Emphasis for the Student Company." *BABC* 51 (June 1988): 10–11.

Describes business writing assignments that encourage students to take group work seriously.

1466. Estrin, Herman A. "Graduate Engineers Evaluate Their In-House Oral Presentation Course." *JTWC* 18 (1988): 135–142.

Describes and evaluates a course that uses presentations made on closed-circuit television.

1467. Figgins, Ross. "The Gutenberg 2001: What Desktop Publishing Could Mean to Business Communicators." *BABC* 51 (June 1988): 1–4.

Discusses the effects of desktop publishing on business communication and business writing instruction.

1468. Galle, William P., Jr., and Olof H. Lundberg, Jr. "Employment Skills in the Basic Business Communication Course." *BABC* 51 (December 1988): 27–31.

Presents results of a survey of ABC members concerning the teaching of employment skills in business communication courses.

1469. Gerson, Steven. "Humanism in Technical/Business Communication: Theory Versus Application." *JTWC* 18 (1988): 345–353.

Argues that students and seminar participants can be taught to humanize correspondence through personalization, which includes considering benefits to readers and embodying the principles of participative management.

1470. Gigliotti, Carol C. "Teaching Intercultural Communication 'Interculturally.'" *BABC* 51 (March 1988): 27–28.

Describes how to plan and conduct a foreign study tour in which students visit foreign companies to observe cultural differences in offices.

1471. Golen, Steven P., and David H. Lynch. "How to Integrate Articles in a Business Communication Class." *BABC* 51 (March 1988): 26–27.

Explains methods of using professional and academic articles in written and oral assignments.

1472. Goodrich, Elizabeth A. "Researching the Organization: The Career Library and the Application Letter." *BABC* 51 (June 1988): 22–23.

Describes how a career library can be used as a resource for a job application assignment in a business writing class.

1473. Gordon, Ronald D. "The Difference between Feeling Defensive and Feeling Understood." *JBC* 25 (Winter 1988): 53–64.

Students' responses to an extensive checklist were used to develop a list of feelings involved when the receiver of a message feels "understood" or "defensive."

1474. Guinn, Dorothy Margaret. "The Case for Self-Generated Cases." *BABC* 51 (June 1988): 4–10.

Explains how business writing students can use "self-generated cases" that pertain to their own fields of study. Gives examples of cases.

1475. Hager, Peter J. "Incorporating the Journal Article into the Business Communication Classroom." *BABC* 51 (June 1988): 11–16.

Describes the stages of an assignment to write a journal article that complements an analytical report assignment.

1476. Haggblade, Berle. "Has Technology Solved the Spelling Problem?" *BABC* 51 (March 1988): 23–25.

Analyzes proofreading errors made in a business report assignment and discusses the effectiveness of electronic spelling checkers.

1477. Hagge, John. "Presenting the Teacher-Based Case: Discourse Analysis in the Business Communication Class." *BABC* 51 (March 1988): 5–12.

Explains how linguistic theory supports the teacher-based case assignment and gives an example of such an assignment.

1478. Harris, Joseph. "Beyond Clarity: An Outer-Directed Approach to Business Writing." *BABC* 51 (March 1988): 1–4.

Explains how composition theory can be used to teach business writing. Describes assignments in an introductory business writing course.

1479. Hilton, Chad. "The Mixed Message: Recognizing and Eliminating This Enemy of Clear Writing." *BABC* 51 (March 1988): 18–20.

Defines the business communication problem of messages with mixed meanings, discusses their causes and effects, and offers possible solutions.

1480. Hollman, Carolyn, and John P. Fleming. "Writing a Notice of a Meeting Memo: A Simulation." *BABC* 51 (December 1988): 33–38.

Presents a business case assignment requiring students to write a memo notifying others of a meeting.

1481. Jordan, Edwina K. "A Letter Writing Unit That Works." *BABC* 51 (September 1988): 16–17.

Describes a business communication assignment. Students keep a journal of business letters based on everyday experience.

1482. Jordan, Edwina K. "Updating the Business Communications Classroom." *BABC* 51 (June 1988): 17.

Describes an assignment in which students summarize magazine articles.

1483. Kam, Hong. "China's Need to Train More Personnel in Business English." *BABC* 51 (September 1988): 27–30.

Describes a program of business English instruction in China.

1484. Kostelnick, Charles. "A Systematic Approach to Visual Language in Business Communication." *JBC* 25 (Summer 1988): 29–48.

Three modes and four levels of visual language provide a 12-cell matrix for systematically describing the visual features of a document.

1485. Mendelson, Michael. "Teaching Arrangement Inductively." *JBC* 25 (Spring 1988): 67–83.

Instead of teaching discourse formulas such as bad news letters, teachers, following Isocrates, should show students various models to let them derive formal options.

1486. Meyers, G. Douglas. "Efficient, Effective Evaluation: Grading Business Communication Assignments with the Primary Trait Scoring Method." *BABC* 51 (June 1988): 18–21.

Describes four steps for using primary trait scoring to evaluate business writing assignments. Gives examples.

1487. Meyers, G. Douglas. "Using Criterion-Based and Reader-Based Peer-Review Sheets." *BABC* 51 (March 1988): 35–39.

Describes the use of peer-review sheets in business writing classes. Gives examples of sheets.

1488. Mitchell, Robert B. "Integrating the Development of Interpersonal Listening, Speaking, and Written Communication Skills: Concluding the Business Communication Course with Realism." *BABC* 51 (June 1988): 27–29.

Describes a team assignment with written and oral components.

1489. Murphree, Carolyn T. "How Far Have You Come, Baby?" *BABC* 51 (March 1988): 29–31.

Discusses career expectations of today's female college students and suggests that business writing assignments can help introduce students to business realities.

1490. Murphy, J. William. "A Four-Step Approach to Improving Student Thinking." *BABC* 51 (June 1988): 26–27.

Describes the steps in assigning a business communication problem that emphasizes critical thinking.

1491. Nielsen, Elizabeth. "Linguistic Sexism in Business Writing Textbooks." *JAC* 8 (1988): 55–65.

Examines 14 current textbooks to show that they do not provide comprehensive instruction for avoiding sexist language. Includes recommendations.

1492. Norman, Rose. "Computer Applications for Business and Technical Writing Courses." *CollM* 6 (May 1988): 177–183.

Describes word-processing exercises used in classes. Recommends that teachers write computer-assisted instructional lessons for advanced writing classes because few commercial packages are available.

1493. Norman, Rose. "Resumex: A Computer Exercise for Teaching Resume-Writing." *TWT* 15 (Spring 1988): 162–166.

Outlines a three-step procedure for revising resumes.

1494. Novak, Mary Ann. "Training Directors' Perceptions of Secretarial and Managerial Training Needs Regarding Written Business Communication." *DAI* 49 (September 1988): 411A.

Analyzes data collected from 172 training directors: demographic information, what training is needed in written business communications, and what partnerships exist between business and colleges.

1495. O'Neill, Sheila. "Tailoring Business Communication Instruction to the Needs of Specialized Professions." *BABC* 51 (December 1988): 8–11.

Explains how to design oral and written business communication courses for specialized areas. Presents courses designed for an environmental health program.

1496. Pomerenke, Paula Jean. "A Business-Based Rationale for Incorporating the Process Approach into University Report Writing Courses." *DAI* 49 (September 1988): 411A.

Examines the composing processes of professional writers to determine if business writing students should be taught the process approach to writing.

1497. Ralston, S. Michael. "Teaching Effective Employment Interviewing." *BABC* 51 (December 1988): 32–33.

Describes the oral and written components of a business communication assignment in job interviewing.

1498. Rawlins, Claudia. "Changes in Corporate Culture and Organizational Strategy: The Effect on Technical Writers." *TWT* 15 (Winter 1988): 31–35.

Advocates shifts in current business and technical writing pedagogy to better prepare students for emerging changes in American corporate culture.

1499. Riley, Kathryn. "Conversational Implicature and Unstated Meaning in Professional Communication." *TWT* 15 (Spring 1988): 94–104.

In the light of Grice's theory, evaluates current accepted pedagogy on bad news messages.

1500. Riley, Kathryn. "Speech Act Theory and Degrees of Directness in Professional Writing." *TWT* 15 (Winter 1988): 1–29.

Develops a matrix for assessing the degree of indirectness appropriate for effective letters of request or for assessing the quality of current pedagogy.

1501. Salerno, Douglas. "An Interpersonal Approach to Writing Negative Messages." *JBC* 25 (Winter 1988): 41–51.

Despite the advice of textbooks to open with a buffer paragraph, an analysis of 22 job rejection letters shows that using a buffer should be a rhetorical variable.

1502. Sawyer, Thomas M. "The Argument about Ethics, Fairness, or Right and Wrong." *JTWC* 18 (1988): 367–375.

Recommends the pattern of logic used by appellate court justices as a way of helping students organize arguments about ethical issues.

1503. Shelby, Annette N. "A Macro Theory of Management Communication." *JBC* 25 (Spring 1988): 13–27.

Regards discourse choices as functions of aim and probable audience response, which are a function of knowledge, self-esteem, apprehension, locus of control, values, and situational variables.

1504. Shenk, Robert. "Ghost-Writing in Professional Communications." *JTWC* 18 (1988): 377–387.

Argues that the practice of writing for one's superiors' signatures is widespread. Suggests ways to help students do this effectively.

1505. Spring, Marietta. "Writing a Questionnaire Report." *BABC* 51 (September 1988): 18–19.

Describes a business communication assignment to write a report based upon the results of a questionnaire.

1506. Sterkel, Karen S. "Integrating Intercultural Communication and Report Writing in the Communication Class." *BABC* 51 (September 1988): 14–16.

Describes a team assignment to write a report on a case involving intercultural issues.

1507. Sterkel, Karen S. "The Relationship between Gender and Writing Style in Business Communication." *JBC* 25 (Fall 1988): 17–38.

Business letters written by 108 students showed no significant differences when 20 stylistic features were analyzed according to the gender of the writer.

1508. Sterkel, Karen S. "The Relationship between Gender and Writing Style in Business

Communications." *DAI* 48 (January 1988): 1585A.

Studies 51 female and 57 male undergraduates in a business communications course. Their writing was evaluated for 20 dimensions of style.

1509. Strode, Mary Lee. "A Memorandum Report Assignment Involving Magazines in Students' Major Fields." *BABC* 51 (June 1988): 17–18.

Describes a report assignment in which students' analyze magazine articles in their major fields of study.

1510. Suchan, James, and Ron Dulek. "Toward a Better Understanding of Reader Analysis." *JBC* 25 (Spring 1988): 29–45.

The treatment of reader-adaptation in business books is poor because demographic heuristics are outmoded, discourse classifications are inadequate, cases are overly simple, and corporate contexts are ignored.

1511. Tebeaux, Elizabeth. "Writing in Academe, Writing at Work: Using Visual Rhetoric to Bridge the Gap." *JTW* 7 (Fall-Winter 1988): 215–236.

Teaching visual rhetoric to employees or to students before they enter the work force improves writing dramatically. Based on experiences with in-house writing instruction.

1512. Timmons, Theresa Cullen. "Consulting in an Insurance Company: What We as Academics Can Learn." *TWT* 15 (Spring 1988): 105–110.

Reports anecdotally on the working process of writers not currently covered by research on writing processes.

1513. Varner, Iris I. "A Comparison of American and French Business Correspondence." *JBC* 25 (Fall 1988): 55–65.

Compares the recommended forms for business letters in two American and two French textbooks.

1514. Varner, Iris I., and Patricia Marcum Grogg. "Microcomputers and the Writing Process." *JBC* 25 (Summer 1988): 69–78.

Eighty-eight business students showed no differences in writing quality or apprehension when using computers, but computer users edited more and spent less total time writing than nonusers did.

1515. Waltman, John L., and Larry R. Smeltzer. "Do Good Grammar Skills Predict Success in a Business Communication Course?" *JBTC* 2 (September 1988): 59–69.

Reviews controversies surrounding grammar instruction and reports on a data-based study, suggesting a positive correlation between grammatical proficiency and course performance.

1516. Weiss, Timothy. "Promoting a Cause." *BABC* 51 (March 1988): 13–17.

Describes an assignment to write a letter promoting a "good cause." This assignment helps students consider the relationship of advertising to social issues.

1517. Weiss, Timothy. "Word Processing in the Business and Technical Writing Classroom." *CC* 5 (April 1988): 57–70.

A study of computer and noncomputer students in a business and technical writing course. Concludes that the computer group wrote significantly better papers.

1518. White, Michael C. "The Tone Scale: A Five-Part Activity for Measuring and Adjusting Tone in Business Correspondence." *BABC* 51 (March 1988): 21–23.

Describes an activity used to teach tone in college business writing classes and in writing workshops for business people.

1519. Yu, Ella Ozier. "Developing Persuasive Strategies: A Different Approach to the Job Application Assignment." *BABC* 51 (June 1988): 24–25.

Describes a recruiting campaign assignment for a business communication course.

See also 472, 499, 1102, 1203, 1432, 1530, 1548, 1555, 1557, 1619

4.2.5 SCIENTIFIC AND TECHNICAL COMMUNICATION

1520. Anderson, W. Steve. "Consulting: What It Has Taught Me about Teaching." *Issues* 1 (Fall 1988): 72–78.

Teaching courses for business and industry helps faculty members understand the work environments students will enter, establishes useful contacts, and provides access to in-house documents.

1521. Angelo, Faye, and Nell Ann Pickett. "Teachers of Technical Communication in Two-Year Colleges: Who, Why, When, and with What Results." *TETYC* 15 (May 1988): 126–134.

Presents results of a survey of technical communication teachers at two-year colleges.

1522. Banset, Elizabeth A. "Technical Writing 200." *JTWC* 18 (1988): 105–106.

A poetic description of some of the obstacles teachers of technical writing encounter.

1523. Barton, Ben F., and Marthalee S. Barton. "Narration in Technical Communication." *JBTC* 2 (January 1988): 36–48.

Observes that nonliterary narrative texts are widely studied, but not by people in technical communication. Argues for the complexity, pervasiveness, and potential advantages of studying narration.

1524. Betza, Ruth. "Rhetorical Awareness in Word-Level Revision of College Writers." *DAI* 48 (June 1988): 3038A.

A study of 22 novice writers in an introductory technical writing course revealed an awareness of rhetorical concerns that is greater than usually assumed.

1525. Birchak, Beatrice Christina. "Coordinating Communication for New Product Development." *TWT* 15 (Winter 1988): 37–41.

Suggests a structure for advanced technical writing courses based on the seven phases of developing new products.

1526. Bishop, Wendy. "Revising the Technical Writing Class: Peer Critiques, Self-Evaluation, and Portfolio Grading." Paper presented at the Penn State Conference on Rhetoric and Composition, State College, Pa., July 1987. ERIC ED 285 178. 26 pages

Describes a process-oriented technical writing course that emphasizes peer evaluation and learning.

1527. Bloomstrand, David. "Procedural Revisions and Updates: Some Applications for Technical Writing Classes." *TWT* 15 (Winter 1988): 42–48.

Details the implementation of a revision assignment comparable to tasks routinely assigned to entry-level technical writers.

1528. Connor, Jennifer J. "Poetry at Work: Historical Examples of Technical Communication in Verse." *JTWC* 18 (1988): 11–22.

Surveys literary and oral functional poetry to increase appreciation for the genre and to encourage technical writers to make use of poetic devices.

1529. Davis, Robert A. "The Evaluation of Reading Levels for the Development of Computer-Aided Instruction." *DAI* 48 (February 1988): 1968A.

Investigates the effects of CAI on knowledge acquisition in a technical curriculum. Evaluates the effects on students of reading levels for some CAI courseware.

1530. Doheny-Farina, Stephen. "A Case Study Approach Using Conflict among Collaborators." *TWT* 15 (Fall 1988): 73–77.

Outlines a writing task that requires group members to negotiate and reconcile differing points of view as part of a collaborative writing assignment.

1531. Graves, Richard L. "What I Learned from Verle Barnes: The Exploratory Self in Writing." *TETYC* 15 (February 1988): 20–24.

Barnes, author of *Portrait of an Estuary*, models the discovery experience and exemplifies the importance of a writer's involvement with the subject.

1532. Harris, John. "The Aversion Factor in Technical Communication." *JTWC* 18 (1988): 199–204.

Suggests ways to overcome aversion to technical tasks.

1533. Holland, Virginia Melissa. "Processes Involved in Writing Procedural Instructions." *DAI* 48 (January 1988): 2124B.

Examines instruction writing, attempting to distinguish between effective and ineffective writing processes.

1534. Horowitz, Renee B. "*Kaizen* in the Classroom: Using Japanese Management Techniques to Improve Technical Communication." *Issues* 1 (Fall 1988): 64–71.

Suggests that some Japanese strategies for achieving *kaizen*, "continual improvement," can be applied to technical writing classrooms, especially as rewards for peer reviewers.

1535. Kalmbach, James. "Technical Writing Teachers and the Challenges of Desktop Publishing." *TWT* 15 (Spring 1988): 119–131.

Discusses three major challenges that desktop publishing presents to technical writing teachers and suggests revising current methodologies.

1536. Lang, Thomas A. "A Technical Writing Laboratory: The Puzzle Exercise." *TWT* 15 (Spring 1988): 132–137.

Describes a classroom exercise that teaches students the difference between their technical tasks as problem solvers and their rhetorical tasks as writers.

1537. MacKenzie, Nancy Rose. "The Effects of Visualization as an Invention Technique in the Composing Processes of Technical Writing Students." *DAI* 48 (February 1988): 2008A.

Examines the uses and effects of writer-based sketches, diagrams, and other drawings as invention strategies.

1538. Maxwell-Paegle, Monica A. "Teaching English to Foreign Students in an American Dental School: A Case Study in Applied Linguistics." *DAI* 49 (July 1988): 84A.

Develops a process-oriented, learner-centered course designed to achieve communicative competence in a specific technical speech community.

1539. Miller, Diane F. *Guide for Preparing Software User Documentation*. Washington, D.C.: Society for Technical Communication, 1988. 78 pages

Discusses audience analysis, information gathering, organization, format, visuals, standard conventions, and terminology.

1540. Morrow, John. "Adapting Cases in Operations Management for Use in the Technical Writing Classroom." *TWT* 15 (Spring 1988): 154–157.

Provides a four-step process for translating cases created for other disciplines into effective writing contexts.

1541. Moxley, Joseph M. "The Myth of the Technical Audience." *JTWC* 18 (1988): 107–109.

Suggests "a few strategies for moving students away from a purely static perception of audience."

1542. Mulcahy, Patricia. "Writing Reader-Based Instructions: Strategies to Build Coherence." *TWT* 15 (Fall 1988): 234–243.

Offers a theoretically grounded paradigm to help technical writers and teachers make instructions for tasks clear, coherent, and comprehensible.

1543. Murray, Margaret Thorell. "The World of Technical Writing Is Round." *TWT* 15 (Spring 1988): 143–153.

Argues that technical writing has a rich rhetorical basis exceeding the formulaic approaches that subsume much current pedagogy.

1544. Popken, Randall L. "A Study of Topic Sentence Use in Scientific Writing." *JTWC* 18 (1988): 75–86.

Finds that writers of scientific articles often use topic sentences, but their frequency and type vary with different sections of the report.

1545. *Proceedings of the Thirty-Fifth International Technical Communication Conference.* Washington, D.C.: Society for Technical Communication, 1988.

A collection of papers presented in Philadelphia, May 1988. Subjects include advanced technology applications; management and professional development; research, education, and training; visual communication; and writing and editing. Authors are not indexed separately in this volume.

1546. Redish, Janice C. "Reading to Learn to Do." *TWT* 15 (Fall 1988): 223–233.

Distinguishes two types of reading tasks— reading to do and reading to learn—and proposes a hybrid for use in developing effective tutorials.

1547. Rude, Carolyn D. "Format in Instruction Manuals: Application of Existing Research." *JBTC* 2 (January 1988): 63–77.

Applies current work in cognitive psychology, instructional technology, and the study of human factors to formatting instructions, specifically typographic cueing and graphic displays.

1548. Safford, Dan. "What I Didn't Teach in Technical Writing." *TETYC* 15 (February 1988): 53–58.

Now working in industry, a teacher realizes he should have emphasized definition of purpose, responsive planning, scheduling, and interpersonal communication.

1549. Sanders, Scott P., and Chris Madigan. "Team Planning a Computerized Technical Writing Course (But We Had So Much in Common)." *CC* 5 (April 1988): 39–50.

Describes planning and team teaching a computer-aided technical writing class.

1550. *SCMLA: Technical Writing.* Stillwater, Okla.: Oklahoma State University, 1987. ERIC ED 292 109. 39 pages

Prints five selected papers from the October 1987 meeting of the South Central Modern Language Association. Papers address topics in technical writing.

1551. Scott, Ann Martin. "Group Projects in Technical Writing Courses." *TWT* 15 (Spring 1988): 138–142.

Advocates the use of group writing assignments because they stimulate inductive learning and reflect writing dynamics typically found in business and industry.

1552. Smith, Frank. "The Preparation and Performance of Technical Writers: A Conversation with Dr. Frank R. Smith." *Issues* 1 (Fall 1988): 5–14.

A practicing technical writer and editor with 30 years' experience offers suggestions for training technical writers in college courses.

1553. Soderston, Candace, and Carol German. "Toward Bridging the Gap between Theory and Practice: Analogy and Person in Technical Communication." *JBTC* 2 (January 1988): 78–102.

Reports the results of a series of experiments that suggest rethinking the use of analogy and direct address as stylistic conventions in scientific discourse.

1554. Spilka, Rachel. "Studying Writer-Reader Interactions in the Workplace." *TWT* 15 (Fall 1988): 208–221.

Analyzes assumptions underlying current pedagogy and describes a heuristic for multiple audience analysis based on observing writers in an engineering firm.

1555. Tebeaux, Elizabeth. "Teaching Professional Communication in the Information

Age: Problems in Sustaining Relevance." *JBTC* 2 (September 1988): 44–58.

Identifies transformations in the workplace and issues brought on by communication technology. Recommends changes in eight areas of professional communication instruction.

1556. Unikel, Graham. "The Two-Level Concept of Editing." *TWT* 15 (Winter 1988): 49–55.

Outlines the editorial structure within one technical publications department and examines the implications for technical writing programs.

1557. Ware, Elaine. "Helping Students to Prepare a Technical Communications Portfolio." *TWT* 15 (Winter 1988): 56–62.

Outlines strategies for helping technical writing students prepare effective writing portfolios prior to employment interviews.

1558. Wong, Irene B. "Teacher-Student Talk in Technical Writing Conferences." *WC* 5 (October 1988): 444–460.

Finds that, when the student knows more about a topic than the teacher does, the student explains the topic to the teacher only 40 percent of the time.

See also 225, 653, 771, 825, 1008, 1065, 1207, 1289, 1451, 1463, 1469, 1492, 1493, 1511, 1517, 1619

4.2.6 WRITING IN LITERATURE COURSES

1559. Bauso, Jean. "The Use of Freewriting and Guided Writing to Make Students Amenable to Poems." *ExEx* 33 (Spring 1988): 32–35.

Offers an assignment based on "Sailing to Byzantium."

1560. Brown-Guillory, Elizabeth. "Integrating Television Game Shows and Reader-Response Criticism." *ExEx* 34 (Fall 1988): 42–43.

Explains how to adapt "To Tell the Truth" into a class game in which five panelists play author while the class attempts to stump them with questions.

1561. Clausen, Christopher. "It Is Not Elitist to Place Major Literature at the Center of the English Curriculum." *CHE* 34 (13 January 1988): A52.

Argues for making traditional "major literature" rather than ethnic or ideological works the focus in college English classes.

1562. Davis, Ellen L., and Dorothy S. Stewart. "Blue Bloods and Indians: Native Americans Revisited." *ExEx* 33 (Spring 1988): 11–16.

Provides synopses of *Love Medicine* and *The Catherine Wheel*. Explains how cultural comparisons may be drawn in class activities and writing assignments.

1563. Demastes, William. "Weighing Huck Finn's Choices and Decisions." *ExEx* 34 (Fall 1988): 39–41.

Identifies passages to help students understand the novel's ethical issues and systems of thought.

1564. Gebhardt, Richard C. "Fiction Writing in Literature Classes." *RR* 7 (Fall 1988): 150–155.

Explains various benefits to students of writing fiction in literature classes. Such assignments develop intuition, heighten appreciation, focus attention, and reinforce expository skills.

1565. Graff, Gerald. "Conflicts over the Curriculum Are Here to Stay; They Should Be Made Educationally Productive." *CHE* 34 (17 February 1988): A48.

Advocates involving students in the literature curriculum controversy through classroom debates and exercises.

1566. Hawkes, Peter. "Teaching Plot." *ExEx* 33 (Spring 1988): 36–38.

Describes a "round robin" group writing assignment that teaches narrative structure.

1567. Heller, Scott. "Some English Departments Are Giving Undergraduates Grounding in New Literary and Critical Theory." *CHE* 34 (3 August 1988): A15-A17.

The English Department at Carnegie Mellon University has replaced traditional genre-based undergraduate literature courses with classes focusing on theme and critical theory.

1568. Holmes, Ken, and Kay Jacob, eds. *The Creative Process in Prose Fiction: Connecting Writing and Literary Studies*. Papers from IATE Summer Institutes. Urbana, Ill.: Illinois Association of Teachers of English, 1988. 64 pages

The editors argue that literature and composition studies must supplement each other. Fifteen essays discuss major authors' prewriting techniques, the study of manuscripts and critical sources, the use of real-life originals for portraits and settings, and revision.

1569. Kurth, Anita. "A Poetry Anthology." *ExEx* 34 (Fall 1988): 37-38.

Provides instructions for a student-produced poetry anthology that contains student-written paragraphs analyzing each poem.

1570. Law, Joe K. "Bloom, Hirsch, and Barthes in the Classroom: Negotiating Cultural Literacy." *FEN* 17 (Fall 1988): 33-36.

Discusses the need to reread rather than consume literature. Provides a strategy for teaching rereading for interpretation.

1571. Madden, Frank. "Computer Software and the Introductory Literature Class." *CollL* 15 (Winter 1988): 1-8.

Briefly discusses available software to be used in teaching literature when the emphasis is upon critical analysis and writing about literature.

1572. Malless, Stan, and Jeff McQuain. *The Elements of English: A Glossary of Basic Terms for Literature, Composition, and Grammar*. Lanham, Md.: University Press of America, 1988. 88 pages

An alphabetical listing of terms arranged in three sections: literature, composition, and grammar. Includes a comprehensive index.

1573. Martin, Bill. "The Meditation Exercise: Searching for Coherence through Literary Response." *ExEx* 33 (Spring 1988): 19-22.

Students, like clergy, should consider a passage in its immediate context as part of a whole work, and for its more general implications.

1574. McLaughlin, Gary L. "Patterns, Images, and Annotations: A Way into Poetry." *ExEx* 33 (Spring 1988): 17-18.

Provides a structured assignment to elicit creative student-written poetry.

1575. *Mightier than the Typewriter: Using the Computer to Teach Writing for Mass Media*. Syracuse, N.Y.: Newhouse School of Broadcasting, 1987. ERIC ED 289 163. 46 pages

Summarizes nine presentations and panels from a December 1986 conference that investigated the power of computers for students and teachers in writing and editing classes. Authors are not indexed separately in this volume.

1576. Myrsiades, Linda S., and Kostas Myrsiades. "A Computer Application for the Study of Oral Literature." *CollL* 15 (Winter 1988): 57-68.

Describes the use of the computer in "identifying and isolating the 'building blocks' of oral structure," the plot units.

1577. Perrin, Noel. "We Could Readmit a Little Pleasure into the Study of Literature." *CHE* 34 (15 June 1988): A44.

Ignored minor masterpieces of American literature should be considered for class reading lists because they are well written and enjoyable to read.

1578. Price, Marian. "Reader Response in the Teaching of Composition." Paper presented at the Annual Meeting of the Florida College

English Association, Ocala, Fla., February 1987. ERIC ED 292 129. 17 pages

Suggests improving writing about literature by applying reader-response theory to writing and discussion.

1579. Rabinowitz, Peter J. "Our Evaluation of Literature Has Been Distorted by Academe's Bias toward Close Reading of Texts." *CHE* 34 (6 April 1988): A40.

Argues for using pluralistic interpretive modes rather than relying on a single method.

1580. Silverstein, Diane. "The Electric Poem." *CollL* 15 (Winter 1988): 25–34.

Discusses how the personal computer is already shaping the ways in which a few poets compose their poems.

1581. Thompson, Edgar H. "Interaction, Performance, and Insight: Giving Life to Literature." *Leaflet* 87 (Spring 1988): 19–23.

Contends that having students visualize scenes in literature and respond through expressive writing helps them interpret what they read.

See also 1410

4.2.7 COMMUNICATION IN OTHER DISCIPLINES

1582. Ambron, Joanna. "Clustering: An Interactive Technique to Enhance Learning in Biology." *JCST* 18 (November 1988): 122–127, 144.

Students use Rico's "clusters" to summarize lectures, integrate reading, and revise assumptions about teaching and learning in biology classes.

1583. Bishop, Wendy. "Teaching Undergraduate Creative Writing: Myths, Mentors, and Metaphors." *JTW* 7 (Spring-Summer 1988): 83–102.

Calls for "debunking myths, refusing to be mentors in inappropriate contexts," and "changing our metaphors from war to peace and harvest to cultivation."

1584. Blair, Catherine Pastore. "Only One of the Voices: Dialogic Writing across the Curriculum." *CE* 50 (April 1988): 383–389.

Argues that true writing across the curriculum should involve dialogue among all departments, with English departments having no special role.

1585. Calman, K. C., R. S. Downie, M. Duthie, and B. Sweeney. "Literature and Medicine: A Short Course for Medical Students." *MEd* 22 (July 1988): 265–269.

Describes a short course, the reading and writing activities associated with it, and its carryover into other medical school courses.

1586. Chamberlin, Ruth Louise. "An Exploratory Study of Learning Logs as a Writing to Learn Strategy in College Classrooms." *DAI* 49 (December 1988): 1357A.

Recommends an increase in appropriate writing in all college classes, on-going inservice work with faculty, and the widest use of learning logs.

1587. Comprone, Joseph J. "Reading Oliver Sacks in a Writing across the Curriculum Course." *JAC* 8 (1988): 158–166.

Uses works such as *The Man Who Mistook His Wife for a Hat* to illustrate negotiating between field-specific and universal discourses.

1588. Connery, Brian A. "Using Journals in the Cross-Curricular Course: Restoring Process." *JAC* 8 (1988): 97–104.

In cross-curricular writing, concerns about the disciplinary content can easily subvert a process orientation. Journal writing should be part of all such courses.

1589. Corse, Larry. "Two Theories of Language and Writing across the Curriculum." *WAC* 5 (May 1988): 10–12.

Rejects the "romantic-ideal" theory of writing in favor of the "individual-meaning-context" theory, which sees writing as essential to a student's understanding a discipline.

1590. Cranfill, R. Caroline, and Robert C. Wess. "Using Drafts in Engineering Report Writing." *WAC* 5 (May 1988): 4–7.

Reports on a class in electrical engineering technology in which students submitted and revised rough drafts for three format reports.

1591. Crismore, Avon. "Initiating Students into Critical Thinking: Reading and Writing about Texts." Paper presented at the MLA Convention, San Francisco, December 1987. ERIC ED 288 202. 18 pages

Offers a method to spur critical thinking through journal responses to textbooks, noting its usefulness for writing across the curriculum.

1592. Dunn, James R. "Improving the Vocabulary and Writing Skills of Black Students Majoring in Biology." *JCST* 17 (March–April 1988): 360–361.

Describes the need for improving vocabulary and writing skills among minority students in science classes. Discusses techniques for doing so.

1593. El Laissi, Moody, and Bobbie El Laissi. "Writing Dialogues of Ideas across the Curriculum." *ArEB* 30 (Winter 1988): 16–17.

Advocates dialogue writing for students so that they may see at least two sides of an issue.

1594. Fontaine, Andre, and William A. Glavin, Jr. *The Art of Writing Nonfiction.* Syracuse, N.Y.: Syracuse University Press, 1988. 232 pages

Discusses the writing of newspaper stories, magazine articles, and books. Describes the writing process as well as the business side of writing and selling. Includes published examples.

1595. Gay, Pamela. "Using Writing to Develop Visual Artists: A Pedagogical Model for Collaborative Teaching and Learning." *Issues* 1 (Fall 1988): 35–49.

Describes how a painting teacher and writing teacher collaborated to make writing an integral rather than an "added on" element of a course.

1596. Glick, Milton D. "Writing across the Curriculum: A Dean's Perspective." *WPA* 11 (Spring 1988): 53–58.

Describes the writing across the curriculum program at the University of Missouri—Columbia. Identifies important elements that allowed the program to gain momentum.

1597. Gordon, Nicholas, and Susan Mansfield. "Computers across the Curriculum: A Confluence of Ideas." *CC* 6 (November 1988): 9–13.

Content area teachers are more likely to accept writing across the curriculum if they view computers as thinking and communicating tools rather than as writing machines.

1598. Gray, Donald J. "Writing across the College Curriculum." *PhiDK* 69 (June 1988): 729–733.

Discusses misunderstandings about writing across the curriculum and the advantages of having college teachers of disciplines other than English teach writing. Cautions against focusing on grammar instead of on communication.

1599. Haber, Marian Wynne. "Ability Grouping in College Beginning Media Writing." *DAI* 49 (July 1988): 6A.

Ability grouped and heterogeneously grouped writing students showed no significant differences in posttest scores.

1600. Hine, Robert V. "When Historians Turn to Fiction." *HT* 21 (February 1988): 215–219.

Looks at the tendencies of historians to fictionalize historical events and figures. Presents the author's own plans for writing a historical novel.

1601. Hotchkiss, Sharon K., and Marilyn K. Nellis. "Writing across the Curriculum: Team Teaching the Review Article in Biology."

JCST 18 (September–October 1988): 45–47.

> Describes the methodology, problems, and results of team-teaching in a sophomore biology class at Clarkson University.

1602. Howard, Rebecca. *"In Situ* Workshops and the Peer Relationships of Composition Faculty." *WPA* 12 (Fall-Winter 1988): 39–46.

> Reports that *in situ* workshops at Colgate University, where a writing professor offers occasional writing instruction in courses across the curriculum, helped to change faculty ideas about writing and writing instruction.

1603. Jensen, J. Vernon. "Teaching East Asian Rhetoric." *RSQ* 17 (Spring 1987): 135–149.

> Outlines a 10-week course in East Asian rhetoric for juniors, seniors, or graduate students.

1604. Kirsch, Gesa. "Writing across the Curriculum: The Program at Third College, University of California, San Diego." *WPA* 12 (Fall-Winter 1988): 47–55.

> Describes the conceptual framework and the curricular and administrative structure of a writing across the curriculum program. Graduate students in the disciplines teach writing sections.

1605. Lariviere, Janis W. "An Outline That Meets the Deadline." *ST* 55 (September 1988): 75–77.

> Describes a multiple-step, self-paced term paper project for honors science classes.

1606. Ledbetter, Cynthia E. "The Five-Slide Essay." *ST* 55 (April 1988): 31–32.

> Suggests teaching patterns of organization for writing in science classes by organizing slide presentations.

1607. MacDonald, Susan Peck. "Susan Peck MacDonald Responds [to Bialostosky, Templeton, Beyer, and Beyer, *CE* 49 (March 1987)]." *CE* 50 (February 1988): 212–220.

> Defends her use of a continuum in discussing problem-definition in academic writing

and reiterates her argument that literature does not lend itself to reductive problem definition.

1608. Maik, Thomas A. "Looking Backward for Signs of the Future." *BADE* 90 (Fall 1988): 59–62.

> Explains how the University of Wisconsin—La Crosse developed minors in expository and creative writing.

1609. McLeod, P. J. "The Impact of Educational Interventions on the Reliability of Teachers' Assessment of Student Case Reports: A Controlled Trial." *MEd* 22 (March 1988): 113–117.

> Finds that evaluating students' case reports is crucial in assessing the ability and development of medical students. Interrater reliability must be controlled for maximum effectiveness.

1610. McMillan, Fay C. "Writing in Different Disciplines: Problems and Possibilities." *WAC* 5 (May 1988): 12–16.

> Evaluates the problems and advantages of writing across the curriculum programs that focus on interdisciplinary writing or discipline-specific assignments.

1611. Menahem, S. "Trigger Segments: Towards Improving Listening Skills." *MEd* 22 (May 1988): 188–192.

> Using short written "trigger" scenarios allows students to observe and practice appropriate responses in patient-physician dialogues.

1612. Merriam, Robert W. "A Function in Trouble: Undergraduate Science Teaching in Research Universities." *JCST* 18 (November 1988): 102–106.

> Institutional pressures to publish and graduate students' disregard for teaching reduce professors' incentives to work closely with students, diminishing their opportunities to co-author scientific papers.

1613. Mitchell, Felicia. "Bridging the Communication Gap between Teacher and Student:

Composing Assignments in the Content Area." Paper presented at the NCTE Convention, Los Angeles, November 1987. ERIC ED 289 178. 17 pages

Studies 130 assignments offered by 35 instructors at the University of Texas—Austin. Two-thirds contained imprecise language or mixed messages.

1614. Moody, Raymond. "Personality Preferences and Foreign Language Learning." *MLJ* 72 (Winter 1988): 389–401.

Argues that required language courses must adapt to personality differences found in this study of elective language learners and other types of students.

1615. Palmini, Dennis J. "Writing about Economics: A Tool to Strengthen Student Understanding." *Issues* 1 (Fall 1988): 15–34.

Summarizes work done in composition, cognitive psychology, and linguistics that link writing and learning. Offers writing assignments to be used in economics courses.

1616. Pond, Elizabeth Farren. "The Development and Validation of a Computer-Assisted Instructional Program in Parent-Child Nursing Designed to Enhance the Critical Thinking Skills of Baccalaureate Nursing Students." *DAI* 49 (September 1988): 423A.

Studies a CAI program designed to enhance the critical thinking skills of baccalaureate nursing students.

1617. Ramsey, Allen. "The Strategy of the Reversed Conference." *WAC* 5 (May 1988): 7–8.

Reports on the use of the reversed conference, in which students assume the teacher's role, at Central Missouri State University.

1618. Reagan, Sally, ed. *Teaching Creative Writing*. Des Moines, Iowa: Iowa Council of Teachers of English (distributed by NCTE), 1987. 81 pages

Twelve theoretical and practical essays on how to help students develop a critical

awareness of fiction, including the ability to use and to critique other students' uses of literary conventions. Also discusses the issues students write about in fiction and ways of teaching fiction to ESL students. Originally published as *Iowa English Bulletin* (Special Issue 1987).

1619. Reese, Stephen D. "New Communication Technologies and the Information Worker: The Influence of Occupation." *JC* 38 (Spring 1988): 59–70.

Professionals, managers, clerical staff, and blue-collar workers hold attitudes toward communication technologies at home and at work that suggest gender and class differences.

1620. Rice, Winthrop Huntington, III. "An ATI Investigation of the Relationship between Locus of Control and Instructional Guidance in the Acquisition of Procedural Knowledge." *DAI* 49 (September 1988): 423A.

Studies the relationship between locus of control and instructional guidance for 79 undergraduates enrolled in a computer literacy course.

1621. Ronald, Kate. "On the Outside Looking In: Students' Analyses of Professional Discourse Communities." *RR* 7 (Fall 1988): 130–149.

Finds that students adopt various stances—the apprentice, the cynic, the insider—when critiquing writing in different disciplines. Advocates greater awareness of social contexts in writing across the curriculum courses.

1622. Rubin, Lois. "Professors Write to Learn about Write-to-Learn." *CollT* 36 (Summer 1988): 94–97.

Discusses the principles and benefits of the write-to-learn approach and describes a faculty development workshop in which writing tasks were planned for various disciplines.

1623. Schierhorn, Ann. "Encouraging Student Writers to Take Risks after Solid Reporting." *JourEd* 42 (Winter 1988): 32–52.

Argues that teachers should require students to take risks, giving examples of the types of risks some students have attempted.

1624. Schuster, Sidney. "Using Writing Strategies to Improve Physics Skills." *WAC* 5 (May 1988): 3–4.

Presents three methods of strengthening logical thinking through writing in physics class.

1625. Shamoon, Linda K., and Robert A. Schwegler. "Sociologists Reading Student Texts: Expectations and Perceptions." *WI* 7 (Winter 1988): 71–81.

Concludes that sociologists' perceptions of student writing are more discipline specific than rhetoric based. Gives suggestions for preparing students for writing in other fields.

1626. Smith, Louise Z. "Why English Departments Should 'House' Writing across the Curriculum." *CE* 50 (April 1988): 390–395.

Proposes that English departments share their knowledge of contemporary textual and composition studies rather than wait for other departments to discover effective methodologies.

1627. Squiteri, Louise. "Cue: How to Get Started Writing in Anatomy and Physiology." *JCST* 17 (February 1988): 279–280, 326.

Describes exercises that integrate reading and writing into student discourse. Used in freshmen science courses, the exercises help to improve students' confidence, organization, and grammar.

1628. Stewart, Roy T., Jr. "Writing across the Curriculum: A Success Story." *WAC* 5 (May 1988): 8–10.

Describes the writing across the curriculum program at Slippery Rock University, offering suggestions for implementing such a program at other institutions.

1629. Stocking, Holly. "Using Personal Narratives as Teaching Tools." *JourEd* 42 (Spring 1988): 58–59.

Describes how personal narratives enlivened a classroom and created a point of view for future writings completed by journalists.

1630. Teppen, Terry C., and Susan Rinker. "First-Person Science." *ST* 55 (September 1988): 72–74.

Discusses a term paper assignment in science classes. Students roleplay famous scientists and then write "autobiographies."

1631. Vigil, Virginia Dorothea. "Authentic Text in the College-Level Spanish Class as the Primary Vehicle of Instruction." *DAI* 49 (September 1988): 451A.

Compares two groups of beginning Spanish students at Austin Community College who used traditional textbooks or authentic texts such as newspapers, poetry, and plays.

1632. Walker, Anne. "Writing across the Curriculum: The Second Decade." *EQ* 21 (1988): 93–103.

Discusses the theory, rationale, merits, challenges, and research that have shaped writing across the curriculum.

1633. Woodward, C. A. "Questionnaire Construction and Question Writing for Research in Medical Education." *MEd* 22 (July 1988): 347–363.

Describes the principles involved in constructing questions, illustrates the techniques, and provides heuristics for writing these instruments.

1634. Yanoff, Karin L., and Fredric D. Burg. "Types of Medical Writing and Teaching of Medical Writing in U.S. Medical Schools." *JMEd* 63 (January 1988): 30–37.

Identifies five important types of writing for physicians and offers suggestions for incorporating writing in medical curricula.

1635. Zajicek, Faith. "Writing through Art, Art through Writing." *ET* 19 (Summer 1988): 15–16.

Gives several suggestions for writing assignments in art class.

See also 117, 153, 951, 1120, 1187, 1286, 1297, 1392, 1557, 1677, 1705, 1781

4.3   ADULT EDUCATION

1636. Carver, L. Sue. *ABE: The Hearing Impaired.* Texas City, Tex.: College of the Mainland, 1987. ERIC ED 287 046. 118 pages

Offers a guide for tutors of adult basic education students who are hearing impaired.

1637. Doran, Linda D. "Access for Adults: The Tennessee State University and Community College System's Initiatives for Serving Academically Underprepared Adults." Paper presented at the American Association for Adult and Continuing Education, Washington, D.C., October 1987. ERIC ED 287 019. 16 pages

Summarizes the efforts of the Tennessee state system to improve adult education.

1638. Enos, Theresa. "Definition, Development, Direction: The Course in Classical Rhetoric." Paper presented at the CCCC Convention, St. Louis, March 1988. ERIC ED 294 214. 11 pages

Presents findings from a survey of courses offered in graduate rhetoric programs.

1639. Thompson, Isabelle. *Writing Instruction in Colleges and Universities: A Survey from 1975–1976 to 1985–1986.* Alexandria, Va.: ERIC Document Reproduction Service, 1987. ERIC ED 286 180. 20 pages

Reports on a survey of 105 universities. Finds that the number of and enrollments in graduate courses in composition have increased, while enrollments in literature courses have remained stable.

See also 407, 642, 661, 1143, 1164, 1512, 1603, 1791, 1794

4.4   ENGLISH AS A SECOND LANGUAGE

1640. Barnett, Marva A. "Reading through Context: How Real and Perceived Strategy Use Affects L2 Comprehension." *MLJ* 72 (Summer 1988): 150–162.

A study showing that, by prereading, comprehension increases as students use and are aware of using strategies to establish a context for reading.

1641. Best, Linda. "Sociolinguistic Theories as Means to Understand and Meet the Needs of ESL College Writers." Paper presented at the CCCC Convention, Atlanta, March 1987. ERIC ED 285 389. 9 pages

Advocates current ESL theory as the best guide to factors influencing ESL college writers.

1642. Betancourt, Francisco, and Marianne Phinney. "Sources of Writing Block in Bilingual Writers." *WC* 5 (October 1988): 461–478.

Writing blocks had different sources for different groups, depending on the language used for writing and the amount of experience the writer possessed.

1643. Braine, George. "Two Commentaries on Ruth Spack's 'Initiating ESL Students into the Academic Discourse Community: How Far Should We Go?' [*TESOLQ* 22 (March 1988)], A Reader Reacts." *TESOLQ* 22 (December 1988): 700–702.

Disagrees with Spack. Contends that integrating academic assignments into ESL writing courses can help students succeed in the university.

1644. Brookes, Gay. "Promising Sets of Practices in the Teaching of Writing to ESL and Native Speaker Students." *DAI* 48 (January 1988): 1679A.

Examines data from seven college classes observed over two months. Identifies six broad areas that characterize good teaching.

1645. Brooks, Elaine. *Case Studies of "Unskilled" ESL College Writers: A Hypothesis about Stages of Development.* New York: New York University, 1985. ERIC ED 289 340. 42 pages

Summarizes a dissertation project studying five ESL writers. Suggests a three-stage model of writing development.

1646. Campbell, Cherry Colleen. "Writing with Others' Words: The Use of Information from a Background Reading Text in the Writing of Native and Nonnative University Composition Students." *DAI* 48 (January 1988): 1679A.

An analysis of 30 writings supplemented by four case studies of writing processes. Finds differences in methods of explaining, summarizing, paraphrasing, quoting, and copying information.

1647. Chan, Michele M. "Learning by Doing, Discussing, and Questioning: A Collaborative Writing Course." Paper presented at the CCCC Convention, St. Louis, March 1988. ERIC ED 296 339. 18 pages

Provides a detailed description of a collaborative writing course taught at the Chinese University of Hong Kong.

1648. Chiste, Katherine Beaty, and Judith O'Shea. "Patterns of Question Selection and Writing Performance of ESL Students." *TESOLQ* 22 (December 1988): 681–684.

A two-year Canadian study of 305 ESL writers and 544 native speakers. ESL writers preferred shorter, earlier positioned questions.

1649. DeWitt, Jean Marie Zaun. "A Description of Functionally Based English as a Second Language Textbooks: Speech, Speech Event, Speech Situation." *DAI* 49 (September 1988): 379A.

Analyzes syntactically organized pre-planned dialogues in textbooks for beginning ESL students.

1650. Diaz, Diana M. "ESL College Writers: Process and Community." *JDEd* 12 (November 1988): 6–12.

Discusses permeable language-centered research as a theoretical framework for analyzing the academic and linguistic needs of ESL writers. Makes suggestions for teaching.

1651. Dickens, Pauline M. Rea, and Edward G. Woods. "Some Criteria for the Development of Communicative Grammar Tasks." *TESOLQ* 22 (December 1988): 623–646.

Analyzes the role of grammar instruction in communicative language teaching. Provides suggestions for designing communicative grammar assignments.

1652. Edlund, John R. "Bakhtin and the Social Reality of Language Acquisition." *WI* 7 (Winter 1988): 56–67.

Discusses Bakhtin's language theory. Illustrates assimilation and the restructuring of an individual's belief system in the writing of nonnative students.

1653. Fink, Darlynn R. "A Descriptive Study of Teacher and Student Questioning Patterns in University ESL and Native Writing Classes." *DAI* 48 (February 1988): 2007A.

Examines teachers' questioning strategies.

1654. Ghazalah, Hasan. "Literary Stylistics: Pedagogical Perspectives in an EFL Context." *DAI* 49 (September 1988): 448A.

Describes literary stylistics as an approach for nonnative students of English literary composition.

1655. Ginn, Doris O. "De-Pidginization: A Rhetoric and Writing Dilemma in Cross-Cultural Communications." *Focuses* 1 (Fall 1988): 41–50.

Explains some cultural problems of second language learners and outlines pedagogical practices for those who teach writing to such students.

1656. Goldman, Susan, and Richard Duran. "Answering Questions from Oceanography Texts: Learner, Task, and Text Characteristics." *DPr* 11 (October–December 1988): 373–412.

Consonant with a proposed model, protocols elicited from native and nonnative speakers of English showed different approaches to answering questions.

1657. Graman, Tomas. "Education for Humanization: Applying Paolo Freire's Pedagogy to Learning a Second Language." *HER* 58 (November 1988): 433–448.

Argues that second language learning can be both transformative and educative. Contends that Freire's critical pedagogy is particularly appropriate for second language learning. Calls for reconceptualizing education.

1658. Guttstein, Shelley P. "Toward the Assessment of Communicative Competence in Writing: An Analysis of the Dialogue Journal Writing of Japanese Adult ESL Students." *DAI* 49 (July 1988): 83A.

Uses holistic assessments, GPA, and the analysis of discourse topic features to assess the communicative competence of Japanese ESL students writing dialogue journals.

1659. Haas, Teri. "Conversation Workshops for Second Language Learners." *WLN* 12 (June 1988): 8–10.

Describes the organization and staffing of groups, the placement of ESL students, and the kinds of topics discussed.

1660. Hadaway, Nancy Lynn. "Writing Apprehension among Second Language Learners." *DAI* 49 (October 1988): 712A.

Using the Daly-Miller Writing Apprehension Scale, questionnaires, and writing samples, this study confirms a significant correlation between L1 and L2 writing attitudes.

1661. Johns, Ann M. "Two Commentaries on Ruth Spack's 'Inititiating ESL Students into the Academic Discourse Community: How Far Should We Go?' [*TESOLQ* 22 (March 1988)]." *TESOLQ* 22 (December 1988): 705–707.

Argues that Spack's article makes her "uneasy" because it is retrogressive.

1662. Kamanya, Ella. "The Nonnative English Writer." *WLN* 12 (June 1988): 7–8.

ESL students, embarrassed and defensive by their lack of fluency, should be encouraged "to think in English" rather than translate from their own language.

1663. Katz, Anne Marie. "Responding to Student Writers: The Writing Conferences of Second Language Learners." *DAI* 49 (December 1988): 1394A.

Describes interactions between conference participants and examines the layers of context that extend from the conference to the classroom.

1664. Kim, Nam-Soon. "Rationale and Design for Large Group Instruction of Korean College Students of English as a Foreign Language for the Development of Communication Skills." *DAI* 48 (April 1988): 2562A.

Offers a context, educational philosophy, and syllabuses that include objectives, content, methods, assessment, and lesson plans.

1665. Lee, Jawon. "Developing Cultural Awareness for EFL Teachers of Korean Students." *DAI* 49 (September 1988): 449A.

Teachers with a knowledge of Korean culture can provide Korean students with appropriate verbal communicative experiences.

1666. Lucas, Tamara Faith. "Personal Journal Writing in an ESL Writing Class: Teaching, Learning, and Adapting to the Genre Conventions." *DAI* 49 (September 1988): 420A.

Examines the journals of nine ESL students and four teachers to determine genre conventions and factors promoting engagement in writing.

1667. Moreno-Montalvo, Marta Mirna. "Developing Communicative Competence through Suggestopedia Techniques: An Exploratory Project with First Year College ESL Students." *DAI* 49 (July 1988): 84A.

Concludes that "suggestopedia techniques" allow ESL students to achieve higher proficiency and greater confidence in English.

1668. Morrow, Phyllis. "Making the Best of Two Worlds: An Anthropological Approach to the Development of Bilingual Education Materials in Southwestern Alaska." *DAI* 48 (March 1988): 2375A.

Describes the design of a bilingual-bicultural program based on the relationship between Yupik and non-Yupik cultures and on the concept of cultural change.

1669. Musallam, Ayshegul. "Attitudinal Effects on the Processing of Written Language by Native and Nonnative Speakers of English." *DAI* 48 (May 1988): 2824A.

Investigates how attitudes and a passage's level of difficulty affect the processing of controversial material.

1670. Norris, David E. "A Charter for ESL Teachers." *AdEd* 61 (September 1988): 105–108.

Reviews British ESL teaching and considers criteria for effective instruction.

1671. Norton, Robert. *A Comparison of Thinking and Writing Patterns in Korea and the U.S.* AFS Occasional Papers in Intercultural Learning, no. 12. New York: American Field Service International/Intercultural Programs, 1987. ERIC ED 190 648. 23 pages

Summarizes a dissertation on purported differences in writing styles between Korean and American essayists. Finds a preference for induction among the former and for deduction among the latter.

1672. Pica, Theresa P. "Communicative Language Teaching: An Aid to Second Language

Acquisition? Some Insights from Classroom Research." *EQ* 21 (1988): 70–80.

Argues that communicative language teaching should be evaluated in light of second language acquisition theory and research.

1673. Ray, Ruth E. "Academic Literacy and Nonnative Writers." *DAI* 48 (May 1988): 2852A.

Documents the difficulties nonnative writers have in meeting English departments' expectations for literacy. Offers cultural reasons for these difficulties.

1674. Richards, Rebecca T. "Thesis/Dissertation Writing for EFL Students: An ESP Course Design." *ESP* 7 (1988): 171–180.

Describes a course using an interactive model of needs analysis and total discourse learning.

1675. Roy, Alice M. "ESL Concern for Writing Program Administrators: Problems and Policies." *WPA* 11 (Spring 1988): 17–28.

Distinguishes three types of second language students—traditional foreign students, recent immigrants, and bilingual students—and considers appropriate programs for each.

1676. Santos, Terry. "Professors' Reactions to the Academic Writing of Nonnative-Speaking Students." *TESOLQ* 22 (March 1988): 69–90.

Surveys 178 UCLA professors' reactions to two ESL compositions written by Chinese and Korean students. Results indicate that certain professors were more lenient than others. Vocabulary errors were judged most serious.

1677. Spack, Ruth. "Initiating ESL Students into the Academic Discourse Community: How Far Should We Go?" *TESOLQ* 22 (March 1988): 29–51.

Maintains that L2 writing instructors should teach general writing principles, especially writing from sources, and should not teach writing in other disciplines.

1678. Spack, Ruth. "Two Commentaries on Ruth Spack's 'Initiating ESL Students into the Academic Discourse Community: How Far Should We Go?' [*TESOLQ* 22 (March 1988)], The Author Responds to Braine." *TESOLQ* 22 (December 1988): 703–705.

Refuting Braine, maintains that composition instructors need specialized, discipline-specific training to teach writing in other fields.

1679. Spack, Ruth. "Two Commentaries on Ruth Spack's 'Initiating ESL Students into the Academic Discourse Community: How Far Should We Go?' [*TESOLQ* 22 (March 1988)], The Author Responds to Johns." *TESOLQ* 22 (December 1988): 707–708.

Disagrees with Johns. Maintains that teaching writing in other disciplines is beyond L2 "teachers' knowledge and abilities."

1680. Swaffar, Janet K. "Readers, Texts, and Second Languages: The Interactive Processes." *MLJ* 72 (1988): 123–149.

Examines the implications of reader response and schemata theory for teaching second language reading. Addresses the impact of syntax as well as semantics on comprehension.

1681. Ward, James H. "Editing in a Bilingual, Bicultural Context." *JTWC* 18 (1988): 221–226.

Editing in bilingual, bicultural contexts is complicated by linguistic interference and culturally conditioned attitudes toward the duties and responsibilities of the editor.

1682. Weissberg, Robert. "Information Transfer in the Teaching of Academic Writing." Paper presented at the Conference of the National Association for Foreign Student Affairs, Long Beach, Calif., May 1987. ERIC ED 292 100. 14 pages

Suggests improving advanced ESL writing assignments by using visual prompts to restate and reorganize information in various types of discourse.

1683. White, Philip Andrew. "An Integration of Social and Linguistic Information in Second Language Acquisition: A Case Study of English-Japanese Conversation." *DAI* 48 (February 1988): 2055A.

Examines current teaching methods from the perspective of conversational turn-taking and turn allocation.

1684. Williams, Mary Karen. "Listening Comprehension: Adult Second Language Learners." *DAI* 49 (December 1988): 1392A.

Seeks to discover information that will improve the selection and design of listening comprehension materials for adult second language learners.

See also 19, 24, 169, 782, 818, 932, 1483, 1538, 1618, 1726, 1764, 1765

4.5 RESEARCH AND STUDY SKILLS

1685. Agesilas, Elie Aurelien. "The Effect of Meaningful Elaborations and Summaries on the Learning and Retention of Prose Materials." *DAI* 48 (May 1988): 2830A.

Compares the performance of students using elaboration of summary techniques with the performance of students using any study technique they wished.

1686. Alexander, James D. "Lectures: The Ethics of Borrowing." *CollT* 36 (Winter 1988): 21–24.

Explores issues surrounding "borrowing" by students, teachers, and scholars in terms of the contexts that define plagiarism in the academic community.

1687. Arrington, Phillip. "A Dramatistic Approach to Understanding and Teaching the Paraphrase." *CCC* 39 (May 1988): 185–197.

Students should practice writing paraphrases that emphasize different ratios in Burke's pentad to learn how to paraphrase for different rhetorical purposes.

1688. Brennan, Sharon McEwan. "An Examination of the Nature of College Studying: The Relationship between Study Practice Use and Summarization of Textual Information." *DAI* 48 (January 1988): 1717A.

Describes the study practices of 49 university sophomores and their perceptions about them. Notes the relationship between study practices and summarizing ability.

1689. Carver, Joan B. "Ideas in Practice: Plan-Making: Taking Effective Control of Study Habits." *JDEd* 12 (November 1988): 26–29.

Explains the plan-making method for helping students clarify and decrease problems related to study habits. The method is also adaptable to other areas of learning.

1690. Closser, Bruce Allison. "An Ethnographic Examination of the Research Paper as Rite of Passage." *DAI* 49 (December 1988): 1358A.

Finds that research papers initiate students into the academic environment, impose the obligations of academic society, and instill academic values.

1691. Cummings, Donald W. *American English Spelling: An Informal Description*. Baltimore City, Md.: The Johns Hopkins University Press, 1988. 608 pages

Demonstrates how spelling is a self-regulating system responsive to phonetic, semantic, etymological, and systemic demands. Introduces a practical procedure for analyzing written words into their basic elements, particles, and processes.

1692. Dalrymple, Prudence. "Retrieval by Reformulation in Two Library Catalogs: Toward a Cognitive Model of Searching Behavior." *DAI* 48 (January 1988): 1568A.

Protocols of two groups of college students engaged in library research reveal an analogy between long-term memory and information retrieval.

1693. DeLoughry, Thomas J. "Self-Detection Programs Help Students Deal with Plagiarism." *CHE* 35 (14 December 1988): A14.

Describes software that deletes words from a manuscript excerpt, then asks the writer to supply them. Authors can usually reproduce their own but not plagiarized words.

1694. Demery, Marie. *Academic Skills Module*. Natchitoches, La.: Northwestern State University, 1988. ERIC ED 289 449. 55 pages

Offers a study skills module for freshmen.

1695. Ellington, Henry. *Some Hints on How to Study Effectively*. Teaching and Learning in Higher Education, no. 25. Aberdeen, Scotland: Scottish Central Institutions Committee for Educational Development, 1987. ERIC ED 289 508. 23 pages

Offers recommendations for improving study skills and the ability to take tests.

1696. Freedman, Morris. "Plagiarism among Professors; or, Students Should Not Be Excused or Treated Gingerly." *CHE* 34 (10 February 1988): A48.

Demonstrates the complexity of plagiarism by identifying modern malefactors. Complains that professors commonly denounce plagiarism without adequately defining it or assisting students in avoiding it.

1697. Fulkerson, Richard. "Oh, What a Cite! A Teaching Tip to Help Students Document Researched Papers Accurately." *WI* 7 (Spring–Summer 1988): 167–172.

Describes an exercise in which students must determine where citations are needed in a mock research paper.

1698. Goodin, M. Elspeth. "The Transferability of Library Research Skills from High School to College." *DAI* 49 (July 1988): 7A.

Library instruction produced higher scores on a posttest, but predicting transferability was not measurable.

1699. Haslam, Elizabeth Long. "The Design, Implementation, and Evaluation of a College Inquiry Writing Course." *DAI* 48 (February 1988): 2008A.

Instruction based on epistemic rhetoric helps teach inquiry and writing in research papers.

1700. Hitchcock, Richard Benner. "The Use of Instructional Activities to Integrate Reading and Writing." *DAI* 49 (September 1988): 449A.

Attempts to determine if instructional activities aided students in transferring meaning from their reading to their writing.

1701. Kantz, Margaret. "Composing from Textual Sources: Rhetorical Stances for Writing Synthesis." *DAI* 48 (March 1988): 2344A.

Successful syntheses of research by undergraduate writers differed from unsuccessful syntheses in several ways. Highest rated essays contained more original and fewer borrowed ideas than essays rated lower.

1702. Kiewra, Kenneth A. "Cognitive Aspects of Autonomous Note Taking: Control Processes, Learning Strategies, and Prior Knowledge." *EdPsy* 23 (1988): 39–56.

Reviews studies of note taking. Offers a research model for investigating the cognitive aspects of autonomous note taking.

1703. Kroll, Barry M. "How College Freshmen View Plagiarism." *WC* 5 (April 1988): 203–221.

Reports that students, especially women, view plagiarism seriously and are concerned about three ethical issues: "fairness, individual responsibility, and ownership."

1704. Kuhlthau, Carol Collier. "Perceptions of the Information Search Process in Libraries: A Study of Changes from High School through College." *IPM* 24 (1988): 419–427.

Concludes that understanding the research process improves the use of libraries. Proposes a six-step information search model and recommends that "mediators" compare the model to students' perceptions.

1705. Lutzker, Marilyn. *Research Projects for College Students: What to Write across the* *Curriculum*. Westport, Conn.: Greenwood Press, 1988. 141 pages

A librarian offers advice about designing, selecting, teaching, and grading plagiarism-proof library assignments. Gives suggestions for teaching resources and documentation.

1706. McCarger, David Frederick. "Differences in Educational Role Expectations, Second Language Learning, and Teacher Evaluation." *DAI* 48 (February 1988): 2147A.

Examines cultural differences in expectations about teachers' and students' roles and how they affect language acquisition.

1707. Nelson, Kathleah Striker. "Prereading Strategies Used by Successful College Students." *DAI* 49 (September 1988): 470A.

Compares the prereading activities suggested by 13 reading methods textbooks with the prereading strategies used by 12 successful college students.

1708. Perrin, Robert. "What'd You Say?: Combatting the Problem of Lazy Listeners." *ExEx* 33 (Spring 1988): 23–27.

Provides eight activities to enhance students' listening skills.

1709. Petterson, Nancy-Laurel. "The Study Lady." *WLN* 12 (June 1988): 14.

Describes an advice column that offers suggestions to help students improve study habits.

1710. St. Onge, Keith R. *The Melancholy Anatomy of Plagiarism*. Lanham, Md.: University Press of America, 1988. 118 pages

A handbook on plagiarism. Offers suggestions on how to avoid plagiarism, how to handle charges of plagiarism, when to charge others with plagiarism, and "how to select and combine optimum defenses for any innocents who may stumble into plagiarism's many traps."

1711. Simbo, F. K. "The Effects of Note Taking Approaches on Student Achievement in

Secondary School Geography." *JEdR* 81 (July–August 1988): 377–381.

Compares three techniques for note taking. The best results were seen among students whose notes were based on outlines the teacher provided.

1712. Solley, Anna Genardi. "Developmental Students' Use of Study Reading Strategies in a Community College Content Course." *DAI* 48 (January 1988): 1635A.

Describes metacognitive processes used by six developmental students as they use written material to meet requirements for an academic course of study.

1713. Stracke, Richard, and Sara Snow. "The Literary Research Paper: Some Operating Principles." *TETYC* 15 (May 1988): 115–119.

Hypothetical scenarios help justify the usefulness of critical research papers, and short-answer exercises introduce students to the library. Students are encouraged to work together and to make short-step revisions.

1714. Williams, Nancy. "Research as a Process: A Transactional Approach." *JTW* 7 (Fall-Winter 1988): 193–204.

Describes an assignment providing time "throughout the semester for shaping perceptions, forming and reforming ideas, taking risks, and focusing," which cultivates positive attitudes toward research.

1715. Woodworth, Margaret K. "The Rhetorical Precis." *RR* 7 (Fall 1988): 156–164.

Explains the purpose of and strategies for using a four-sentence paragraph to summarize the essence of a discourse. Cites positive results.

See also 1611, 1633

4.6   OTHER

1716. Baran, Avi, and Lori Van Houten. "Lessons Taught and Lessons Learned: A Story of

Differential Teacher Adaptations of Lessons for High- and Low-Ranked Hearing Impaired Students." *DPr* 11 (April–June 1988): 117–138.

Teaching strategies differed greatly between high-ranked and low-ranked groups, with low-ranked groups covering less material in a lesson.

1717. Boynton, Robert. "Somewhere over the Rainbow: Textbooks and English Classes." *EEd* 20 (December 1988): 206–214.

Makes nine suggestions that could bring traditional textbooks closer to the kinds of textbooks that "well informed" educators would find reasonable.

1718. Fine, Michelle. "Sexuality, Schooling, and Adolescent Females: The Missing Discourse of Desire." *HER* 58 (February 1988): 29–53.

Sees the rhetoric of sex education, prevailing discourses of female sexuality in schools, as anti-sex, thereby exacerbating young women's vulnerability. Argues for regarding sex education as intellectual empowerment.

1719. Hidalgo, Manuel. "Motivating Minority Students: Publishing *Amigos Juntos/Friends Together*." *CollT* 36 (Winter 1988): 9–11.

Describes publishing students' writings in a summer transition program for minority students entering college.

1720. Long, Maxine M. *Teaching Writing to Learning-Disabled Students: A Pilot Study*. Batavia, N.Y.: Genesee Community College, 1988. ERIC ED 296 374. 25 pages

Reports on a pilot study that examines the influence of team teaching, computers, and conferencing on learning-disabled students.

1721. Longo, Judith A. "The Learning Disabled: Challenge to Postsecondary Institutions." *JDEd* 11 (Spring 1988): 10–14.

Discusses case studies of successful learning-disabled students and suggests ways of helping them to cope with academic tasks.

1722. McCauley, Lynne. *Intellectual Skills Development Program: Annual Report, 1986–1987*. Kalamazoo, Mich.: Western Michigan University, 1987. ERIC ED 288 478. 65 pages

Reviews the Intellectual Skills Development Program at Western Michigan University. Includes the results of writing evaluations.

See also 1122

5

Testing, Measurement, and Evaluation

1723. Ahmed, B., L. B. Ahmed, and M. M. Al-Jouhari. "Factors Determining the Performance of Medical Students of the Faculty of Medicine, University of Kuwait." *MEd* 22 (November 1988): 506–508.

Concludes that the strongest predictor of students' success was proficiency in spoken and written English.

1724. Allen, Jo. "A Machiavellian Approach to Grading Writing Assignments." *TWT* 15 (Spring 1988): 158–160.

Outlines a method for democratically establishing the evaluative standards to be used in class.

1725. Bailey, Kathleen M., ed. *Language Testing Research: Selected Papers from the Colloquium.* Monterey, Calif.: Defense Language Institute, 1987. 187 pages

Offers 10 papers from a conference on language testing. Papers are abstracted separately as ERIC ED 267 645 and ERIC ED 287 283 through ERIC ED 287 291.

1726. Birdsong, David, and Margaret Ann Kassen. "Teachers' and Students' Evaluations of Foreign Language Errors: A Meeting of Minds?" *MLJ* 72 (Spring 1988): 1–12.

A study showing that second language teachers agree with their students about the seriousness of errors, even though the severity of their judgments may differ.

1727. Carlson, Sybil B. "Writing Samples Viewed from Different Perspectives: An Approach to Validity." Paper presented at the AERA, New Orleans, April 1988. ERIC ED 295 995. 41 pages

Studies the objective description and identification of variables that distinguish reasoning skills.

1728. Clark, Francelia. "Studying the Longitudinal Study. Introduction: Do Impromptu Essays Show Changes in Critical Thinking over the Span of College? Cautions and Insights from a Pilot Case Study." Paper presented at the CCCC Convention, Atlanta, March 1987. ERIC ED 293 120. 23 pages

A pilot study suggests that impromptu essays written over the span of college years reveal critical thinking, although better cognitive-developmental indices are needed.

1729. Cole, Suzanne. "Using Required Departmental Grading Profiles." Paper presented at the NCTE Convention, Los Angeles, November 1987. ERIC ED 289 179. 9 pages

Reports on a project at a Texas community college, where a committee devised grading standards.

1730. *College-Bound Seniors Report, 1985–86*. Hartford, Conn.: Connecticut State Board of Education, 1987. ERIC ED 289 400. 29 pages

Reports on the SAT performance of college-bound high school seniors.

1731. Connors, Robert J., and Andrea A. Lunsford. "Frequency of Formal Errors in Current College Writing; or, Ma and Pa Kettle Do Research." *CCC* 39 (December 1988): 395–409.

Reports on a study ranking the errors students make most often and the errors teachers most frequently mark.

1732. Crouse, James, and Dale Trusheim. *The Case against the SAT*. Chicago: University of Chicago Press, 1988. 224 pages

Summarizes the results of a six-year research project on the origins and uses of the SAT by American colleges and universities. Argues that, despite the SAT's ability to predict educational success, the test is unnecessary.

1733. Daiker, Donald A. "The Student Essay as Dubloon: Discrepancies in Holistic Evaluation." *JTW* 7 (Fall–Winter 1988): 127–141.

Reports on Miami University's study of essays that produced widely diverging assessments from trained readers. Suggests

three appeals procedures for composition classes.

1734. Davis, Kevin. "Improving Students' Writing Attitudes: The Effects of a Writing Center." *WLN* 12 (June 1988): 3–6.

Describes a method of measuring apprehension toward writing. Reports a positive effect of peer response on writers, whether in class or in a writing center.

1735. Dindia, Kathryn. "A Comparison of Several Statistical Tests of Reciprocity of Self-Disclosure." *ComR* 15 (December 1988): 726–752.

In comparing several statistical tests of reciprocity of self-disclosure, finds little evidence for reciprocity.

1736. Dragga, Sam. "The Effects of Praiseworthy Grading on Students and Teachers." *JTW* 7 (Spring–Summer 1988): 41–50.

An empirical study of commentary that praises. Considers the caliber of writing and students' and teachers' attitudes. Suggests that teachers receive training "on explicit criteria for praiseworthy writing."

1737. Edelsky, Carol, and Susan Harmon. "One More Critique of Reading Tests—With Two Differences." *EEd* 20 (October 1988): 157–169.

Argues that tests can never test reading and writing because the conception of reading and writing inherent in such tests is faulty.

1738. Ehrman, Madeline, and Rebecca Oxford. "Effects of Sex Differences, Career Choice, and Psychological Type on Adult Language Learning Strategies." *MLJ* 72 (Autumn 1988): 253–265.

A study claiming that, in addition to sex and occupation, the Myers-Briggs Type Indicator can predict whether an individual will be a good language learner.

1739. Fitzgerald, Kathryn R. "Rhetorical Implications of School Discourse for Writing Placement." *JBW* 7 (Spring 1988): 61–72.

Argues that "the rhetorical problems of basic writers are as fundamental to their difficulties in college writing as their syntactical and mechanical errors." Includes assessment criteria.

1740. Fleming, P. R. "The Profitability of 'Guessing' in Multiple-Choice Question Papers." *MEd* 22 (November 1988): 509–513.

Over a two-year period, students who were encouraged to guess strategically at unknown items on multiple-choice tests steadily increased their scores.

1741. Fuller, David. "A Curious Case of Our Responding Habits: What Do We Respond to and Why?" *JAC* 8 (1988): 88–96.

Teachers in a workshop were given either handwritten or typed versions of a text, revealed later as Hemingway's. Their evaluation and comments varied dramatically.

1742. Gao, Jie, and Marie Jean Lederman. "Instruction and Assessment of Writing in China: The National Unified Entrance Examination for Institutions of Higher Education." *JBW* 9 (Spring 1988): 47–60.

Describes writing instruction in Chinese middle schools. Discusses writing tasks and scoring procedures for the national examination and compares assessment problems shared by Chinese and American institutions.

1743. Gohmann, Stephen E. "Comparing State SAT Scores: Problems, Biases, and Corrections." *JEdM* 25 (Summer 1988): 137–148.

Suggests that comparing SAT scores among states leads to biased results because of sample selection. Proposes a method for solving the selection problem.

1744. Gorman, Tom P., Alan C. Purves, and R. Elaine Degenhart, eds. *The IEA Study of Written Composition I: The International Writing Tasks and Scoring Scales*. Oxford, England: Pergamon Press, 1988. 214 pages

Presents the rationale for and theoretical background of a study sponsored by the International Association for the Evaluation of Educational Achievement, created to examine the educational performance of students around the world. Describes the tasks and scoring scales used to assess students' writing. Authors are not indexed separately in this volume.

1745. Hancock, Lee Weber. "College Writing: Finding an Assessment Process for Community College Students." *DAI* 48 (March 1988): 2263A.

Examines the effectiveness of a holistically scored departmental essay test used to supplement instructors' grading.

1746. Haswell, Richard H. "Contrasting Ways to Appraise Improvement in a Writing Course: Paired Comparison and Holistic Impression." Paper presented at the CCCC Convention, St. Louis, March 1988. ERIC ED 294 215. 22 pages

Compares different images of writing produced by different assessment methods.

1747. Haswell, Richard H. "Critique: Length of Text and the Measurement of Cohesion." *RTE* 22 (December 1988): 428–433.

Critiques research that correlates the length of a student writer's text with measures of cohesion.

1748. Haswell, Richard H. "Dark Shadows: The Fate of Writers at the Bottom." *CCC* 39 (October 1988): 303–315.

Analyzes the organization and verbal wit of low-scoring papers, concluding that "bottom writers" displayed more knowledge and variety than is commonly recognized.

1749. Hays, Janice N. *The Impact of Friendly and Hostile Audiences on the Argumentative Writing of a Group of High School Seniors and College Students: A Perry Scheme Perspective*. Alexandria, Va.: ERIC Document Reproduction Service, 1987. ERIC ED 292 095. 60 pages

Finds that intellectual performance on the Perry Scheme was a more significant predictor of holistic scores on argumentative essays than were demographic variables.

1750. "The International Baccalaureate." *EngT* 4 (April 1988): 33–37.

An interview with Robert Blackburn. Discusses an international qualifying program for university entrance, which includes a language component.

1751. Kaminsky, Sally, Elaine Hrach, and Rose Harrison. "Positive Reinforcement and Self-Evaluation Accuracy Influence on Reading and Writing." *AdLBEd* 12 (1988): 33–42.

Since accurate self-evaluation and improvement in reading and writing correlate, reinforcement should encourage students' self-evaluation rather than being merely positive.

1752. Koenig, Judith Anderson, and Karen Mitchell. "An Interim Report on the MCAT Essay Pilot Project." *JMEd* 63 (January 1988): 21–29.

Concludes that a 45-minute essay has been most successful. Data are still being gathered to study native versus second language performance, reliability as a predictor, cost, and curricular implications.

1753. Lederman, Marie Jean. "Why Test?" *JBW* 7 (Spring 1988): 38–46.

Recommends essay tests as *"rites de passage* to help our students live well" in a complicated world. Compares problems of testmakers in China and America.

1754. Lee, James F., and Diane Musumeci. "On Hierarchies of Reading Skills and Text Types." *MLJ* 72 (Summer 1988): 173–187.

Asserts that the ACTFL Proficiency Guidelines falsely assume a hierarchy of text types and reading skills, and so do not predict reading proficiency.

1755. Livingston, Samuel. "The Effects of Time Limits on the Quality of Student-Written Essays." Paper presented at the AERA, Washington, D.C., May 1987. ERIC ED 286 936. 20 pages

Finds little effect of increased writing time on holistically scored essay placement tests, except that high-ability students benefited from a 10-minute planning period.

1756. Lombard, George F. F. "Evaluation, Proper and Improper, Part I." *ETC* 45 (Spring 1988): 36–42.

Evaluation is context dependent. It should be feedback-directed and open-ended, moving toward a structurally accurate reflection of internal and external events.

1757. Lombard, George F. F. "Evaluation, Proper and Improper, Part II." *ETC* 45 (Summer 1988): 132–137.

Argues that we must understand processes of misevaluation occurring during decision making in order to make accurate judgments.

1758. Lucas, Catharine Keech. "Toward Ecological Evaluation." *CSWQ* 10 (January 1988): 1–3, 12–17.

Discusses the implications of the shift in writing assessment from learning done in the service of evaluation to evaluation done in the service of learning.

1759. Lydic, David Lynn. "Relational Mapping as a Measure of Writing Ability in College Freshmen." *DAI* 49 (December 1988): 1395A.

Compares relational mapping and traditional t-unit analysis as ways to evaluate students' writing.

1760. Mann, Rebecca. "Measuring Writing Competency." Paper presented at the Southeastern Conference on English in the Two-Year College, Louisville, February 1988. ERIC ED 295 695. 18 pages

Analyzes the merits and limitations of objective tests and direct evaluation of writing samples.

1761. Martin, Wanda. "A Study of Reader Process in the Evaluation of English Placement Essays." *DAI* 48 (February 1988): 2009A.

Investigates scorers' interests and concerns in holistic evaluations. Suggests that readers construct an "imagined writer" on which they base placement.

1762. Moore, Debra Elaine. "IQ and Achievement: Verbal-Performance Differences as Moderators." *DAI* 49 (July 1988): 63A.

Explores the relationship of verbal IQ and performance IQ to achievement.

1763. Orbach, Linda B. "A Comparison of the Pass-Fail Rates of Traditional and Nontraditional Students on an English Composition Exit Examination." *DAI* 49 (November 1988): 1074A.

Performance on the examination may indicate academic integration and persistence.

1764. Perkins, Kyle. "A Proposed Research Program for ESL Composition Evaluation." Paper presented at the NCTE Convention, San Antonio, November 1986. ERIC ED 290 155. 28 pages

Proposes a comprehensive research program for studies evaluating ESL composition.

1765. Pharis, Keith E. "A Study of Faculty Perceptions of Foreign Graduate Student Writing." *DAI* 48 (January 1988): 1682A.

Investigates how reliably faculty members evaluated eight student essays and what criteria they used to judge quality.

1766. Piper, Terry, and William Ross McEachern. "Content Bias in Cloze as a General Language Proficiency Indicator." *EQ* 21 (1988): 41–49.

Questions the use of cloze procedures to determine general language ability after testing 20 adult learners in the People's Republic of China.

1767. Pitts, Beverley J. "Peer Evaluation Is Effective in Writing Course." *JourEd* 42 (Summer 1988): 84–88.

Describes five types of guides that can help peers review a piece of writing and aid the writer during revision.

1768. Pressley, Michael, and Elizabeth S. Ghatala. "Delusions about Performance on Multiple-Choice Comprehension Tests." *RRQ* 23 (Fall 1988): 454–464.

Finds that university students were better able to predict their performances on tests with analogies and opposites in vocabulary than on tests involving reading comprehension.

1769. Rose, Mike. "Narrowing the Mind and Page: Remedial Writers and Cognitive Reductionism." *CCC* 39 (October 1988): 267–302.

Argues that poor school performance should not be explained by any one theory of cognition, such as cognitive style, hemisphericity, Piaget's work, or orality-literacy theory.

1770. Ross, Roberta S. *Formative Evaluation of College Composition: A Formula for Revision and Grading*. College Park, Md.: University of Maryland Department of English, 1988. ERIC ED 289 554. 31 pages

Freshmen composition students were given grading criteria and assigned to direct instruction or peer-critique groups. Results show no significant difference in grade or attitude.

1771. Rozakis, Laurie. "Holistic Evaluation: A Primer." *ExEx* 34 (Fall 1988): 11–18.

Explains, justifies, and provides examples of holistic scoring for essays.

1772. Santos, Terry. "Professors' Reactions to the Academic Writing of Nonnative-Speaking Students." Paper presented at the TESOL Meeting, Anaheim, Calif., March 1986. ERIC ED 285 380. 76 pages

When 178 faculty members evaluated two compositions, they gave higher ratings for language than for content.

1773. Schlieper, Reinhold. "Computer-Assisted Composition: Grade Calculation." *CAC* 3 (Summer 1988): 1–10.

Discusses a computer-assisted, analytical theme-grading procedure that correlates with sections in the *Harbrace Handbook*.

1774. Schmitt, Alicia P. "Language and Cultural Characteristics That Explain Differential Item Function for Hispanic Examinees on the SAT." *JEdM* 25 (Spring 1988): 1–13.

Investigates the characteristics of items influencing differences in performance of Hispanic examinees on the SAT.

1775. Sipple, JoAnn. "Teacher Protocols: A New Evaluation Tool for Writing across the Curriculum Programs." Paper presented at the CCCC Convention, Atlanta, March 1987. ERIC ED 285 150. 20 pages

Analyzes protocols of faculty planning a writing assignment aloud. Shows the positive effect of a writing seminar on participants.

1776. Stach, Carl Louis. "The Component Parts of General Impressions: Predicting Holistic Scores in College-Level Essays." *DAI* 48 (January 1988): 1683A.

Three college faculty members holistically rated 150 university essays and later scored them for seven primary traits. This study analyzes 13 variables as potential predictors for holistic scores.

1777. Stock, William P., Juan Flores, and Linnea M. Agcack. *A Study of English Placement Test Subscores and Their Use in Assigning CSU, Fresno, Freshmen Beginning English Courses.* Fresno, Calif.: California State University—Fresno, 1986. ERIC ED 289 453. 81 pages

Follows students placed in developmental and regular composition courses over an academic year, concluding that the initial placement essay is a valid measure.

1778. Tawake, Sandra K. "Cognitive Factors Influencing Writing Performance in Five Modes of Discourse." *DAI* 48 (June 1988): 3066A.

Finds that TSWE scores correlate positively with some modes of discourse and negatively with other modes.

1779. Thayer, Frank. "Remedial Courses for Writing Skills Proven Effective." *JourEd* 42 (Summer 1988): 71–72.

Reports on a study suggesting that a students' scores on the Test of Standard English Usage can be increased by attending a remedial program.

1780. Tripp, John D., and Nan Webb. *Student Development in 1990: New Developments in Testing.* Charlotte, N.C.: Central Piedmont Community College, 1987. ERIC ED 287 552.

Surveys testing and placement instruments, recommending pre- and postmatriculation competency testing.

1781. Trylong, Vicki Long. "Aptitude, Attitudes, and Anxiety: A Study of Their Relationships to Achievement in the Foreign Language Classroom." *DAI* 48 (April 1988): 2564A.

Correlates data collected from 216 students in the first course in French at a state university. Includes scores on written examinations and oral quizzes.

1782. Wainer, Howard. "How Accurately Can We Assess Changes in Minority Performance on the SAT?" *AmP* 43 (October 1988): 774–778.

Interprets changes in minority students' scores from 1980 to 1985.

See also 16, 169, 435, 1192, 1254, 1291, 1486, 1599, 1609, 1793

5.2 EVALUATION OF TEACHERS

1783. Haggard, Carrol Ray. "Instructor Feedback Elicitation Style: Collecting Process Information on Teacher Effectiveness." *DAI* 48 (June 1988): 3009A.

Examines verbal feedback from students in 73 classrooms. Finds that the Assessment of Instructor Feedback Elicitation Style is a valid and reliable instrument.

1784. Hynds, Susan. "Throw Away the Fish, Eat the Plank: Developing the Writer through the Text." *JTW* 7 (Spring–Summer 1988): 75–81.

Teachers should use "texts as springboards and training aids for development of students as both writers and human beings." Gives nine questions for teacher self-evaluation.

1785. Rash, Wesley Joaquin. "The Relationship of Perceived Teaching Effectiveness to Formal Training as Determined by Student Ratings of Graduate Teaching Assistants." *DAI* 49 (September 1988): 400A.

Using a rating scale of 19 items relating to teaching effectiveness, 1763 students at the University of Idaho evaluated 64 teaching assistants.

1786. Sachs, Harley L. "The Publication Requirement Should Not Be Based Solely on 'Refereed' Journals." *CHE* 35 (19 October 1988): B2.

Advocates teachers' publishing in more widely read national magazines rather than in esoteric periodicals read by only a few.

1787. West, R. F. "The Short-Term Stability of Student Ratings of Instruction in Medical School." *MEd* 22 (March 1988): 104–112.

Students are only moderately consistent in their evaluation of teachers. Thus data from their evaluations should be used with caution in tenure and promotion decisions.

See also 1204, 1706

5.3   EVALUATION OF PROGRAMS

1788. Bernhardt, Stephen A. "Teaching College Composition with Computers: A Program Evaluation." Paper presented at the CCCC Convention, St. Louis, March 1988. ERIC ED 295 191. 43 pages

Presents a writing program evaluation from Southern Illinois University. Focuses on computer instruction.

1789. Grable, John R. "Remedial Education in Texas Two-Year Colleges." *JDEd* 12 (November 1988): 2–5, 29.

A statewide study assessing the effectiveness of postsecondary remedial education programs. Presents recommendations for improvement.

1790. Krendl, Kathy A., and Julie Dodd. *Assessing the National Writing Project: A Longitudinal Study of Process-Based Writing.* Bloomington, Ind.: ERIC/RCS, October 1987. ERIC ED 289 167. 39 pages

Reports on a three-year study in Tennessee. Evaluates the effects of process-based training on high school students' writing. Finds significant positive results.

1791. McQueen, Sandra Marilyn. "The Development of an Evaluation Model and Instrument for Nonresidential Educational Programs for Older Adults." *DAI* 49 (September 1988): 421A.

Develops an evaluation model and instrument for educational programs for older adults. Bases the model on characteristics of the older learner, andragogical processes, and evaluation paradigms.

1792. Morrisey, Thomas. "A Preview of Plattsburgh's WAC Assessment Program." *CompC* 1 (December 1988): 4–5.

Describes the history and goals of an assessment project in the College of Arts and Sciences at SUNY—Plattsburgh.

1793. Nash, James. "Posttesting for Basic Composition in New Jersey." *CompC* 1 (November 1988): 6–7.

Criticizes New Jersey's use of a test designed for student placement as a posttest assessing program efficiency.

1794. Tanous, Cynthia. *Adult and Community Education Program Review Instrument.* Augusta, Maine: Maine State Department of Educational Services, 1986. ERIC ED 289 044. 60 pages

Provides a guide for program review.

1795. Wakefield, Gay. "Caution: Public Relations Education Ahead." *CSSJ* 39 (Summer 1988): 88–98.

Advocates accrediting degree programs regardless of disciplinary affiliations. Calls for strengthening educators' credentials, improving advising, and standardizing the core curriculum.

5.4 OTHER

1796. DeLoughry, Thomas J. "Plan for Scholars to Review Peers' Academic Software Is Announced by College Computing Consortium." *CHE* 34 (17 February 1988): A13, A18.

EDUCOM, a consortium of 500 colleges, proposes to review educational software, identifying useful programs and assisting authors in receiving academic recognition.

1797. Fetterman, David M. *Qualitative Approaches to Evaluation in Education: The Silent Scientific Revolution.* New York: Praeger, 1988. 312 pages

Thirteen essays compare, contrast, and explain qualitative approaches to educational evaluation. Covers ethnography, naturalistic inquiry, generic pragmatic (sociological) qualitative inquiry, connoisseurship and criticism, and several new qualitative approaches.

1798. Lim, Tock Keng. "Relationship between Standardized Psychometric and Piagetian Measures of Intelligence at the Formal Operations Level." *Intell* 12 (April–June 1988): 167–182.

Concludes that a general factor underlies both types of tests. Psychometric tests should be broadened to include the Piagetian concept of intelligence.

Subject Index
Name Index

Subject Index

Numbers in the righthand column refer to sections and subsections (see Contents). For example, entries containing information on achievement tests appear in Section 5, Subsection 5.1 (Evaluation of Students). When the righthand column contains only a section number, information on the subject appears in several subsections. Entries addressing assignments in the classroom, for example, appear in several subsections of Section 4, depending on the kind of course for which the assignments are appropriate.

Name Index

This index lists authors for anthologized essays as well as authors and editors for main entries.

WITHDRAWN